Space, Place, and Religious Landscapes

Bloomsbury Studies in Material Religion

Bloomsbury Studies in Material Religion is the first book series dedicated exclusively to studies in material religion. Within the field of lived religion, the series is concerned with the material things with which people do religion, and how these things – objects, buildings, landscapes – relate to people, their bodies, clothes, food, actions, thoughts, and emotions. The series engages and advances theories in 'sensuous' and 'experiential' religion, as well as informing museum practices and influencing wider cultural understandings with relation to religious objects and performances. Books in the series are at the cutting edge of debates as well as developments in fields including religious studies, anthropology, museum studies, art history, and material culture studies.

Christianity and the Limits of Materiality, edited by Minna Opas and Anna Haapalainen
Figurations and Sensations of the Unseen in Judaism, Christianity and Islam, edited by Birgit Meyer and Terje Stordalen
Food, Festival and Religion, Francesca Ciancimino Howell
Material Devotion in a South Indian Poetic World, Leah Elizabeth Comeau
Museums of World Religions, Charles D. Orzech
Qur'anic Matters, Natalia K. Suit
The Religious Heritage Complex, edited by Cyril Isnart and Nathalie Cerezales

Space, Place, and Religious Landscapes

Living Mountains

Edited by
Darrelyn Gunzburg and Bernadette Brady

BLOOMSBURY ACADEMIC
LONDON • NEW YORK • OXFORD • NEW DELHI • SYDNEY

BLOOMSBURY ACADEMIC
Bloomsbury Publishing Plc
50 Bedford Square, London, WC1B 3DP, UK
1385 Broadway, New York, NY 10018, USA
29 Earlsfort Terrace, Dublin 2, Ireland

BLOOMSBURY, BLOOMSBURY ACADEMIC and the Diana logo are trademarks of
Bloomsbury Publishing Plc

First published in Great Britain 2021
This paperback edition published in 2022

Cover design: Maria Rajka
Cover image: Cwm Idwal Path, Snowdonia, Wales
© Chris Hepburn / Getty Images

A catalogue record for this book is available from the British Library.

A catalog record for this book is available from the Library of Congress.

Library of Congress Control Number: 2020945429

ISBN: HB: 978-1-3500-7988-5
PB: 978-1-3501-8642-2
ePDF: 978-1-3500-7989-2
eBook: 978-1-3500-7990-8

Series: Bloomsbury Studies in Material Religion

Typeset by Newgen KnowledgeWorks Pvt. Ltd., Chennai, India

To find out more about our authors and books visit www.bloomsbury.com
and sign up for our newsletters.

Contents

Figures

Maps

Tables

Contributors

Fiona Bowie is a research affiliate at the School of Anthropology and Museum Ethnography, Oxford University. Her diverse research interests include Cameroon, African religions and the Cameroonian diaspora, gender, religion and identity, Christian spirituality, ethnographic studies of the afterlife, and parapsychological phenomena. She has published widely in these fields, most recently in relation to spirit possession and spirit release therapy in the UK. Bowie is currently engaged in a new project on religion in Wales. Her widely used textbook on the *Anthropology of Religion* has been translated into over a dozen languages, and is going into its third edition (2020).

Bernadette Brady holds a PhD in anthropology (2012) and MA in cultural astronomy and astrology (2005). She is currently a tutor in the Sophia Centre for the Study of Cosmology in Culture at the University of Wales Trinity Saint David, UK. Her research interests are the role of fate in contemporary astrology, the religious and cultural significance of stars and star phases, and the union of mythology with landscape in its potential to capture earlier astronomies. Recent publications include work in Egyptian astronomy (2012), the orientation of the Solsticial Churches of North Wales (2017), and the solar discourse in Cistercian Welsh abbeys (2016). Apart from journal papers she has also authored *Cosmos, Chaosmos and Astrology* (2014).

Jon Cannon, Fellow of the Society of Antiquaries of London (FSA), is a research associate of the History of Art department at the University of Bristol, and Canon Historian at Bristol cathedral. As an author and historian, his academic focus is on medieval church architecture. He has published several books on religious buildings, and his broadcasting work on the subject includes BBC4's *How to Build a Cathedral*. His *Stones of Britain: Geology and History in the British Landscape* will be published in 2020.

Alan Ereira is Professor of Practice at University of Wales Trinity Saint David. His career has been as a TV producer specializing in history. He has been involved with the Kogi people of Colombia since 1989, for whom he established the Tairona Heritage Trust. His most recent book is *The Nine Lives of John Ogilby* (2019), and he is currently writing a cultural history of gold.

J. Anna Estaroth is currently undertaking a PhD in Skyscape Archaeology of Orkney and Shetland with the University of the Highlands and Islands. Her research interests include the analysis of Neolithic and Bronze Age structures, from a phenomenological perspective, incorporating current theories of the anthropology of wonder. Her work on the Clava Cairns of Scotland has been published in the *Journal of Mediterranean Archaeoastronomy and Archaeometry*.

Darrelyn Gunzburg, PhD from University of Bristol, is a medievalist and art historian, and a tutor for the Sophia Centre for the Study of Cosmology in Culture at the University of Wales Trinity Saint David. She has published widely in the fields of the cultural astronomy of medieval Italian frescos, in the orientation of Cistercian abbey churches in Wales, UK, and Europe and their theological relationship to landscape, in how meaning is derived from natal horoscopes in contemporary Western astrology, as well in the areas of loss and grief.

Christos Kakalis is Lecturer in Architecture at the School of Architecture, Planning and Landscape of Newcastle University. He holds a PhD in Architecture from the Edinburgh School of Architecture and Landscape Architecture (ESALA) for which he received the David Willis Prize (2010) and the Richard Brown award (2011). His work focuses on the conditions of embodied experience of the architecture and natural landscape and he has published on themes related to religious architecture and landscapes, architectural experience, and architectural typology.

Lionel Obadia, PhD, is Professor in Anthropology at the University of Lyon, France, and in other French universities (EHESS, EPHE, SciencePo). His specialism is in the anthropology of religion, Asian religions, and globalization. He has conducted fieldwork in France, Europe (on Buddhism in the West), Nepal (on Buddhism and Shamanism), and South India. He is also interested in magic and witchcraft, and his last book was on *Satan* (2016). He now heads the Department of Social Sciences and Humanities at the French Agency for Research (ANR).

Frank Prendergast is emeritus research fellow at Technological University Dublin in the College of Engineering and Built Environment. He holds a PhD from the School of Archaeology, University College Dublin. His research interests focus on cultural astronomy related to interpretative archaeology pertaining to the Irish Neolithic, Bronze Age, and Iron Age. More recent research by him addresses the growing threat to archaeological landscapes from light pollution (2019) and the loss of the dark sky at these places. He has published on megalithic tomb and monument alignment, methodological and theoretical approaches, and advised heritage bodies on the environmental impacts from modern infrastructure on culturally sensitive landscapes containing prehistoric monuments.

Christopher Tilley is Professor of Anthropology in the Department of Anthropology, University College London. He has written extensively about phenomenological approaches to landscape and material culture. His recent books are *An Anthropology of Landscape: The Extraordinary in the Ordinary* (2017), *Landscape in the Longue Durée* (2017), and *London's Urban Landscape: Another Way of Telling* (2019).

Amy R. Whitehead is Senior Lecturer in Social Anthropology at Massey University in Aotearoa, New Zealand. Her research is concerned with the material and performance cultures of religions, and she contributes to debates in the ontological turn to (religious) things, indigenous religions, and vernacular religion. She is committed to developing new critical discourses and approaches to animism and the fetish, and has published widely in these fields of interest. At present, she is the managing series editor for Bloomsbury Studies in Material Religion where she continues to be inspired by the excellent works being carried out by others.

Foreword

Christopher Tilley

As I am writing this I can see the ridge top of the South Downs through my study window. The highest point is to the north and the horizon line veers and dips gradually down to the south before fading out into the Ouse valley near to the sea. The highest point of the ridge is little more than a few hundred metres high, yet appears like a mountain chain seen from below, such is the abruptness and declivity of the uninterrupted slope, rising aloof from the hedged fields below. Threaded like pearls by Neolithic long barrows and far more numerous Bronze Age round barrows the ridge forms a memorious ancestral landscape in which temporality has seemingly been arrested. Monuments that once gleamed starkly white from the chalk of which they were constructed are now green and demure. Culture has now slipped backwards in time to become an indelible part of what we might term 'nature' on the ridgeway. In so doing the past has become present and, in the process, acquired a new sensibility and a new meaning. Apart from a few wind-blown hawthorn bushes crowning the ridge top the stark boldness and purity of form of the downland ridge is visually arresting: the fluted sides, smooth precipitous slopes dizzying from above, the rounded hollows, flattened cols, sinuous curves, and finger-like projecting spurs. As a result, in ordinary and everyday human sensory experience, these hills become truly mountains of, and for, the mind, good to think with and act in relation to. This is a union of the visible and the invisible, the material and the immaterial in experience. The eye of the beholder is always a thinking and an embodied eye.

As a number of authors in this collection of papers point out there is no point whatsoever in attempting to objectively define what a mountain might be. Height is only one consideration among many and declivity and shape are equally important. Ambience and aura may be far more significant than both to the manner in which mountains are individually and socially experienced and whether or not they are understood as living and animate beings with a spiritual essence and sacred power. This is often a matter of their relational qualities in terms of the wider landscapes in which they are found. A river flowing from a mountain may well be part of what it is as will be changing vegetational patterns, flora and fauna held to be characteristic, springs, bogs, lakes, caves, areas of tumbled stone, smoothly declining slopes, or sheer scarp edges. Moreover, the essence and character of mountains differ in terms of the rocks of which they are composed – singular or uniform, complex or reticulated.

Mountains will always be different according to how we approach them or leave them and the impact that directionality and the process of ascent and descent have on us. The same place may look and feel utterly different when approached from one valley, or plain, or direction and another. Above all, their multiple experiential sensory dimensions contribute to their singularity, varying according to the seasons of the year, the rhythms of the weather, the times of the day, or the movements of celestial bodies in relation to them. Rather than being static things, mountains are always in motion: being and becoming, defined by flux.

Cézanne was famously much concerned with how to paint the mountain in the south of France that he saw near to his home in Aix-en-Provence, Sainte-Victoire. He painted it over sixty times. In each painting there is a different mountain expressed on canvas in terms of colour, composition, and form. Using small brush strokes and viewing the mountain from different places and angles, he built up complex fields of vision of its changing forms over many years. However, he was never satisfied with the result to the extent that in his old age he wondered whether there was something wrong with his eyes. He wanted to paint the mountain exactly as he experienced it from below. In this, thought and feeling were linked. His concern with colour was paramount and went far beyond the visual. He was trying to convey the depth, smoothness, softness, and hardness of the mountain as part of the material experiential landscape. He even claimed one could see its odour in its colours and forms. In essence he wanted to capture the manner in which the world emerged through colour. So, he was as much interested in the deep geological formations of the mountain, its bones, as the manner in which the patterns of the rocks were manifested on the surface. The mountain 'thinks itself in me' and 'I am its consciousness' he would say.

From a phenomenological perspective what we witness here is Cézanne's immersion in what he was painting. The mountain was part of him and he was part of it; subject and object were mutually constitutive. His desire to paint as exactly as possible what he experienced involved a clear bracketing of prejudicial assumptions with what was primary or secondary in human experience, that for example a measurement of height might be more significant than an expression of colour. So, it is no surprise that he rejected the Renaissance rules of linear perspective. They only provided a mathematically inspired illusion of reality for 'correct' representation and perspective of the mountain landscape. Renaissance perspective painting is the visible manifestation of scientism, technological reductionism, and abstracted rationalist thought. It is incapable of representing the world as people actually experience it because ultimately it is inhuman, god-like, trying to capture and pin down a static image of the world that actually does not exist.

Cézanne teaches us that the human perception of the mountain arises not from the workings of a disembodied analytical mind paying abstracted attention to composition, outline, light, and shadow but from a lived human relation and bodily presence in the world. In his case this is expressed primarily through the medium of paint and colour. The whole point of Cézanne's art was not so much to simply represent the phenomenal mountain world as it appeared to him, but to make that world visible to an observer of his canvas. This was to make the mountain anew through the manner in which it was represented. Ultimately, it is to accept that representations whether they be in the form of images or words are just that: they are always partial, ambiguous, changing, perspectival, undertaken from a point of view, shaped, and being shaped.

In an analogous way the archaeological and anthropological study of mountains and the landscapes of which they form a part is not ultimately aiming to describe in an analytical fashion what we individually experience, or what is experienced by others, in an 'objective' manner somehow devoid of subjectivity and emotion. They necessarily involve a re-description and re-enchantment of the world that is out there. Describing the world as faithfully as possible in text, that I take to be the general goal of a phenomenology of landscape, is not a mimetic act. It goes far beyond the idea that we could ever capture a mirror image of the world in text and language or images. Instead it develops through the subjective and interpretative process of fashioning thick descriptions of the manner in which matter and mind intersect. These descriptions are necessarily always re-descriptions, hopefully allowing us to understand places from a fresh perspective and see and feel something that is new in them in the process. We always select out of the visible and the material world from a point of view. We may thus understand it differently and inevitably do so from multiple perspectives. We can never exhaust the complexity of the world in our descriptions because we inevitably select out of it what we deem to be important according to our values and concerns and the interpretative philosophical traditions available to us. Thus, in all our accounts some aspects of the mountain world inevitably become foregrounded and others backgrounded, but we hopefully reach a new and profounder understanding. Such accounts and descriptions of place do not precede a higher level of activity that we might include analysis because they themselves actually produce that of which we speak and write. Mountains do not define or make themselves. They require us to make them what they are, to write their narratives and stories and frame them in terms of the manner in which they are experienced and understood.

As this volume well exemplifies, mountain narratives involve considerations of their biographical significance, the manner in which they become part and parcel of people's lives and entangled in how they think and act. Furthermore, mountains are always social things, their understanding and use is negotiated, bound up with the people who live in or visit them. This is fundamentally linked with perceptual sensory experience. We cannot experience mountains in any manner that we might like. Their very materiality both grounds and constrains the way in which people give them human significance and meaning, through their relationship to myths, cosmologies, and world views. They actively provide food for thought in their sensuous materiality. They simultaneously provide touchscapes, visionscapes, soundscapes, smellscapes, and tastescapes. These intersect with their bodily experience to create a synaesthetic understanding. These can be worked and reworked in relation to people's lives, their interests and aspirations facilitating knowing how to go on in the world, and the routines of everyday life. Equally, they can be manipulated in order to maintain structures of power and social dominance. All these scapes are themselves intimately related to the bodily kinesthetics of movement up and down, across and between and within mountain terrain. The essence of a mountain may thus be held to reside as much in the taste of the cheeses made in these high places as in their deep geology and the contortions and colours of the rocks of which they are composed.

As the individual chapters demonstrate mountains clearly possess relational agency in relation to people's lives: they have profound power and effects on thought and action and the meanings people give to their lives, and those of others. Advocating a relational ontology, that provides a foundation for all phenomenological thought, requires us to understand the manner in which mountains touch us, in both a literal and metaphorical sense, as we simultaneously touch them. This notion of touching and being touched equally applies to all the scapes mentioned above and manifests itself through the kinesthetics of embodied experience. Here we can refer to being touched by things visually and the touch of sound and smell and taste that viscerally work through the body and stimulate human emotion, reverence, fear, and awe and wonder. As the relationality is reciprocal and always occurs contextually through time and memory, place and landscape, it cannot be predicted in advance. As such mountains may, or may not, be deemed sacred places. Whether they are deemed as sacred, or profane, changes over time and in relation to how they are used and valued and by whom: what activities they are involved in. For example, if the mountain is a 'task-scape' related to earning a living by those who dwell there (as e.g. a hunter, a tourist guide, a forestry or agricultural worker) or a 'leisure-scape' used for personal satisfaction or aesthetic fulfilment by tourists and other outsiders. Consequently, mountains are always contested and potentially conflictual places because they are understood and valued, or otherwise, from different points of view.

In contemporary society mass tourism and development may successively degrade notions of the sacred, the liminal, and the numinous. These are often associated with high places, frequently accredited with spiritual power, simply because they are often set apart from the routines of everyday life. Alternatively, they may result in an essentially romantic re-enchantment of the mountain world as 'other' as various contributors point out. Mountains may have a prosaic significance as places to be 'bagged and conquered' by the walker or the climber in the least time possible. Or they may be subject to sacralization as places for pilgrimage, religious contemplation, and aesthetic appreciation. This may stimulate an array of emotional responses such as a feeling of being purified as one ascends, or notions of a heightened ascetic or religious insight as one approaches the peak. Different ways of walking and modes of ascent clearly manifest themselves in sacred and ritual, or prosaic and mundane responses to the mountain world. Common to both is the visceral agency and power of the mountain itself mediated through an embodied kinesthetics in which it directly exerts its influence impinging on the muscles and sinews, the lungs and the heart, and the other internal organs of the body.

Mountains like other places *gather*. They gather together histories, people, events, associations, cosmologies, rituals, spirits, myths and stories, mist and clouds, ice and rain and snow, the sun, the moon, and the stars. They often do so in peculiarly dramatic and memorable ways because they are visible from afar, punctuate the skyline, and connect the earth to the heavens acting as an *axis mundi* in relation to which people understand themselves. This book is quite appropriately, therefore, also a form of gathering that productively explores the multiple and often interconnected ways in which these high places act as mediums for bringing together persons and collectivities, structure and practice, power and politics, the religious and the everyday.

Introduction

Darrelyn Gunzburg and Bernadette Brady

Nan Shepherd, in her book *The Living Mountain*, first published in 1977, and to whom we pay homage in the subtitle of this book, wrote of how a mountain became a living presence through a combination of the geology from which it was formed and the ecology that inhabited it.[1] The rocks, soil, water, frost, air, and sun, woven together with the vegetation that grew from the soil and the life forces that breathed the air, the birds that flew through the trees and the insects that scurried across the rocks, even the saxifrage that broke the rock as it pushed through to gain life, all contributed in a commensal connection to a webbed existence that gave the mountain its presence. 'But why should I make a list?' she continued. 'It serves no purpose, and they are all in the books. But they are not in the books for me – they are in living encounters, moments of their life that have crossed moments of mine.'[2] Like Shepherd, this book recognizes these 'moments of crossing' between mountains and humans. We have chosen to call them 'conversations'.

In the past, mountains have been viewed for how they sit in their landscapes, how rapidly or abruptly they rise from their surrounding topography, the heights they reach, and whether their elevation in their adjacent terrain make them impressive. Geology sees the origins of mountains as being created by volcanoes or folds in the earth's crusts or by breaks in the crust where blocks of rock thrust out of the surface or, finally, by erosion where the mountain is a skeleton laid bare in a landscape. Part of the story of a mountain is its story of creation and its journey through its life. Some mountains are skeletons and reduce in height, like old men or women slowly rolling back into the earth, while others are young and growing. Mountains are, therefore, material entities that exist in a different time frame to our own; they exist in deep time. Hence we do not see this change and if they were alive, they would not see us – our story is too short to register in their time frame. We, however, see them. We see them as unchanging entities guarding, protecting, or threatening, entities that have always been there and always will be there, eternal and, at times, dangerous and as such we name them. We name them regardless of height or geological features. Such names are the beginnings of the narrative a mountain has with its human community and the complexity of a mountain that has 'faces' can be reflected in its name. The highest peak on earth, for example, is located in Nepal and named Mount Everest by those who seek to conquer it. In contrast, the Tibetan people who live and move through the forest of mountains at its base know this mountain by two names, Sagarmatha, 'Peak of Heaven', as well as the more human-touchable name of Chomolungma (Chinese, Zhmulangma), 'Goddess Mother of the World (or Valley)'. These Tibetan names show both respect for its great height, the summit of the Himalaya, and one of the mountain's other 'faces', that of a protective mother goddess.

The narrative, however, moves beyond a personal name, as moods and personalities are also ascribed to mountains. Weather changes on a mountain can talk of the mountain turning angry, or as Emily Dickinson wrote in her poem, *Ah Teneriffe* (1914), the mountain wore its ice as a warrior, 'Still – Clad in your Mail of ices – ', and concluded her poem with a call, or prayer, directed to the entity itself: 'Ah Teneriffe! I'm kneeling – still – '.[3] Such personality-inspired ways of addressing mountains are so ubiquitous that, when considering the role of mountains in culture, the fact that they carry these names and personalities often goes unrecognized. The overt reaction is that mountains are a geological feature and, as such, cannot and should not be attributed with any living traits.

With or without a personality, however, a mountain mediates between land and sky. High or small, they are all material metaphors of liminal spaces, guardians, gateways, and bridges from one realm to another. Their physical magnitude can lend them notions of reverence and this feature alone can bring them into the sphere of material religion. This is a feature that can be exploited for religious purpose, not only for the isolation of a monastic group that seeks closeness to the divine but also for the amplification of the divine. Corcovado Mountain in Rio de Janeiro, Brazil, was exploited by Paul Landowski in the 1920s when he used its summit as the place for his 30-metre-high statue of *Christ the Redeemer* to add a Christian conversation to the way the mountain overlooked the city below and appeared to reach out and protect it. The prayer flags of the Himalaya are the way the Buddhist monks use the holiness offered by the mountains' high places to blow prayers around the globe. To view mountains just as static, neutral, high platforms, for retreat or amplification, however, is, we suggest, to miss a large part of the conversation.

In 2007, Christopher Tilley within the discipline of archaeology focused on stones and raised the idea of 'the processual significance stones have in relation to persons and sociopolitical relations'.[4] Tilley, working in the field of post-processual archaeology, a movement in archaeological theory that emphasizes the subjectivity of archaeological interpretations, argued that the idea of materiality questioned 'why certain kinds of stone and their properties become important to people' and that the complex processes that answered such questions went way beyond the studies undertaken by geologists who were concerned only with the material properties rather than what stones mean. 'All materials have their properties which may be described', Tilley wrote, 'but only some of these materials and their properties are significant to people. The concept of materiality is one that needfully addresses the "social lives" of stones in relation to the social lives of persons'.[5] The material make-up of a stone, he noted, did not give it its value. Rather, it was its use and place in the community which gave it worth. In the same way the height of a mountain is a measure of its height, not a measure of its presences, personality, and relationship to its community.

In parallel to this shift in archaeology, in the last three decades there has also been a shift within studies of religion. S. Brent Plate argued that there has been a change of emphasis from ideas acting as the generators of religion to that of the material world itself. This move occurred as scholars began to focus on the physical aspects of religion and a more lived approach to its expression – the importance of the body and its senses, the performative aspects of ritual, the relevance and history of the book, to name a few. In this way spaces, physical objects, and bodies became the shapers of ideas, beliefs, and creeds and gave rise to practices and traditions. It is worth repeating Plate's working definition of material religion: '(1) an investigation of the interactions between human bodies and physical objects, both natural and human-made; (2) with much of the interaction taking place through sense perception; (3) in special and specified spaces and times; (4) in order to orient, and sometimes disorient, communities and individuals; (5) towards the formal strictures and structures of religious traditions'.[6] Plate's definition coheres with the focus of this volume, and, following Plate, might be adapted as 'an investigation of the interactions between human bodies and mountains, with much of the interaction taking place through sense perception in special and specified times in order to orient communities and individuals towards the formal strictures and structures of religious traditions'.

Mountains, therefore, have at least two faces. One can be defined by their geological origin myth, and another, by their personality myth. Nowhere was this more vividly on display than the events of late June 2018. In Thailand, there is a mountain range known as Doi Nang Norn. Geology labels the mountain range as karstic, or soluble rock, meaning that the mountains are full of caves and underground drainage systems. However, the other origin myth is that of a young princess and the forbidden love of a stable boy. The tragic end of the story occurs when the princess, hiding in one of the caves, commits suicide. Her body becomes the mountain range and her blood the water that flows through it. Into this duel set of narratives stepped twelve young Thai footballers and their coach. On 23 June 2018, they went exploring Tham Luang Khun Nam Nang Norn cave— 'the great cave of the sleeping lady'. The cave twists and turns for 10 kilometres under a mountain range that separates Thailand and Myanmar. While they were inside, the rain that had fallen in the previous days started to drain into the caves and they became trapped 4 kilometres from the cave entrance. The boys and their coach took shelter on a small rocky shelf. Surrounded by darkness, unable to return to the world outside, their coach, a former monk, taught the boys to meditate in order to stay calm and conserve strength. Meanwhile, a rescue plan involving US air force rescue specialists, and cave divers from the UK, Belgium, Australia, Scandinavia, and many other countries, was taking place. The planning involved huge engineering and geological knowledge and expertise. At a local level, the community turned to the other conversation with the mountain, the story of the princess and her death. Every day, at the mouth of the cave, fruits, incense, and candles were offered to the cave and the mountain, 'to show respect to the spirit that protects the cave' as the coach's godmother expressed it.[7] This was a direct request to the princess to protect the twelve boys and their coach, for it was thought that the boys may have offended her by intruding into the cave. After two weeks, the mountains gave the boys back to the world, brought about by a combination of the hard work of the rescue teams and, perhaps, the mountain princess hearing the pleas of the villagers. As with any return to safety, however, a re-entry ritual was required. For those who viewed the mountain as a neutral object, there were the rituals of the interviews, with the world's cameras probing into the well-being of the boys and their experience. The mountain viewed as a living entity was also acknowledged. The boys were ordained for nine days as Buddhist monks, so they could repay a spiritual obligation to the Thai diver who died in the rescue operation and be spiritually cleansed. The repayment of the debt occurred outwardly through meditation, prayer, and cleaning the temple. However, as Seewad Sompiangjai, grandfather of one of the rescued boys, observed, 'They should spend time in a monastery. It's for their protection. It's like they died but now have been reborn.'[8]

This contemporary story captures the essence of the conversations we humans have with mountains that this volume addresses. In doing so, it locates mountains as material objects which, as Plate argued, are objects that contribute to the physical expression of religious belief and life, but also as objects that, as Tilley argued for stone, can have a 'social life' which engages with the social life of the person.[9] It is time for mountains to be acknowledged in the emerging field of material religion. Edwin Bernbaum captured both the phenomenology of place and the active agency of places when he wrote, 'The sacred does not simply present itself to our gaze: it reaches out to seize us in its searing grasp.'[10] This is a theme into which our contributing authors delve deeply, when mountains and their stories hold us in their 'searing grasp'.

Part 1, Prehistoric Conversations, is explored by Frank Prendergast and J. Anna Estaroth. Both authors approached mountains that contained hilltop cairns as a way of understanding how prehistoric peoples may have connected with the mountainous landscape through burial practices. Prendergast's encounters with Ireland's Neolithic hilltop passage tombs were undertaken between 2004 and 2007, inspired by the work of renowned Irish field botanist, ecologist, and conservationist Robert Lloyd Praeger (1865–1953) who had observed that, on the island of Ireland, the different landscapes tended to push the cultures of the prehistoric past into the mountain fringe. Prendergast, however, approached the research as a surveyor, cultural astronomer, and archaeologist, walking the same landscape as Praeger, but focusing on the role played by topographical height in the construction of passage tombs. Prendergast was surprised to find how impactful moving up or down a mountain to reach the tombs felt, akin to moving through layers of liminality, and he likened his internal experience to one of passing through metaphysical thresholds created in the mind. On such elevationally high and unprotected places, the perception of being close to an intangible portal to an otherworld was, for Prendergast, emphatic and perceptible.

This theme of liminality to an otherworld was one also found by J. Anna Estaroth in researching the Clava cairns of the Central Highlands of Scotland, and the landscape dominated by mountains of the River Nairn valley. The cairns were thought to be places of transition as they were where the *Sìth* or fairy folk, who were thought to reside under the earth and within the mountains, could enter and exit the *Sìthean* realm. Thus Clava cairns were considered dangerous and associated for centuries with altered experiences of time and timelessness. As a way of exploring and investigating the relationship between the *Sìthean* realm and time, Estaroth undertook fieldwork in the Clava landscape between

December 2014 and October 2016 specifically to survey the mountains. She found that, since the moon was sufficiently low at these northerly latitudes, and appeared to come down to earth, the shadows cast by the hills onto certain cairns implied deep-seated ideas about sacredness.

In Part 2, Medieval Conversations, Jon Cannon and Darrelyn Gunzburg encounter the agency of mountains in connection with architecture built on them in the medieval period that created places of worship. Cannon first encountered Brentor in Devon in January 1974 when he was 11 years old. The phenomenological impact of the tiny church of St Michael atop the rocky outcrop, a response to both architecture and place, to things both artificial and natural, was so profound that it became, in Cannon's words, 'a hunt for the Divine, by which I mean some kind of sentience that unites and transcends all creation'. This powerful conversation was felt as a call to vocation and, in endeavouring to understand the nature of mountains and sacred architecture that was built on them, informed his career pathway. In unpacking the phenomenological impact on him at such a young age of what was, in effect, a small but dramatic hill with a simple church at its peak, Cannon offers insights into the power of place and what might constitute sacred landscape.

Gunzburg's chapter is also an exploration of the creation of a sacred and religious landscape, this time through the lens of one man, St Francis of Assisi, one of a handful of historical figures associated with a town and a mountain. As the generator of a new mendicant order, St Francis' body after death became of vital importance. The final burial site on the side of Mt Subasio beyond the town of Assisi was initially considered to be a wild place, 'the Hill of Hell'. The bones of a saint sanctify place, however, and thus the site was transformed into a place of veneration. Gunzburg argues that, in receiving the bones of St Francis, the mountain became a reliquary, a placeholder for the experience of holiness or the sacred as reflected in the life of St Francis. This interment, she concludes, changed forever the quality of the conversation pilgrims had, and continue to have, with this mountain.

Part 3, Animistic Conversations, explores the non-human entities that inhabit mountains. Fiona Bowie's perspective looks specifically at Mount Everest, (Sagarmatha/Chomolungma), in the Himalaya, and Mount Fuji in Japan. Her chapter is built on the idea, suggested by the theosophist Annie Besant and elaborated in the writings of Cynthia Sandys, that each mountain contains a key energy signal that reflects the sum of the spirit activity in that landscape. Bowie used both conventional ethnographic and historical data alongside mediumistic communications in her research and this approach enabled her to ask new questions regarding the entanglement of thought, body, and place. She concludes that learning to live and work with these forces not only signifies particular challenges, but that a conversation with a mountain that recognizes that the world of spirits, deities, and cosmic forces forms part of a universal imaginary is a necessary part of the 'spiritscape' of anthropology.

In a similar way Whitehead's chapter takes both a personal and an animist relational approach to Roan Mountain, part of the Appalachian Mountains of North-East Tennessee. Raised in the shadow of Roan Mountain, Whitehead grew up recognizing that, for her, the mountain was 'kin' and contained an interactive presence that informed her identity through a weave of stories and felt presences of otherworldly beings. She argues that, while Roan Mountain appeared to be a solid fixture in the vast landscape of East Tennessee, it rendered itself fluid in terms of the relational and spatial dynamics experienced by those humans and non-humans who were present and participating in the relating. Roan Mountain, she maintains, thus formed Appalachian-specific nature religions. She concludes by suggesting that the language of animism is an appropriate tool with which to consider mountains as a central form of religious materiality.

Part 4, Storied Conversations, begins with Bernadette Brady's consideration of Pen y Fan and Corn Du, the two highest peaks of the Brecon Beacons in southern Britain, and part of a mountain range of six main peaks which geographically defines the border between South and Mid Wales. Brady's research weaves together local folklore, the annual movement of the stars against the mythic landscape, the contemporary use of the place, and the location's larger cultural themes of the dragon of Wales and its links to kingship. She argues that all of this creates the potency of place which, using Aristotle's thinking on proper place, points to an ongoing symbiotic relationship that exists between mountains and humans. She argues that it is only our ontologies that cast landscape as an inactive canvas and concludes that as an area becomes entwined with cultural layers, so its potential to influence human activity increases, and thus humanity increasingly seeks to maintain the place names and stories of the location.

Christos Kakalis explores the sacred topography of Mount Athos, a peninsula in north-eastern Greece which, since 1988, has been classified as a world heritage UNESCO monument. A male monastic community ruled by twenty coenobitic monasteries lives on this mountain. In the eighteenth and nineteenth centuries, many printed copper engraving representations of Mount Athos were produced and these engravings, Kakalis argues, offered recipients a tangible connection to the physical and metaphysical dynamics of this religious mountain. The way that the prints were made gave the mountain cultural and symbolic agency as a hierophanic topos and triggered the imagination of the viewer, inviting him/ her into an active dialogue with the landscape. Kakalis concludes that Mount Athos thus offers insights into the way a mountain exerts agency via its printed representations and gives an insight into material religion.

In Part 5, Contemporary Conversations, Lionel Obadia evaluates the way that the mountains of the Himalaya are viewed. While mountains are sites for the everyday life and experiences of those who live there, the Western imagination has conceived of the Himalaya as a sacred place where human beings have sacred experiences. Through ethnographic fieldwork, undertaken among mountain dwellers and itinerant visitors between late 1999 and the mid-2000s, Obadia deconstructs such generalizations, recognizing that not all mountainous landscapes are equal in terms of sacredness. Instead, he argues, mountain spaces are complex, combining a multiplicity of references and frameworks from the diverse cultures and people dwelling in or traversing them and creating a hybrid network of meanings. He concludes that, as socially produced spaces, mountains of the Himalaya have become places where indigenous secularity and Western sacredness improbably mix and merge.

Alan Ereira brings the volume to a close with his experience as a documentary filmmaker summoned by a mountain to hear its message. The mountain is the Sierra Nevada de Santa Marta, on Colombia's Caribbean coast, the highest coastal mountain in the world, populated by the indigenous people of the mountain, the Kogi. Through his work as a BBC documentary film-maker, Ereira began a connection with the Kogi and their Mamas, men trained in divination who mediate between the community and other planes of existence. In 2009 he received a call from the mountain via the Kogi. After several days' arduous journey, he reached the ritual meeting places on the mountain and listened while the Mamas delivered the mountain's message, a warning to stop destroying the mountain and, by implication, the life of the world.

This volume was conceived as an opportunity to fuse ideas of space, place, and material religion with cultural environmentalism and take an interconnected approach to mountains as material religio-landscapes. In this way it fills the gap between lived religious traditions, personal reflection, phenomenology, historical context, environmental philosophy, myths, ritualscapes, and performativity by asking the specific question of whether bonding and reverence to a mountain is constructed by people, intrinsic to the mountain, or whether this is a mutual endeavour. Such questions further the current debates in ontology and new animism studies and also advance Viveiros de Castro's 'perspectivity' in suggesting that mountains may be capable of a point of view.

As Robert Macfarlane wrote, 'I am interested, you could say, not only in what we make of places, but also in what places make of us.'[11] In defining material religion as active engagement with mountain-forming/human-shaping landscapes, our aim is that the research/ideas presented here will also be widely applicable to other forms of material religion.

We wish to thank all of the authors who submitted essays for this volume. It has been our great pleasure to work with each and every one of you and your conversations with these mountains have informed and deepened our understanding. The words of Mama Pedro Juan quoted by Alan Ereira are transcribed from the recording made by him for the documentary ALUNA, copyright of which is owned by the Tairona Heritage Trust. We are indebted to the trust for permission granted on behalf of the trustees for use of the extract. This volume would not have come to fruition without the support of Amy Whitehead and Lalle Pursglove at Bloomsbury Academic to whom we offer our grateful thanks.

Notes

1   Nan Shepherd, *The Living Mountain: A Celebration of the Cairngorm Mountains of Scotland* (Edinburgh: Canongate, 2011), 48.

2   Shepherd, *Living Mountain*, 67.

3   Emily Dickinson, *The Complete Poems of Emily Dickinson*, ed. Thomas H. Johnson (Boston, MA: Little, Brown, 1955), Poem 666, 331.

4   Christopher Tilley, 'Materiality in Materials', *Archaeological Dialogues* 14 (2007): 16–20: 17.

5   Tilley, 'Materiality in Materials', 17.

6   S. Brent Plate, ed., *Key Terms in Material Religion*, Religious Studies (London: Bloomsbury Academic, 2015), 5.

7   Helier Cheung and Tessa Tessa Wong, 'The Full Story of Thailand's Extraordinary Cave Rescue', 14 July 2018. https://www.bbc.co.uk/news/world-asia-44791998.

8   'Thai Cave Boys Ordained in Buddhist Ceremony', 24 July 2018. https://www.bbc.co.uk/news/world-asia-44933744.

9   Tilley, 'Materiality in Materials', 17.

10 Edwin Bernbaum, *Sacred Mountains of the World* (San Francisco, CA: Sierra Club Paperback Library, 1992), xvi.

11 Robert Macfarlane, Fellow and Part II Director of Studies in English, on his studies, writing, teaching, and research at Emmanuel College, https://www.emma.cam.ac.uk/contact/fellows/spotlight/?id=39 (accessed December 2017).

Bibliography

Bernbaum, Edwin. *Sacred Mountains of the World*. San Francisco, CA: Sierra Club Paperback Library, 1992.

Cheung, Helier, and Tessa Tessa Wong. 'The Full Story of Thailand's Extraordinary Cave Rescue', 14 July 2018. https://www.bbc.co.uk/news/world-asia-44791998 (accessed 18 July 2018).

Dickinson, Emily. *The Complete Poems of Emily Dickinson*, edited by Thomas H. Johnson. Boston, MA: Little, Brown, 1955.

Plate, S. Brent, ed. *Key Terms in Material Religion*, Religious Studies. London: Bloomsbury Academic, 2015.

Shepherd, Nan. *The Living Mountain: A Celebration of the Cairngorm Mountains of Scotland*. Edinburgh: Canongate, 2011.

'Thai Cave Boys Ordained in Buddhist Ceremony', 24 July 2018. https://www.bbc.co.uk/news/world-asia-44933744 (accessed 6 December 2019).

Tilley, Christopher. 'Materiality in Materials'. *Archaeological Dialogues* 14 (2007): 16–20.

Part One

Prehistoric conversations

1

The archaeology of height – cultural meaning in the relativity of Irish megalithic tomb siting

Frank Prendergast

Introduction

Robert Lloyd Praeger (1865–1953) was a renowned Irish field botanist, ecologist, and conservationist. In his lifetime, he traversed Ireland 'from end to end, and from sea to sea' to 'appraise the many monuments of man's industry and faith'. He encountered the numerous prehistoric hilltop cairns, the unusual nature of the island's topography, and wrote how 'ancient crumplings of the earth's crust' resulted in the formation of mountainous landscapes in the coastal perimeter and a 'broad low plain in the centre'. His acute eye observed how the different landscapes would have affected patterns of human settlement in the prehistoric past, 'tending to push pre-existing cultures not into an inaccessible centre, as in most islands, but into the mountain-fringe'. His journeys were described in *The Way That I Went*, first published in 1937.[1] Between 2004 and 2007 I followed in the footsteps of Praeger. My journeys were to reappraise the island's much-studied Neolithic passage tombs, similarly distributed from 'end to end' and 'from sea to sea'. As a surveyor, cultural astronomer and archaeologist, I had many and different questions to ask and answer using methodological advances undreamt of by Praeger almost a century ago. My approaches, referencing a developed body of archaeological literature, used field astronomy, geographical information science tools, statistical modelling, and network analysis of recorded intervisibility between the prehistoric tombs. These methodologies were integrated into a phenomenological approach drawing on my field walking to nearly three hundred sites dispersed across the island.

A brief portrait of a landscape and people

The story of Ireland's mythical mountains cannot be isolated from the natural processes that created and moulded the landscape of this island. Formation of the oldest rocks, formed about two billion years ago in the Precambrian Era, began the complex processes of mountain building that continued until the end of the Palaeozoic Era.[2] The legacy of those geological events is the igneous, sedimentary, and metamorphic rocks collectively termed 'bedrock'. Earlier humans exploited these lithic resources to construct their stone monuments. Geodiversity as a term and concept best describes such relationships, how people culturally engaged with the physical elements of their landscape.

The earliest that human inhabitants could have arrived on these shores must post-date the ending of the last ice age. Recent studies of the glacial geomorphology of the last ice sheet, analysis of high-resolution satellite digital elevation models of the land and seabed surrounding Britain and Ireland, and ground-based geological investigations support this claim.[3] The results show that in *c.*20000 BCE, and while much of southern Britain was free of glaciation, an ice sheet of variable thickness to approximately 900 metres still blanketed the whole of Ireland. It extended offshore beyond the present coastline onto the continental shelf – less to the west and more significantly to the south. There was ice-free terrain (nunataks) here during the last glacial maximum but this was limited in extent and encountered only at very high elevations.[4] Such evidence demonstrates the hostility of the environment for human settlement here prior to the ending of the last cold stage in *c.*12000 BCE.

A gradual warming of the climate in the later Palaeolithic induced the northwards retreat of the ice sheet and, with it, a marked change in the physical landscape of Ireland and northern Europe generally. Temperate woodland and a diverse range of flora and fauna gradually replaced more barren open tundra and steppes. For humans who had already migrated north-westwards to these shores, this beneficial environmental change propelled a transition from a hunter-gatherer mode of subsistence, first evident during the Late Palaeolithic *c.*9000 BCE–8000 BCE, to nomadic pastoralism and, eventually, settlement and an economy based on farming.[5] Thus began the appropriation, cultivation, and spiritual imbuement of landscapes from the Early Neolithic (4000 BCE–3600 BCE) onwards.

The processes of human settlement would have evolved in a horizontal and vertical sense. The horizontal socialization of landscapes at mostly lower elevations would have created clearly defined communal areas that offered security, greater potential for tillage, and delineated spaces for communal gatherings. As will be shown, observed distribution patterns of passage tombs suggest a preference for burials belonging to that tradition in upland and mountainous topographies. Relevantly, Jason Toohey stated, 'Mountain peaks and other high points on the landscape hold special places in the ritual and political landscapes of many ancient and contemporary cultures.'[6]

The Neolithic in Ireland had begun by *c*.4000 BCE and is defined by Gabriel Cooney as typified by 'economic criteria, material culture and monumental parameters'.[7] If the period could be described in one paragraph, then palaeoenvironmental and archaeological data show that its beginning in Ireland after *c*.4000 BCE was characterized by woodland clearance, extensive settlement, farming, and a distinctive rectangular timber house horizon (traces of 110 have been discovered to date).[8] The domestication of animals, cereal planting, fabrication of distinctive pottery styles, and the trading of prestige polished stone and flint axe-heads and mace-heads are just some of the indicative material cultural markers for this period of Ireland's prehistoric past. Significantly, the ensuing centuries also witnessed the construction of megalithic tomb building. Three different traditions encompassed the majority erected in the Neolithic: court, portal, and passage types. Each exhibited distinct design styles and differing spatial distribution patterns. However, the topographical 'canvas' which the tomb builders encountered and appropriated needs to now be explored.

Hill or mountain? Beyond etymology

Geographers and cartographers use a variety of quantitative and non-quantitative definitions to distinguish a mountain from a non-mountain environment with resulting widespread disparity in perceptions of what constitutes a mountain. Ordnance Survey Ireland does not have a convention to differentiate a hill from a mountain. Instead, it allows local place names to dictate their classification. This conundrum has now been resolved in the first global-scale assessment of mountain ecosystems by the United Nations Environmental Programme (UNEP). It classifies 27 per cent of the Earth's land surface as mountainous and uses six defined categories based on elevation and gradient to do so. The lowest has a vertical range of 300–1,000 metres and, importantly, for this chapter's discussion, UNEP adopts the 300-metre contour as the defining boundary to distinguish a hill from a mountain.[9] The latest cartographic representation of the

Table 1.1 Height classification of Irish summits

Elevation in metres	Number of hills and mountains
≥200	1,400
≥300	1,158
≥400	954
≥500	570
≥600	288
≥700	115
≥800	41
≥900	14
≥1,000	3

broad-scale physical landscape of Ireland in the form of a physiographic map follows the UNEP convention.[10]

Ireland has an area of approximately 88,000 square kilometres with an extensive central lowland of predominantly sedimentary limestone bedrock (the largest such continuum in Europe). A mostly continuous coastal perimeter of uplands, hills and mountains surrounds the interior. Three-quarters of the landmass lies below the 150-metre contour with only 5 per cent above the 300-metre contour.[11] Much of the variation in topographical relief is attributable to the variable resistance of the different rock types to erosion rather than to any uplift caused by past tectonic events. The analysis shown here of Irish summit elevations provided by Stuart Simon reveals the exponential-like decrease in the number of peaks relative to an increase in elevation above mean sea level (Table 1.1).[12]

These maximum elevations in Table 1.1 may seem small compared to those encountered globally, but this belies the perception of their visual impact on the viewer. To illustrate the phenomenological point, *Slieve na Calliagh* (or Loughcrew Hills) in Co. Meath rise abruptly out of the central lowland. This is an archaeological and cultural landscape of international renown with thirty-two prehistoric monuments comprising Neolithic passage tombs, cairns, and unclassified megalithic structures located on the slopes and summits.[13] The highest hill is 276 metres and crowned by a passage tomb considered focal to the whole complex. Yet this landscape is visible over great distances and has the allure of being mountainous to an observer located anywhere in the surrounding flat countryside (where the average elevation is less than 100 metres). This raises a key question relating to the interchangeability of 'hill' and 'mountain' as terms.

A quantitative approach to distinguish a hill from a mountain offers numerical certainty for definition purposes, but such rigour misses the more nuanced enlightenment gained from a qualitative approach. Roderick Peattie provided this when he stated, 'Mountains should be impressive; they should enter into the imagination of the people who live in their shadows. Unfortunately, it is next to impossible to include such intangibles in a definition. Mountains have bulk; mountains also have individuality.'[14] Peter Wilson advised that criteria other than elevation (flora, fauna, climate, and agricultural activities) also define hills and mountains.[15] Drawing on the work of others, Wilson added another subjective criterion to define a mountain – 'separateness', meaning the 'minimum amount of height-gain from the highest adjacent col'. For these reasons, hills which exhibit Peattie's 'intangibles', and Wilson's 'separateness', clearly evident at *Slieve na Calliagh*, are legitimately regarded here as mountainous.

Tiered landscapes and human settlement

The geological processes described earlier produced three characteristic prevailing landscape types – coastal, lowland, and upland.[16] Coastal landscapes possess considerable resources including freshwater from rivers, fish, shellfish, seaweed, and the potential for settlement, trading, and defence. Lowland landscapes dominate the centre of the island where glacial till in excess of 50 metres in thickness is a characteristic feature, as are the numerous areas of wetlands (bogs, fens, marshes, swamps). Upland is a commonly used term to depict all high or hilly terrains generally above 150–200 metres and is characterized by the absence of glacial drift. This boundary is an arbitrary limit above which, in Ireland, tillage is seldom undertaken.[17] The lower average elevation of the central lowland in comparison to its more mountainous bounding perimeter also gives this island a somewhat shallow saucer-shaped profile in cross-section. Consequently, many of its streams and rivers initially flow towards inland lakes rather than towards the sea.[18] In the age of megalithic tomb building, the central lowland was characterized by waterlogged ground, and large expanses of lakes and soils of low nutrient value. These conclusions are partly based on pollen diagrams which offer a palynological record that is detailed enough to allow a confident reconstruction of the environment and associated human activities at that time.[19] The common consensus is that the central lowland was a less preferential zone for settlement and habitation purposes during the prehistoric past and partially explains the perceived near absence of burial tombs and timber houses throughout this region. Map 1.1a illustrates this argument by using the locations of c.830 extant megalithic tombs (court, portal, and passage) and the discovered subsurface traces of 110 Neolithic rectangular houses. Despite the lack of knowledge of the number of tombs destroyed in the intervening millennia, the apparent distribution pattern of the extant structures shown in Map 1.1a demonstrates a clear but noticeable avoidance of the central lowland. This represents a significantly different pattern of settlement from the one expected under a random model of tomb distribution. Logically, the more elevated and better-drained terrain offered a more sustainable environment for settlement and farming. Higher locales also coincide with geologically more favourable sources for the raw materials required to construct any type of megalithic monument. For burial tombs located in geologically less favourable terrain devoid of glacial erratics, arduous journeys to distant mountainous areas were required to source, quarry, and transport the raw lithic materials, often over considerable distances.[20] The conclusion from this evidence is that tombs were deliberately located in areas where tree cover was less enveloping; tombs were located closer to areas of favourable geology and readily available sources of suitable stone for building; and tombs were preferentially located in areas of higher elevation for improved visibility, intervisibility, and to enhance their symbolism and visual signature from afar. These cultural inferences, while pragmatic, do not capture the entire range of site selection criteria used for tomb building. As this chapter will explore, high places and mountains can also act like a magnet, drawing humans towards their slopes and summits. When located there, the feeling I experienced of power over the lowland below, and the sensation of being connected to a spiritual world overhead, was tangible. My observations at these liminal thresholds therefore raise the question as to whether the experience of being situated in these high places has anything to do with why burials were located there in the Neolithic.

Mountainous landscapes – sacred landscapes

The relief of mountains surrounding the central lowland of Ireland has two particular regions of importance in terms of extant aggregations of passage tombs. These are the Wicklow Mountains on the east coast and the Ox Mountains and Bricklieve Mountains in the north-west. The latter, on the Atlantic coast of Co. Sligo, has one of the richest concentrations of passage tombs in Western Europe. Evidence of human activity in that region dates to the earliest phase of

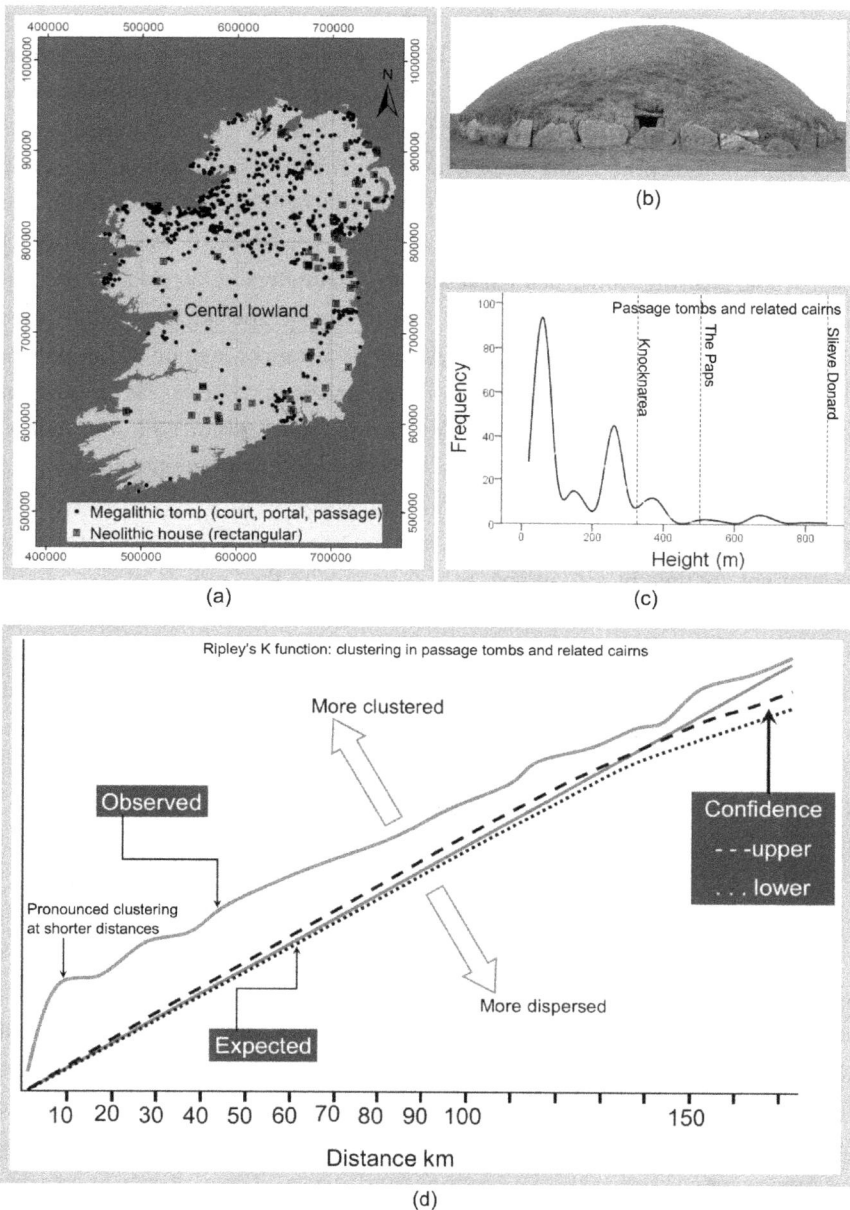

Map 1.1 (a) Distribution map of Irish megalithic tombs; (b) Knowth 12; (c) Frequency graph; (d) Ripley's K Function test for clustering in Irish passage tombs. Graph: Frank Prendergast using own data in ArcGIS 10.4.1 (TU Dublin License).

the Neolithic after *c.*4000 BCE.[21] This archaeological landscape extends across the Ox Mountains in the south to the Dartry Mountains to the north. Between lies the *Cúil Irra* Peninsula, renowned for the dramatic flat-topped Knocknarea Mountain (327 metres) lying at its western end. Seventy extant passage tombs lie clustered on its hinterland, slopes, and top. The most dominant and visually striking is the gigantic Maeve's Cairn (SMR: SL014-076003-) perched on the summit (Map 1.1c; and see Figure 1.1c). This round cairn was built using locally sourced limestone, has basal and top diameters of 60 and 24 metres, respectively, and a height of 10 metres. The volume of the cairn is 14,700 cubic metres, making it clearly visible on the skyline at distances of up to 80 kilometres as observed during my fieldwork. Using previous criteria for mountain classification, Knocknarea and Maeve's Cairn together exhibit 'impressiveness', 'bulk', 'individuality', and 'separateness'.[22] Such is the prominence and impact of this cairn on the viewer that Stefan Bergh was moved to hypothesize, 'The monument becomes a link to the gods, and the few initiated in the secrets of the monument are thereby also in charge of contact with the Gods.'[23]

Intensive interest in the *Cúil Irra* Peninsula and the surrounding region by Bergh and others gives important insights on one of Ireland's most renowned cultural landscapes. My focus was on the broader character and symbolism of the tombs and their landscapes at an island scale as a way of assessing the attraction such mountains had on humanity's desire to use height in connection with death – potentially bringing added insights to our prehistoric cultural heritage.

A *corpus* of monuments – towards an archaeology of height

Turning now to other tombs found in these landscapes, the term 'megalithic tomb' is generic and commonly used to describe any type of stone-built chambered monument erected in the Neolithic and Bronze Age. Diagnostic architectural elements include lintelled entrance passages, forecourts, simple or complex burial chambers, and, frequently, an enclosing kerb delimiting a covering mound of earth, loose stone, and turves. The central role of Irish examples, at least, was for the placement of mortuary deposits of cremated and unburnt bone, and grave goods in some cases. Importantly, the term 'cemetery' for a cluster of prehistoric tombs, suggesting an area for the disposal of human remains, is now outmoded.[24] The term 'complex' reflects more accurately the range of ceremonial purposes that these groups of monuments played.[25]

Descriptively, court tombs (which number c.230 in the height analysis) are trapezoidal in plan with an unroofed forecourt at the broader end of a long barrow. The roofed segmented burial gallery on the tomb's long axis contained the inhumed and cremated remains of the dead. They broadly date to 3700 BCE–3570 BCE. Portal tombs (which number 191) have a short chamber formed by two portal stones, two side stones and a back stone. The characteristic roof stone slopes from the front towards the rear of the monument. The available evidence indicates that these monuments had repeated episodes of inhumed burials *c.*3800 BCE–3200 BCE. Passage tombs (which number 221) have their burial chambers set at the end of an access passage within a round covering cairn delimited by an enclosing earthfast kerb of contiguous stones (Map 1.1b). The predominant burial rite was cremation, but the presence of unburnt bone (including from children) and the skulls and long bones from adults is also evident.

Developed passage tombs are architecturally elaborate and exhibit extraordinary embellishment with engraved or picked art in many cases. Michael Herity observed that passage tombs contained a distinctive assemblage of artefacts and grave goods that are unlike anything found in either of the contemporaneous court or portal tomb types.[26] Where there is spatial overlap between the three types, I have discovered that passage tombs are always elevationally above court and portal types.[27]

Landscapes and tombs – a summary spatial analysis

Theoretical approaches to how and why humans defined and used social space are of enduring interest to scholars of anthropology, archaeology, and geographical science. Fred Hamond suggested that the processes of site selection in a landscape were complex.[28] At least three related factors were involved – the initial strategy or idea, the influence of the environment within which decisions were made, and past experiences (or tradition). Andreas Koch argued that sociality and spatiality were linked reciprocals with a 'mutually dependent relationship between the social construction of spatiality and the spatial construction of sociality'.[29] Relevantly, Timothy Darvill defined landscape 'as a term appropriate to a humanistic understanding of the environment'.[30] A landscape, then, is an amalgamation of the natural and what it becomes once it is appropriated, built on, and ritualized. It is also multidimensional with layers of meaning and usage incorporating natural, social, ideological, ritual, and sacred elements.

For this discussion, social landscapes in the prehistoric past are what people tangibly encountered in terms of perceived constraints delimited by physical barriers, including mountainous terrain.[31] In contrast, ideological, ritual, or sacred landscapes are suggested here as intangible entities and therefore difficult to describe, locate, and interpret. The role of hills and mountains in that ideological framework then becomes a key question. Methodologically, spatial analysis of megalithic tomb distribution has several advantages. It can give a better understanding of prehistoric settlement preferences and bring specific landscapes and prominent topographical features into ideological focus for further scrutiny. For these reasons I set about analysing tomb locations for comparative evidence indicative of preferences in their adjacency and elevation. My field methodology used autonomous GPS, a prismatic compass and inclinometer. Post-processing and analysis of the data used spreadsheet calculations, geostatistical tools, geographical information system (GIS), and social network analysis.

Spatial distribution patterns

My first point of analysis was to consider spatial distribution patterns, the way the tombs were laid out in the landscape. Map 1.1a illustrates how the central lowland of the island was devoid of all types of megalithic tomb except for a small number of passage tombs and related structures on elevated ground or hills in that region. This represents a significantly different pattern of distribution than would be expected under a random model. Various sociological and environmental factors can account for this apparent avoidance. These include geomorphological factors, dense tree cover, distance from mountains, and restricted visibility and intervisibility with other tombs. As the central lowland accounts for approximately 17 per cent of the landmass, I next sought evidence of tomb clustering and how this phenomenon might associate more with hilly or mountainous terrain.

Spatial point pattern analysis of tomb clustering

My second point of investigation was to use spatial point pattern analysis to determine the degree of clustering in tomb locations.[32] My work used various methods including complete spatial randomness tests, nearest-neighbour analysis, class proximity tests, and spatial density analysis.[33] These showed that court tombs and portal tombs are three times more likely to cluster with each other than with passage tombs. Expressed differently, there is significant evidence that passage tombs exhibited very strong territorial segregation and avoided court and portal tombs as neighbours, both in elevation and adjacency in plan. I then used the more powerful Ripley's K function test, as modified by Dixon, to test for spatial randomness.[34] This technique examined the spatial character of the three tomb data sets at defined spatial scales of distance separation. Any non-random findings in their distributions could reflect the influence of natural or human agencies in such distributions. From an archaeological perspective, these might include deliberate spatial ordering. The results showed that while clustering was evident in all three classes of Neolithic tomb, passage tombs exhibited the greatest degree of this phenomenon. This outcome is illustrated in Map 1.1d for the network of passage tombs taken as a whole and shows how clustering changes with increasing or decreasing distances between the tombs. At a national scale, my work also revealed that the majority of passage tomb clusters occurred on locally elevated terrain and on the slopes and summits of mountains.

Height analysis of tombs

Interest in Irish megalithic tomb heights is of enduring interest to archaeologists and folklorists alike, so my third point of investigation was to analyse the heights of the tombs. Gabriel Cooney and Eoin Grogan noted how the prehistoric burial tombs of Co. Leitrim and beyond are discernibly upland as well as lowland in distribution.[35] Seán Ó Nualláin showed that the siting and altitudinal preferences of Irish megalithic tombs indicated that court and portal tombs had a lowland bias, with 60 per cent of court tombs and 70 per cent of portal tombs lying below the 120-metre contour.[36] In a further assessment of passage tomb height, Bergh noted that 16 per cent lie above the 300-metre contour and this preference for height was what typologically set them apart.[37] Charles Mount came to a similar conclusion using evidence from a pollen study undertaken in the Bricklieve Mountains of Co. Sligo where many passage tombs are located.[38] Eamon Cody concluded, 'What remains to be explained is the relationship between the builders of the various megalithic tomb types and this leaves open the question of what role relative height may have played in the siting of tombs.'[39]

Table 1.2 Descriptive statistics for sampled Irish megalithic tomb heights

Tomb type	N	Range	Minimum	Maximum	Mean and SDEV
Court	264	312	5	317	114 ± 4
Portal	182	243	13	256	96 ± 5
Passage	217	857	0	857	166 ± 10
Passage and hilltop cairns	274	857	0	857	172 ± 9
Linkardstown	17	260	20	280	102 ± 18
Wedge	410	343	8	351	150 ± 4

Table 1.2 shows summary height statistics for the majority of megalithic tombs compiled from my field surveys and inventory sources. It is clear that passage tombs exhibit the greatest range in height – from sea level to the summits of very high mountains. Neolithic single burial tombs (known as Linkardstown type) and Bronze Age wedge tombs are included in Table 1.2 merely to capture height statistics for all prehistoric tomb traditions on the island.

N = number of tombs with available heights. Range = difference between highest and lowest tomb. Minimum, Maximum = elevation of the lowest/highest tomb. Mean and SDEV = arithmetic mean height and standard deviation of mean height. All heights are in metres.

The chi-square test was used to examine the hypothesis that there is no significant difference between the mean heights of the different tomb types. The null hypothesis (H0) is that the tombs are randomly located in height. The resulting test statistic is 9.49 at the 0.05 significance level and the result ($\chi^2 = 30.2$, $p < 0.001$) suggests that the null hypothesis is rejected. My analysis also showed that the height distribution of passage tombs is discernibly bimodal with peaks in the height histogram at approximately 60 and 250 metres (Map 1.1c). Cooney came to a broadly comparable conclusion using a similar methodology.[40] What this means in common parlance is that passage tombs with higher elevations, although fewer, could embrace a different ideology associated with specific social and burial traditions and preferences associated with uplands and mountain tops.

Cosmic levels and place

The idea that prehistoric burial tombs were placed on the highest point of the middle cosmic level to be furthest from the underworld and closest to the upper heavenly tier is a common one embraced by anthropologists such as Robert Hertz and ethnographers such as Edward Tregear.[41] That argument could be refuted by the ready availability of suitable stone prevalent at the majority of burial sites. Importantly, however, recent archaeological and geological research demonstrated how passage tombs in the Boyne Valley, Co. Meath, were constructed with exotic stone, such as granite, greywacke, quartz, and incorporated as structural stones. These were not procured from the local bedrock or from local glacial erratics, were transported over great distances, and were clearly imbued with high symbolism.[42] Relatedly, W. R. Lethaby indicated, 'The main purpose and burthen of sacred architecture – and all architecture, temple, tomb, or palace, was sacred in the early days – is thus inextricably bound up with a people's thoughts about God and the universe.'[43] This is phenomenology, the subjective treatment of experienced phenomena, here applied to the materiality of landscape and its impact on the senses. This includes the 'edge condition', a well-known architectural term that, inter alia, describes the metaphysical junction between the built environment and the perceived natural world, or a space.[44] If borrowed as a term for this discussion, the concept of 'edge' suggests a liminal zone where the human senses and the visual perception of space and boundary can be at their most acute and intense. This is especially the case at the junction of summit and sky where the heightened sensory perception of being closest to the intangible otherworld is emphatic.

Genius loci is another emotion that describes the character, essence, and quality of a place. Literally meaning 'Spirit of Place', it first appeared as a votive inscription on an Ancient Roman Altar Stone (43 CE–410 CE) dedicated to Jupiter, the God of the Sky.[45] The Norwegian architect Christian Norberg-Schulz was the modern proponent of the term in the context of moving design theory in his own discipline from the quantitative towards the qualitative. He advocated 'place' as the root of all design inspiration and equated architectural structural design in its time with *genius loci*. Relevantly, he interpreted the architecture of early civilisations as a 'concretization of the understanding of nature … in terms of things, order, character, light and time'. He viewed ancient people's relationship with buildings and artefacts as imbued with life and magical power and how their buildings located on mountain summits defined a significant boundary or 'edge', as I have already discussed. Norberg-Schultz viewed mountains as natural archetypal elements exhibiting natural force, bulk, solidity, and permanence; sacred architecture placed on mountains absorbed these symbolic qualities and epitomized 'the marriage of heaven and earth'.[46] The anthropologist Roderick Sprague, drawing on Hannon, also observed the strong cultural tendency to place 'cemeteries' on hilltops, not only because of better drainage and remoteness from farming activity but also because of their closeness to the deities and the afterlife.[47] In a sense then, mountains, prominent hills and summits are the nexus between heaven and earth. In my final section, I illustrate my ideas with selected examples of hills and mountains chosen from across the island.

Phenomenology of high places

Like Praeger did a century ago, I too walked this same landscape from 'end to end' and from 'sea to sea'. Although his perspectives had a mainly botanical focus, nevertheless the experiences I gained during my fieldwork gave me perceptions and feelings for these special locations which had much in common with Praeger. In his time, computer-aided visualizations of the land were inconceivable and even in the modern era such approaches can never replicate the sensory experience of actually being on a mountain. In that environment, the full force of nature's elements exposes our body and mind to a range of physical and emotional effects. Emotionally, the dynamic of moving up or down a mountain is to move through layers of liminality and is an experience sharpened by the indefinable but conscious state of passing through metaphysical thresholds created in the mind. The countless climbs I undertook to reach the tombs gave me a primal and visceral understanding of the meaning of tiered cosmic levels – the ancient world view of heaven, earth, and underworld commonly attributed to ancient cosmological traditions.

What is also very apparent when climbing to such places is not only the realization of the inordinate physical effort required to reach them in many cases but also the rapidity with which a commanding view is achieved, even when the increment in elevation can be comparatively small. Arguably then, it is not the value of absolute height above sea level but height relative to the lowland below that is the measure or metric that captures and sharpens that experience. Relevantly, Yi-fu Tuan suggested that the mind was psychologically detached from the norms of everyday when located at height.[48] What I found, however, was that as I attained significant height, my mind became acutely prone to sensations of awe and fear, induced by ascending steep terrain, the exposed aspect, and the related feeling of my human vulnerability and sense of isolation. Two paradoxically similar yet different sites in terms of their landscape character exemplify how gradient, in a phenomenological sense, is more significant than absolute height.

The first is the round Neolithic cairn located on the summit of Donald's Hill (403 metres) in the townland of Drumsurn Upper, Co. Derry

(SMR: LDY017:017). The second is the destroyed passage tomb located on the summit of Slieve Donard (853 metres) in the townland of Ballaghbeg, Co. Down (SMR: DOW049:011). The latter has the distinction of being the highest passage tomb in north-west Europe (Figure 1.1a). Each monument commands an extensive and panoramic view of the horizon, is located on a summit, but has a considerably different elevation above sea level. The sensation of height induced by vertically ascending some 200 metres from the lowland over a gradient of 44 per cent onto the summit of Donalds Hill is extreme. The proximity of the intangible and imaginary boundary created by the low cloud that prevailed at the time of my visit further accentuated my sense of detachment from the world below. There was also an elusive feeling of being seemingly close to an otherworld, or domain, as I approached and moved through the cloud ceiling. The ascent to the summit of Slieve Donard, twice the elevation of Donalds Hill, was experientially far less dramatic. My field notes describing these comparative climbing experiences indicate how the much more severe gradient encountered on Donalds Hill left me petrified with fear and feelings of vertigo. While Slieve Donard is indisputably a mountain, the diminutive Donalds Hill certainly qualifies it as a mountain by exhibiting all of the intangible qualities earlier alluded to by Peattie.[49]

These experiences suggested to me that, regardless of the height of a place, the motivation to build prehistoric burial tombs on summits likely emanated from a primal cultural need to exploit the proximity of the middle cosmic level (earth) to the highest cosmic level (sky) as part of the burial ritual. Such a belief would then be part of their cosmology, defined by Darvill as 'the world view and belief system of a community based upon their understanding of order in the universe'.[50] Drawing on Darvill and other sources, Tore Lomsdalen advanced the meaning of the term as 'a holistic worldview, a belief system that encompasses all aspects of human society, their environments and the observable, but intangible sky'.[51] These ideas, along with my own experiences and research, could begin to account for the siting of many Irish passage tombs on the summits of prominent hills and mountains – into the sky.

From end to end – Ireland's sacred and mythical mountains

Myth underpins many of Ireland's mountain festival traditions and how people engaged with mountains in the historic period, especially for seasonally timed ascents. Máire MacNeill documented seventy-eight festive assemblies on heights with no recognized connection to religion.[52] Many coincided with the annual gathering of the crops at harvest time. Seventeen, however, were converted to Christian devotion and became pilgrimages, attesting to their likely prehistoric, or later pagan, origins. Croagh Patrick Mountain, Co. Mayo (764 metres), is a prime exemplar, being a Christian ritual landscape and an important focus of religious pilgrimage over the last fifteen hundred years.[53] The discovery of remains of a dry stone oratory on the summit, radiocarbon dated to 430 CE– 890 CE, attests to the mountain's enduring religious associations and gives credence to the rich oral tradition linking it with St Patrick.[54] That summit oratory, conceivably, might have replaced or covered an earlier prehistoric tomb or cairn and, if so, the possibility that a Neolithic or Bronze Age structure preceded Christian pilgrimage architecture on the summit. The discovery of two astronomically aligned Bronze Age stone rows linking the setting sun at winter solstice with the lower slopes of Croagh Patrick could suggest a cultural reverence for the mountain in the prehistoric past and lend support to such a hypothesis.[55]

Apart from Croagh Patrick, several other mountains and hills deserve consideration from the perspectives of eminent height, distinctiveness, mythology, or religiosity. Significantly, three of the following five examples each has a passage tomb(s) located on the summit.

Slieve Donard – a mountain and tomb that touch the sky

The two extant prehistoric cairns on the summit of Slieve Donard have an elevation of 853 metres (Figure 1.1a). The dimensions of the larger 'Great Cairn' were recorded in *c.*1826 prior to its deliberate destruction during triangulation surveys for the mapping of Ireland.[56] A survey drawing survives in the National Archives of Ireland and indicates the presence of a large round kerbed mound – a likely passage tomb. Harris and Smith described later Christian pilgrimages on Slieve Donard and the religious appropriation of its then intact prehistoric monuments:

> St. *Domangard*, corruptly written Donard, a Disciple of St. *Patrick*, spent the life of a Hermit on this Mountain, and built a Cell or Oratory on the Top of it towards the close of the 5th Century; for he died (according to the martyrology of *Taulaght*) in the Year 506. … the Patron day seems to be the 25th of July, St. *Jame's* Day; for then the bigoted Members of the Church of *Rome* in this

(a)

(b)

(c)

Figure 1.1 Photographs of three sacred mountains in Ireland: (a) Slieve Donard Co. Down; (b) The Paps, Co. Kerry; and (c) Knocknarea Mountain and Maeve's Cairn, Co. Sligo. Photos: Frank Prendergast.

Neighbourhood climb up this Mountain to do Penance, and pay their Devotion perhaps to both Saints.[57]

MacNeill also documented pilgrimages onto the summit of Slieve Donard on the last Sunday of July (Garland Sunday) from 1645 onwards – evidence of the enduring sacredness of the highest peak with a passage tomb in Ireland.[58] Although my journey to the summit of Slieve Donard was not for pilgrimage, the arduous ascent (and descent) always had the potential for danger from the elements and the topography – offsetting any gain from spiritual salvation, if that had been the purpose of my visit!

The Paps – paired sacred mountains

Although Mangerton Mountain (843 metres) is the highest peak of the Derrynasaggart Mountains in Co. Kerry, 'The Paps' (694 metres and 690 metres) in the same range are more renowned because of their obvious human breast-like profile symbolizing fertility to most observers (Figure 1.1b). The two crowning prehistoric cairns emphasize their apparent femininity (SMR: KE076-019----, KE076-036----). According to Frank Coyne, the name 'Paps of Anu' derives from *Anu* or *Danu*, the legendary name of the mother goddess of the *Tuatha Dé Danann*, a mythological race credited with magical powers and wisdom and believed to have first inhabited Ireland in earliest times. What is more certain and beyond conjecture is that these paired cairns are likely to be of Neolithic origin due to their collapsed centres, and traces of an external drystone-walled kerb at the base of each cairn.[59] The summits are linked by a linear row of upright earthfast jagged stones demarcating a possible ceremonial route or link of prehistoric origin. Pending a full archaeological excavation, it is legitimate to suggest that The Paps were paired sacred mountains in the prehistoric past with a deep mythology that has perpetuated through time by finding expression in the place names attaching to some local topographic features such as valleys, rivers, and lakes. Recent research undertaken by Frédéric Armao on the nearby inter-visible archaeological hilltop complex known as *Cathair Crobh Dearg* supports this claim.[60] Drawing on Coyne and on his own archaeological, mythological, folkloric, and ethnographic analysis of the site, Armao described The Paps and *Cathair Crobh Dearg* as a 'dual site' whose paired functions were ritual, ceremonial, and religious since antiquity.

Knocknarea Mountain and Maeve's Cairn –
a 'Mimetic Hill' on a mountain

The flat-topped Knocknarea Mountain (327 metres) in the *Cúil Irra* region of Co. Sligo (described in an earlier section) with the gigantic 'Maeve's Cairn' (SMR: SL014-076003-) perched on its summit (Figure 1.1c) is, according to Bergh, key to understanding the wider symbolism of the physical landscape and the cosmology of the Neolithic population at that time.[61] The mountain is a spectacular focal point in the region and it is here, Bergh noted, that Neolithic farmers first constructed numerous passage tombs in a linear arrangement on the summit during the first half of the fourth millennium BCE. Though unexcavated because of the enormous quantity of loose limestone forming the cairn, several kerbstones are visible around the base of the structure, indicative of a probable concealed passage tomb. The later addition of a complex system of banks on the eastern flanks of the mountain seems to enclose the sacred space of the summit, which 'effectively transformed the entire mountain into a monument'.[62] The truncated cone-shaped Maeve's Cairn, named after the legendary warrior queen of the province of Connaught, mirrors the natural shape of the mountain on which it sits. To my eye, this is the finest example of mimetic prehistoric architecture on the island. Such a striking example provides powerful visual evidence that built form made to evoke already sacred natural form was an apparent deliberate act to imbue and amplify the symbolism of the cairn by absorbing the height, bulk, and power of the mountain into the morphology and function of the cairn itself. One can speculate that the mountain and cairn were a virtual ladderway to the intangible dome of the sky and the supernatural spirit world of the gods. From the summit of Knocknarea I was rewarded with commanding views of the Ox Mountains and the many islands that dot Clew Bay in the wild Atlantic Ocean far below, a lofty setting for the dead, imbued with the drama and power associated with height.

Knocknashee Hill – 'The hill of the fairies'

My visit to Knocknashee Hill (276 metres) in south-west Sligo, on 1 August 2015 immediately followed fieldwork at Knocknarea. Seen from afar, this hill has the appearance of a truncated cone with a large oval-shaped tabletop plateau towering impressively above the lowland 200 metres below. Recent archaeological assessment has increased the total number of roundhouse foundations to almost fifty.[63] Along with two passage tombs and a hillfort, this summit was therefore an important settlement site and a ceremonial tribal centre in the prehistoric past. Importantly, the anglicized form of the hill's name derives from the Irish Gaelic *Cnoc Sí*. Translated, this means 'Hill of the Fairy Mound', a reference to the passage tombs. The folklorist Tok Thompson referred to the term *sí* as meaning 'spirits of the mounds', to having its own 'discursive and epistemological properties' and being mentioned in late seventh-century Irish writings.[64]

From a phenomenological perspective, having spent many hours exploring this summit, Knocknashee Hill seemed the embodiment of a magical landscape as its mythological name suggested. The sheer bulk and impressiveness of its geological form seemed to radiate power across the hinterland. From the summit, I experienced the fundamental human trait for distant gazing afforded by such vantage. I could sense how height and the penetrating power of vision and view as paired entities gave me a sense of control and dominance over the awe-inspiring landscapes before me. It was also apparent that summits enhanced with any type of religious edifice from antiquity onwards could be numinous – possessing a strong spiritual quality and a divine power.

In building monumental architecture on this elevated place in the Neolithic, it seemed to me the structures and the place were imbued with layers of meaning and symbolism now lost to us over the intervening millennia. Yet standing in this place, I felt completely immersed in my own cultural identity, and how I was immutably linked to my own ancestors. Perhaps all was not lost then.

Ardpatrick Hill – a sacred mountain to climb

Ardpatrick Hill (227 metres) is an ancient pilgrimage summit at the northern end of the Ballyhoura Mountains, Co. Limerick. The place name in Irish is *Ard Pádraig* meaning 'the high place of *Pádraig*', a saint who remains tremendously important in the history and religious traditions of the island. The site has commanding views across the hinterland. In the glossary of words commonly found in Irish place names, *Ard* occurs in 940 cases attesting to a cultural reverence attaching to height.[65] This conical hill is crowned with a complex of recorded structures including a pre-Romanesque ruined church (SMR: LI056-002008-) dedicated to St Patrick, a round bell tower (SMR: LI056-002003-) built between the tenth and twelfth centuries and a still-in-use eighteenth-century graveyard (SMR: LI056-002009).[66] A continuing custom is to carry coffins over the steep 20 per cent gradient from the modern church located in the lowland below. The locally held belief is that by the time the deceased has reached the hilltop graveyard following the arduous ascent, 'their soul is already halfway to Heaven'.[67] Ardpatrick is diminutive compared to my earlier examples and exhibits the qualitative features of impressiveness, distinctiveness, or separateness only to a lesser degree. Nonetheless, it is a significant example of a 'Living Mountain' linking topography, tradition and the eternal cycle of death, burial, and the afterlife.

Conclusions

Ascending any mountain experientially moves the climber or worshipper from the familiar lowland domain to a metaphysical realm above. By focusing on the parameter of topographical height, my understanding of prehistoric passage tomb siting has broadened. From the numerous climbs required to reach each of these iconic monuments, it was unavoidably apparent to me, standing in those places, that hill and mountain summits are prime locations to experience a wide range of emotions, especially the 'edge condition' and 'spirit of place' as discussed earlier. On such elevationally high and exposed places, the perception of being close to an intangible portal to an otherworld is emphatic and perceptible – the gateway to the imagined abode of afterlife and spirit world, perhaps.

More than a century ago, Praeger began his journeys, partly inspired by the island's rich heritage of prehistoric megalithic tombs and structures. In 2004, I began my own island-wide journeys, but with an interdisciplinary focus on its enigmatic passage tombs. My analysis included landscape setting, spatial cohesion, intervisibility, axial orientation, and alignment on topographical and celestial targets. No other study had collectively considered these themes at an island scale. Drawing on that work, in this chapter I have concentrated on cultural and phenomenological factors to explore the apparent lure that mountain slopes and summits held for Neolithic people and their burial traditions. My statistical analysis shows that eminence and topographical height were dominant themes in the construction of many passage tombs. This is also evident in a comparison of passage, court, and portal tomb elevations. My research, a combination of the statistics and the phenomenological, has shown that the apparent and emphatic relationship of many passage tombs with summits, whether on locally high ground, uplands, or mountains, strongly suggests a burial strategy intimately connected with a preference for proximity to the upper cosmological tier, the so-called 'otherworld'. This could imply that cosmic order and cosmological principles were added determining cultural factors for placing the remains of the dead in realms that were closer to an imagined otherworld of the gods above. In my view, numinous summits still retain a spiritual quality which emanates from the prehistoric past and this is surely the essence of any nation's cultural identity and inherited tradition.

Notes

1   Robert Lloyd Praeger, *The Way That I Went: An Irishman in Ireland* (Dublin: Hodges Figgis, 1937), 2–3.

2   Andrew Sleeman, Brian McConnell, and Sarah Gately, *Understanding Earth Processes, Rocks and the Geological History of Ireland* (Dublin: Geological Survey of Ireland, 2004), 76.

3   Chris D. Clark, Jeremy C. Ely, Sarah L. Greenwood, Anna L. C. Hughes, Robert Meehan, Lestyn D. Barr, Mark D. Bateman, et al., 'Britice Glacial Map, Version 2: A Map and GIS Database of Glacial Landforms of the Last British – Irish Ice Sheet', *Boreas* 47, no. 1 (2017): 11–27, e1–8, 23. https://onlinelibrary.wiley.com/doi/epdf/10.1111/bor.12273 (accessed June 2019).

4   Robert T. Meehan, 'Glacial Geomorphology of the Last Irish Ice Sheet', in *Advances in Irish Quaternary Studies*, ed. P. Coxon, S. McCarron and F. Mitchell (Amsterdam: Springer, 2017), 67–101, 156, 165.

5   Marion Dowd and Ruth F. Carden, 'First Evidence of a Late Upper Palaeolithic Human Presence in Ireland', *Quaternary Science Reviews* 139 (2016): 158–63, at 161; M. McClatchie, A. Bogaard, S. Colledge, N. J. Whitehouse, R. J. Schulting, P. Barratt, and T. R. McLaughlin, 'Neolithic Farming in North-Western Europe: New Archaeobotanical Evidence from Ireland', *Journal of Archaeological Science* 51 (2014): 206–15, at 213.

6   Jason L. Toohey, 'Feeding the Mountains: Sacred Landscapes, Mountain Worship, and Sacrifice in the Maya and Inca Worlds', *Reviews in Anthropology* 42 (2013): 161–78, at 162.

7   Gabriel Cooney, *Landscapes of Neolithic Ireland* (London: Routledge, 2000), 12.

8   T. Rowan McLaughlin, Nicki J. Whitehouse, Rick J. Schulting, Meriel McClatchie, Philip Barratt, and Amy Bogaard, 'The Changing Face of Neolithic and Bronze Age Ireland: A Big Data Approach to the Settlement and Burial Records', *Journal of World Prehistory* 29 (2016): 117–53, at 123.

9   S. Blyth, B. Groombridge, I. Lysenko, L. Miles, and A. Newton, *Mountain Watch: Environmental Change and Sustainable Development in Mountains.*

UNEP-WCMC Biodiversity Series 12, 74, https://www.unep-wcmc.org/resources-and-data/mountain-watch--environmental-change-sustainable-development-in-mountains, UNEP-WCMC, 2002 (accessed October 2018).

10　Xavier M. Pellicer, Monica Lee, and Robert Meehan, 'Physiographic Units Map of Ireland'. Geological Survey of Ireland, https://www.gsi.ie/en-ie/events-and-news/news/Pages/Physiographic-Units-Map-of-Ireland.aspx (accessed October 2018).

11　F. H. A. Aalen, Kevin Whelan, and Matthew Stout, *Atlas of the Irish Rural Landscape* (Cork: Cork University Press, 1997), 7.

12　Simon Stuart, 'The Irish 150 Metre Mountain & Hill Database', https://mountainviews.ie/mv/irl150setup.htm (accessed November 2018).

13　Frank Prendergast, 'The Loughcrew Hills and Passage Tomb Complex', in *Irish Quaternary Association Field Guide No. 29: North Meath*, ed. Bettina Stefanini and Gayle Mc Glynn (Dublin: Irish Quaternary Association, 2011), 42–54, at 46.

14　Roderick Peattie, *Mountain Geography: A Critique and Field Study* (Cambridge, MA: Harvard University Press, 1936), 5.

15　Peter Wilson, 'Listing the Irish Hills and Mountains', *Irish Geography* 34, no. 1 (2001): 89–95, at 90.

16　Jasper Knight, 'The Ice Age Inheritance of the Irish Landscape', in *Natural and Cultural Landscapes: The Geological Foundation*, ed. M. A. Parkes, Conference Proceedings, 9–11 September 2002, Dublin Castle (Dublin: Royal Irish Academy, 2004), 29–32, at 29.

17　Frank Mitchell and Michael Ryan, *Reading the Irish Landscape* (Dublin: Town House and Country House, 1997), 71.

18　Marinus L. Otte, 'Introduction', in *Wetlands of Ireland: Distribution, Ecology, Uses and Economic Value*, ed. Marinus L. Otte (Dublin: University College Dublin Press, 2003), 15–19, at 16.

19　Michael O'Connell, 'Early Land Use in North-East County Mayo: The Palaeoecological Evidence', *Proceedings of the Royal Irish Academy* 90C (1990): 259–79, at 263; Nicki J. Whitehouse, Rick J. Schulting, Meriel McClatchie, Phil Barratt, T. Rowan McLaughlin, Amy Bogaard, Sue Colledge, et al., 'Neolithic Agriculture on the European Western Frontier: The Boom and Bust of Early Farming in Ireland', *Journal of Archaeological Science* 51 (2014): 181–205, at 186.

20　Geraldine Stout and Matthew Stout, *Newgrange* (Cork: Cork University Press), 2008, 7.

21　Stefan Bergh, *Landscape of the Monuments: A Study of the Passage Tombs in the Cúil Irra Region, Co. Sligo, Ireland*, Arkeologiska Undersökningar; Skrifter Nr. 6 (Stockholm: Risantikvarieämbetet, 1995), 38–47; Stefan Bergh, *Heritage Guide No. 78: Neolithic Cúil Irra, Co. Sligo–Knocknarea/Carrowmore/Carns Hill* (Bray: Archaeology Ireland, 2017), 2.

22　Peattie, *Mountain Geography*, 20.

23 Bergh, *Landscape of the Monuments*, 156.

24 Gabriel Cooney, 'The Role of Cremation in Mortuary Practice in the Irish Neolithic', in *Transformation by Fire: The Archaeology of Cremation in Cultural Context*, ed. Ian Kuijt, Colin P. Quinn, and Gabriel Cooney (Tucson: University of Arizona Press, 2014), 189–206.

25 Cooney, *Landscapes of Neolithic Ireland*, 148.

26 Michael Herity, *Irish Passage Graves: Neolithic Tomb-Builders in Ireland and Britain 2500 B.C.* (Dublin: Irish University Press, 1974), 8.

27 Frank Prendergast, *Linked Landscapes: Spatial, Archaeoastronomical and Social Network Analysis of the Irish Passage Tomb Tradition*, unpublished PhD thesis (University College Dublin, 2011), 141.

28 Fred Hamond, 'The Colonisation of Europe: The Analysis of Settlement Processes', in *Pattern of the Past: Studies in Honour of David Clarke*, ed. Ian Hodder, Glynn Isaac, and Norman Hammond (Cambridge: Cambridge University Press, 1981), 211–50, at 223.

29 Andreas Koch, 'Autopoietic Spatial Systems: The Significance of Actor Network Theory and System Theory for the Development of a System Theoretical Approach of Space', *Social Geography* 1, no. 1 (2005): 5–14, at 5.

30 Timothy Darvill, *The Concise Oxford Dictionary of Archaeology* (Oxford: Oxford University Press, 2002), 220.

31 Prendergast, *Linked Landscapes*, 56.

32 Peter J. Diggle, *Statistical Analysis of Spatial Point Patterns*, 2nd ed. (London: Arnold, 2003); Brian D. Ripley, *Spatial Statistics* (New York: Wiley, 1981); David Wheatley and Mark Gillings, *Spatial Technology and Archaeology: The Archaeological Applications of GIS* (London: Taylor & Francis, 2002).

33 Prendergast, *Linked Landscapes*.

34 Philip M. Dixon, 'Ripley's K Function', in *Encyclopedia of Environmetrics*, ed. Abdel H. El-Shaarawi and Walter W. Piegorsch (Chichester: John Wiley, 2002): 1796–1803, at 1796.

35 Gabriel Cooney, 'Some Aspects of the Siting of Megalithic Tombs in County Leitrim', *Journal of the Royal Society of Antiquaries of Ireland* 109 (1979): 74–91, at 79; Gabriel Cooney, 'Megalithic Tombs in Their Environmental Setting: A Settlement Perspective', in *Landscape Archaeology in Ireland*, BAR British Series 116, ed. Terence Reeves-Smyth and Fred Hammond (Oxford: BAR, 1983), 179–94, at 183–5; Gabriel Cooney and Eoin Grogan, *Irish Prehistory: A Social Perspective* (Dublin: Wordwell, 1999), 61–3.

36 Seán Ó Nualláin, 'Irish Portal Tombs: Topography, Siting and Distribution', *Journal of the Royal Society of Antiquaries of Ireland* 113 (1983): 84.

37 Bergh, *Landscape of the Monuments*, 130–5.

38　Charles Mount, 'The Environmental Siting of Neolithic and Bronze Age
　　Monuments in the Bricklieve and Moytirra Uplands, County Sligo', *Journal of Irish*
　　Archaeology 7 (1996): 1–11, at 9.

39　Eamon Cody, *Survey of the Megalithic Tombs of Ireland, Volume VI: County Donegal*
　　(Dublin: Stationery Office, 2002), 289.

40　Cooney, 'Megalithic Tombs in Their Environmental Setting', 179–94, at 183–5.

41　Robert Hertz, *Death and the Right Hand*, trans. Rodney and Claudia Needham
　　(Aberdeen: Cohen and West, [1907] 1960), 96; Edward Tregear, *The Maori Race*
　　(Wangunui: A. D. Willis, 1904).

42　Mary Corcoran and George Sevastopulo, 'Provenance of the Stone Used in the
　　Construction and Decoration of Tomb 1', in *Excavations at Knowth 6: The Passage*
　　Tomb Archaeology of the Great Mound at Knowth, ed. George Eogan and Kerri
　　Cleary (Dublin: Royal Irish Academy, 2017), 505–68, at 505.

43　W. R. Lethaby, *Architecture Mysticism and Myth* (New York: Macmillan, 1892), 2.

44　Kent C. Bloomer and Charles W. Moore, *Body, Memory, and Architecture* (New
　　Haven, CT: Yale University Press, 1977), 77.

45　Roman Inscriptions of Britain, https://romaninscriptionsofbritain.org/
　　inscriptions/792 (accessed October 2018).

46　Christian Norberg-Schulz, *Genius Loci: Towards a Phenomenology of Architecture*
　　(London: Academy Editions, 1980), 10, 50–5, 66.

47　RoderickSprague, *Burial Terminology: A Guide for Researchers* (Walnut Creek,
　　CA: Alta Mira Press, 2005), 166; Thomas J. Hannon, 'The Cemetery: A Field of
　　Artifacts', in *Forgotten Places and Things: Archaeological Perspectives on American*
　　History, ed. Albert E. Ward (Albuquerque, NM: Center for Anthropological
　　Studies, 1983), 263–5, at 264.

48　Yi-fu Tuan, *Passing Strange and Wonderful: Aesthetics, Nature, and Culture*
　　(Washington, DC: Shearwater Books, 1993), 137.

49　Peattie, *Mountain Geography*, 20.

50　Darvill, *Concise Oxford Dictionary of Archaeology*, 103.

51　Tore Lomsdalen, 'Different Approaches to Cosmology in Archaeology and Their
　　Application to Maltese Prehistory', in *The Marriage of Astronomy and Culture: Theory*
　　and Method in the Study of Cultural Astronomy, ed. Nicholas Campion
　　(Lampeter: Culture and Cosmos & Sophia Centre Press, 2017), 105–30, at 108.

52　Máire MacNeill, *The Festival of Lughnasa: A Study of the Survival of the Celtic*
　　Festival of the Beginning of Harvest (London: Oxford University Press, 1962), 68.

53　Chris Corlett, 'Prehistoric Pilgrimage to Croagh Patrick', *Archaeology Ireland* 11,
　　no. 2 (1997): 8–11, at 9.

54　MacNeill, *Festival of Lughnasa*, 71; Brian Lacey, *Pocket History of Irish Saints*
　　(Dublin: O'Brien Press, 2003), 30–6, at 32.

55 Frank Prendergast, 'The Stone Rows of the West of Ireland: A Preliminary Archaeoastronomical Analysis', in *Proceedings of the International Conference Oxford VI and SEAC 99, La Laguna*, June 1999, ed. César Esteban and Juan Antonio Belmonte (La Laguna: OACIMC, 2000), 35–42, at 39.

56 J. H. Andrews, *A Paper Landscape: The Ordnance Survey in Nineteenth-Century Ireland*, 2nd ed. (Dublin: Four Courts, 2001), 163.

57 Walter Harris and Charles Smith, *The Ancient and Present State of the County of Down* (Dublin: William Williamson, 1757), 121.

58 MacNeill, *Festival of Lughnasa*, 109.

59 Frank Coyne, *Heritage Guide No. 10: The Paps of Anu – Two Sacred Mountains in County Kerry* (Bray: Archaeology Ireland, 2000), 3.

60 Frédéric Armao, 'Cathair Crobh Dearg: From Ancient Beliefs to the Rounds 2017', *Estudios Irlandeses* 12, no. 2 (2017), 8–31, at 9.

61 Stefan Bergh, 'Transforming Knocknarea – the Archaeology of a Mountain', *Archaeology Ireland* 14, no. 2 (2000), 14–18, at 14.

62 Bergh, *Heritage Guide No. 78*, 3.

63 Dirk Brandherm, Cormac McSparran, Thorsten Kahlert, James Bonsall, Anthony Wilkinson, and Tatjana Kytmannow, 'The Hill of the Faireys', *Archeology Ireland* (Autumn 2018), 30–3, at 31.

64 Tok Thompson, 'The Irish Sí Tradition: Connections between the Disciplines, and What's in a Word', *Journal of Archaeological Method and Theory* 11, no. 4 (2004), 335–68, at 342.

65 Fiontar, *Placenames Database of Ireland* (Dublin City University), https://www.logainm.ie/en/inf/proj-about (accessed November 2018).

66 Tomás Ó Carragáin, *Churches in Early Medieval Ireland: Architecture, Ritual and Memory* (New Haven, CT: Yale University Press, 2010), 131–2; Leo Swan, '2.1 Ecclesiastical Settlement in Ireland in the Early Medieval Period', Paper presented at the Actes du IIIe congrès international d'archéologie médiévale (Aix-en-Provence, 28–30 Septembre 1989), 1994, Société d'Archéologie Médiévale, 50–56, at 53. https://www.persee.fr/doc/acsam_0000-0000_1994_act_3_1_1042.

67 RTE Radio 1, *Ardpatrick Graveyard*. Podcast audio. Countrywide, 2019. https://www.rte.ie/radio1/countrywide/programmes/2019/0105/1020444-countrywide-saturday-5-january-2019/ (accessed January 2019).

Bibliography

Aalen, F. H. A., Kevin Whelan, and Matthew Stout. *Atlas of the Irish Rural Landscape*. Cork: Cork University Press, 1997.

Andrews, J. H. *A Paper Landscape: The Ordnance Survey in Nineteenth-Century Ireland*, 2nd ed. Dublin: Four Courts, 2001.

Armao, Frédéric. 'Cathair Crobh Dearg: From Ancient Beliefs to the Rounds 2017'. *Estudios Irlandeses* 12, no. 2 (2017): 8–31.

Bergh, Stefan. *Landscape of the Monuments: A Study of the Passage Tombs in the Cúil Irra Region, Co. Sligo, Ireland*, Arkeologiska Undersökningar; Skrifter Nr. 6. Stockholm: Risantikvarieämbetet, 1995.

Bergh, Stefan. 'Transforming Knocknarea – the Archaeology of a Mountain'. *Archaeology Ireland* 14, no. 2 (2000): 14–18.

Bergh, Stefan. *Heritage Guide No. 78: Neolithic Cúil Irra, Co. Sligo –Knocknarea/ Carrowmore/Carns Hill*. Bray: Archaeology Ireland, 2017.

Bloomer, Kent C., and Charles W. Moore. *Body, Memory, and Architecture*. New Haven, CT: Yale University Press, 1977.

Blyth, S., B. Groombridge, I. Lysenko, L. Miles, and A. Newton. *Mountain Watch: Environmental Change and Sustainable Development in Mountains*. UNEP-WCMC Biodiversity Series 12. https://www.unep-wcmc.org/resources-and-data/ mountain-watch--environmental-change-sustainable-development-in-mountains, UNEP-WCMC, 2002.

Brandherm, Dirk, Cormac McSparran, Thorsten Kahlert, James Bonsall, Anthony Wilkinson, and Tatjana Kytmannow. 'The Hill of the Faireys'. *Archeology Ireland* 32, no. 3 (Autumn 2018): 30–3.

Clark, Chris D., Jeremy C. Ely, Sarah L. Greenwood, Anna L. C. Hughes, Robert Meehan, Lestyn D. Barr, Mark D. Bateman, et al. 'Britice Glacial Map, Version 2: A Map and GIS Database of Glacial Landforms of the Last British – Irish Ice Sheet'. *Boreas* 47, no. 1 (2017): 11–27, e1–8. https://onlinelibrary.wiley.com/doi/ epdf/10.1111/bor.12273.

Cody, Eamon. *Survey of the Megalithic Tombs of Ireland*. Volume VI: County Donegal. Dublin: Stationery Office, 2002.

Cooney, Gabriel. 'Some Aspects of the Siting of Megalithic Tombs in County Leitrim'. *Journal of the Royal Society of Antiquaries of Ireland* 109 (1979): 74–91.

Cooney, Gabriel. 'Megalithic Tombs in Their Environmental Setting: A Settlement Perspective'. In *Landscape Archaeology in Ireland*, BAR British Series 116, edited by Terence Reeves-Smyth and Fred Hammond, 179–94. Oxford: Archaeopress, 1983.

Cooney, Gabriel. *Landscapes of Neolithic Ireland*. London: Routledge, 2000.

Cooney, Gabriel. 'The Role of Cremation in Mortuary Practice in the Irish Neolithic'. In *Transformation by Fire: The Archaeology of Cremation in Cultural Context*, edited by Ian Kuijt, Colin P. Quinn and Gabriel Cooney, 189–206. Tucson: University of Arizona Press, 2014.

Cooney, Gabriel, and Eoin Grogan. *Irish Prehistory: A Social Perspective*. Dublin: Wordwell, 1999.

Corcoran, Mary, and George Sevastopulo. 'Provenance of the Stone Used in the Construction and Decoration of Tomb 1'. In *Excavations at Knowth 6: The Passage*

Tomb Archaeology of the Great Mound at Knowth, edited by George Eogan and Kerri Cleary, 505–68. Dublin: Royal Irish Academy, 2017.

Corlett, Chris. 'Prehistoric Pilgrimage to Croagh Patrick'. *Archaeology Ireland* 11, no. 2 (1997): 8–11.

Coyne, Frank. *Heritage Guide No. 10: The Paps of Anu – Two Sacred Mountains in County Kerry*. Bray: Archaeology Ireland, 2000.

Darvill, Timothy. *The Concise Oxford Dictionary of Archaeology*. Oxford: Oxford University Press, 2002.

Diggle, Peter J. *Statistical Analysis of Spatial Point Patterns*, 2nd ed. London: Arnold, 2003.

Dixon, Philip M. 'Ripley's K Function'. In *Encyclopedia of Environmetrics*, edited by Abdel H. El-Shaarawi and Walter W. Piegorsch, 1796–803. Chichester: John Wiley, 2002.

Dowd, Marion, and Ruth F. Carden. 'First Evidence of a Late Upper Palaeolithic Human Presence in Ireland'. *Quaternary Science Reviews* 139 (2016): 158–63.

Fiontar (Dublin City University). 'Placenames Database of Ireland'. http://www. logainm.ie/en/inf/proj-about (accessed 10 August 2019).

Hamond, Fred. 'The Colonisation of Europe: The Analysis of Settlement Processes'. In *Pattern of the Past: Studies in Honour of David Clarke*, edited by Ian Hodder, Glynn Isaac and Norman Hammond, 211–50. Cambridge: Cambridge University Press, 1981.

Hannon, Thomas J. 'The Cemetery: A Field of Artifacts'. In *Forgotten Places and Things: Archaeological Perspectives on American History*, edited by Albert E. Ward, 263–65. Albuquerque, NM: Center for Anthropological Studies, 1983.

Harris, Walter, and Charles Smith. *The Ancient and Present State of the County of Down*. Dublin: William Williamson, 1757.

Herity, Michael. *Irish Passage Graves: Neolithic Tomb-Builders in Ireland and Britain 2500 B.C.* Dublin: Irish University Press, 1974.

Hertz, Robert. *Death and the Right Hand*, translated by Rodney and Claudia Needham. Aberdeen: Cohen and West, [1907] 1960.

Knight, Jasper. 'The Ice Age Inheritance of the Irish Landscape'. In *Natural and Cultural Landscapes: The Geological Foundation*, edited by M. A. Parkes. Conference Proceedings, 9–11 September 2002, Dublin Castle, 29–32. Dublin: Royal Irish Academy, 2004.

Koch, Andreas. 'Autopoietic Spatial Systems: The Significance of Actor Network Theory and System Theory for the Development of a System Theoretical Approach of Space'. *Social Geography* 1, no. 1 (2005): 5–14.

Lacey, Brian. *Pocket History of Irish Saints*. Dublin: O'Brien Press, 2003.

Lethaby, W. R. *Architecture Mysticism and Myth*. New York: Macmillan, 1892.

Lomsdalen, Tore. 'Different Approaches to Cosmology in Archaeology and Their Application to Maltese Prehistory'. In *The Marriage of Astronomy and*

Culture: *Theory and Method in the Study of Cultural Astronomy*, edited by Nicholas Campion, 105–30. Lampeter: Culture and Cosmos and Sophia Centre Press, 2017.

MacNeill, Máire. *The Festival of Lughnasa: A Study of the Survival of the Celtic Festival of the Beginning of Harvest*. London: Oxford University Press, 1962.

McClatchie, M., A. Bogaard, S. Colledge, N. J. Whitehouse, R. J. Schulting, P. Barratt, and T. R. McLaughlin. 'Neolithic Farming in North-Western Europe: New Archaeobotanical Evidence from Ireland'. *Journal of Archaeological Science* 51 (2014): 206–15.

McLaughlin, T. Rowan, Nicki J. Whitehouse, Rick J. Schulting, Meriel McClatchie, Philip Barratt, and Amy Bogaard. 'The Changing Face of Neolithic and Bronze Age Ireland: A Big Data Approach to the Settlement and Burial Records'. *Journal of World Prehistory* 29 (2016): 117–53.

Meehan, Robert T. 'Glacial Geomorphology of the Last Irish Ice Sheet'. In *Advances in Irish Quaternary Studies*, edited by P. Coxon, S. McCarron and F. Mitchell, 67–101. Amsterdam: Springer, 2017.

Mitchell, Frank, and Michael Ryan. *Reading the Irish Landscape*. Dublin: Town House and Country House, 1997.

Mount, Charles. 'The Environmental Siting of Neolithic and Bronze Age Monuments in the Bricklieve and Moytirra Uplands, County Sligo'. *Journal of Irish Archaeology* 7 (1996): 1–11.

Norberg-Schulz, Christian. *Genius Loci: Towards a Phenomenology of Architecture*. London: Academy Editions, 1980.

O'Connell, Michael. 'Early Land Use in North-East County Mayo: The Palaeoecological Evidence'. *Proceedings of the Royal Irish Academy* 90C (1990): 259–79.

Ó Carragáin, Tomás. *Churches in Early Medieval Ireland: Architecture, Ritual and Memory*. New Haven, CT: Yale University Press, 2010.

Ó Nualláin, Seán. 'Irish Portal Tombs: Topography, Siting and Distribution'. *Journal of the Royal Society of Antiquaries of Ireland* 113 (1983): 75–105.

Otte, Marinus L., 'Life in Wetland Environments'. In *Wetlands of Ireland: Distribution, Ecology, Uses and Economic Value*, edited by Marinus L. Otte, 15–19. Dublin: University College Dublin Press, 2003.

Peattie, Roderick. *Mountain Geography: A Critique and Field Study*. Cambridge, MA: Harvard University Press, 1936.

Pellicer, Xavier M., Monica Lee, and Robert Meehan. 'Physiographic Units Map of Ireland'. Geological Survey of Ireland. https://www.gsi.ie/en-ie/events-and-news/news/Pages/Physiographic-Units-Map-of-Ireland.aspx (accessed 20 August 2019).

Praeger, Robert Lloyd. *The Way That I Went: An Irishman in Ireland*. Dublin: Hodges Figgis, 1937.

Prendergast, Frank. 'Linked Landscapes: Spatial, Archaeoastronomical and Social Network Analysis of the Irish Passage Tomb Tradition'. Unpublished PhD thesis. University College Dublin, 2011.

Prendergast, Frank. 'The Loughcrew Hills and Passage Tomb Complex'. In *Irish Quaternary Association Field Guide No. 29: North Meath*, edited by Bettina Stefanini and Gayle Mc Glynn, 42–54. Dublin: Irish Quaternary Association, 2011.

Prendergast, Frank. 'The Stone Rows of the West of Ireland: A Preliminary Archaeoastronomical Analysis'. In *Proceedings of the International Conference Oxford Vi and Seac 99, La Laguna*, June 1999, edited by César Esteban and Juan Antonio Belmonte, 35–42. La Laguna: OACIMC, 2000.

Ripley, Brian D. *Spatial Statistics*. New York: Wiley, 1981.

Roman Inscriptions of Britain. https://romaninscriptionsofbritain.org/inscriptions/792 (accessed 15 August 2019).

RTE Radio 1. *Ardpatrick Graveyard*. Podcast audio. Countrywide, 2019.

Sleeman, Andrew, Brian McConnell, and Sarah Gately. *Understanding Earth Processes, Rocks and the Geological History of Ireland*. Dublin: Geological Survey of Ireland, 2004.

Sprague, Roderick. *Burial Terminology: A Guide for Researchers*. Walnut Creek, CA: Alta Mira Press, 2005.

Stout, Geraldine, and Matthew Stout. *Newgrange*. Cork: Cork University Press, 2008.

Stuart, Simon. 'The Irish 150 Metre Mountain & Hill Database'. https://mountainviews. ie/mv/irl150setup.htm (accessed 1 August 2019).

Swan, Leo. 'Ecclesiastical Settlement in Ireland in the Early Medieval Period'. In *L'environnement Des Églises Et La Topographie Religieuse Des Campagnes Médiévales. Actes Du Iiie Congrès International D'archéologie Médiévale* (Aix-Enprovence, 28–30 Septembre 1989), edited by Société d'Archéologie Médiévale, 50–56. https:// www.persee.fr/doc/acsam_0000-0000_1994_act_3_1_1042, Société d'archéologie médiévale, 1994.

Thompson, Tok. 'The Irish Sí Tradition: Connections between the Disciplines, and What's in a Word?'. *Journal of Archaeological Method and Theory* 11, no. 4 (2004): 335–68.

Toohey, Jason L. 'Feeding the Mountains: Sacred Landscapes, Mountain Worship, and Sacrifice in the Maya and Inca Worlds'. *Reviews in Anthropology* 42 (2013): 161–78.

Tregear, Edward. *The Maori Race*. Wangunui: A. D. Willis, 1904.

Tuan, Yi-fu. *Passing Strange and Wonderful: Aesthetics, Nature, and Culture*. Washington, DC: Shearwater Books, 1993.

Wheatley, David, and Mark Gillings. *Spatial Technology and Archaeology: The Archaeological Applications of GIS*. London: Taylor & Francis, 2002.

Whitehouse, Nicki J., Rick J. Schulting, Meriel McClatchie, Phil Barratt, T. Rowan McLaughlin, Amy Bogaard, Sue Colledge, et al. 'Neolithic Agriculture on the European Western Frontier: The Boom and Bust of Early Farming in Ireland'. *Journal of Archaeological Science* 51 (2014): 181–205.

Wilson, Peter. 'Listing the Irish Hills and Mountains'. *Irish Geography* 34, no. 1 (2001): 89–95.

2

How the shadow of the mountains created sacred spaces in Early Bronze Age Scotland

J. Anna Estaroth

Introduction

The mountainous Highlands of Scotland have lost part of their past, socially, culturally, and ecologically, through mass emigration, land clearance, and deforestation. Yet they retain elements of the past through megalithic monuments, legends, and fossils. This loss and part-preservation is exemplified by the enigmatic Clava cairns of the Central Highlands. The name Clava derives from the Clava valley with the best-preserved cairns at Balnuaran of Clava (hereafter Balnuaran) (Map 2.1). Clava refers to the cairns themselves and specifically this River Nairn valley, which has multiple cairns. Alexander MacGregor explained that Clava is Scottish Gaelic for good, meaning the stones of the Good Neighbours or fairy folk: places where the *Sìth* (pronounced shee) could enter and exit the *Sìthean* (pronounced shee-an) realm, tracing these tales back to 1200 CE, although possibly sixth century CE in origin or even earlier.[1] The *Sìth* were thought to reside under the earth and within the mountains. Indeed, George Bain described Clava cairns as places of transition, liminal in nature, and dangerous to frequent, in case of transportation to the *Sìthean* otherworld, which operated at a different time.[2] This connects Clava cairns with notions of second sight, or more correctly two-sightedness, which Alexander Mackenzie defined as the ability to see what occurs in this place and time, while being aware of what occurs in the *Sìthean* otherworld.[3] The classic authority on second sight and the Gaelic fairy world was Robert Kirk who said the *Sìth* 'live much longer than wee', and multiple legends describe humans who physically transferred to the otherworld, apparently for days, returning a hundred years later.[4] Therefore,

Clava cairns were associated for centuries with notions of time – both altered experiences of time and as locations of timelessness. Current calendrical notions of time often relate to the sun (year) and moon (month); and although *Sithean* legends postdate cairn building, they hint at something as relevant then as today – sol/lunar orientations at significant times of the year.

This landscape is dominated by mountains, scarred during the ice age and traversed by rivers largely flowing from south-west to north-east, which, Alan McKirdy explained, was the direction of glacial melt when the ice age ended.[5] As these mountains are where the moon visually appears to enter and exit the earth in a unique way, they give the impression of offering themselves as a source of power, which in turn appears to transfer to the cairns and thence to humans. Placing myself into that mountainous landscape, a vibrant boundary between land and sky, I undertook fieldwork between December 2014 and October 2016, in order to explore the skyscapes of the region's rivers for comparison with Balnuaran. By exploring the Clava landscape, my primary aim with this research was to investigate the relationship between the mountains and the moon, and thus between the *Sithean* realm and time.

I was also interested in investigating the Clava cairns from an archaeological perspective, within their environment and their relationship with the sky, how they orientate to the sun and moon on the horizon. Midsummer and midwinter solstices occur when the sun, viewed from the earth, appears to be at a standstill on the horizon, prior to reversing direction. The moon also appears to reverse direction along the horizon, in a cyclical dance. In the northern hemisphere the moon reaches the most southerly extreme in summer and its most northerly extreme in winter on specific years, known as major limit years (hereafter major limit). Halfway through this cycle, it reaches the least southerly and least northerly positions, during minor limit years (hereafter minor limit). Clava cairns were built in the Early Bronze Age as ring cairns and passage graves. Richard Bradley noticed that they share similar architectural features with Knocknarea in Ireland and Maeshowe in Orkney.[6] Bradley also recognized that midwinter sunset orientations, at Balnuaran's passage graves, resemble the earlier, Neolithic structures of Maeshowe, Durrington Walls, and Stonehenge.[7] However, the comparable major limit backdrop connects them with Gerald Hawkins' explorations at *Tursachan Calanais* or Callanish I (hereafter Calanais).[8] Clive Ruggles referred to the full moon occurring nearest midsummer during major limit as 'midsummer full moon' (hereafter midsummer full moon) with both Ruggles and Aubrey Burl describing Clava cairn lunar orientations.[9] Burl recognized that many Clava cairns are sol/lunar-orientated, but at Balnuaran many scholars have focused almost exclusively on midwinter sunset alignments, without considering potential lunar directions.[10] Ruggles argued that Balnuaran was exceptional – mainly due to the size, shape and coloured stone arrangements.[11] Thus, the secondary aim of my research was to explore Balnuaran's uniqueness from a lunar perspective and to see whether my finding of midsummer full moon hill shadow earmarked Clava valley as exceptionally sacred space, in comparison with other Clava cairns.[12]

Other Scottish monuments exhibit interesting lunar phenomena. James Cornell described the midsummer full moon as skimming, as it travelled along the tops of the southerly hills at Calanais.[13] During major limit years the moon is high in the sky near midwinter and low near midsummer, when it often appears to skim along the horizon, sometimes disappearing altogether behind sufficiently high mountains. This cycle occurs regularly every 18.61 years. Attending the last Calanais skimming moon event in 2006 stimulated my interest in this phenomenon. The full moon dramatically appeared to journey along the hilltops vanishing into Mount Clisham, looking as though the moon was kissing the earth. Ruggles observed that the midsummer full moon looks largest near the horizon and 'there is a feeling of the celestial and terrestrial coming together, being in direct association' and, for me, this cogently described my experience of that event.[14] Scotland's northern latitude and the earth's curvature combine to produce an exceptionally low midsummer full moon, which disappears or reappears as southerly hills intervene, hills which resemble a reclining figure at Calanais.

Whether the shape of the hills or the Moon's apparent journey along them was most significant to the builders at Calanais is unknown. Discussing this landscape, Colin Richards, Adrian Challands, and Kate Welham stated that the builders lived in 'a vibrant living material world, where people not only encountered things and substance perceived to be animate', they connected with potentially ancestral relations so that the agency engages both the human and natural world and in these circumstances 'people were not merely part of landscapes; they were participants in an intimate and reciprocal relationship'.[15] With this in mind I journeyed along the Clava region's rivers, with often steep-sided valleys, where lunar skimming might occur, becoming familiar with the regional topography and gathering data enabling comparisons with cairn sites. I wanted to test how the midsummer full moon was perceived on the southerly horizon, for the whole Clava region, in order to ascertain whether Balnuaran's darkness was normal for these latitudes and in this district. Therefore, both my primary and secondary aims focus on the southern horizon: whether hilltops generated visible moonlight or darkness at cairns. However, my tertiary goal was in considering in what way these phenomena might have been experienced by Bronze Age people, generating a subsidiary objective: to try to ascertain whether different Clava cairn styles (passage grave versus ring cairn) had different functions or seasonal significance.

Clava cairns and the landscape of the *Sìth*

Clava cairns were recognized by Audrey Shore Henshall as predominantly riverine and their territory is primarily around Inverness, although it also stretches southwards along the river Spey (Map 2.1).[16] Mountainous terrain could have prevented them being built elsewhere, or rivers may have been integral to their accessibility, providing pilgrimage routes and potentially playing a part in their ceremonial life. Clava cairns are a concise cultural group with Henshall listing forty-three monuments.[17] They comprise a central chamber or open space, a cairn (with or without a passage), a peristalith, and a platform surrounded by a free-standing stone circle. Only one cairn, Belladrum North, has no known circle. Their defining feature is that both the circle orthostats (large stone

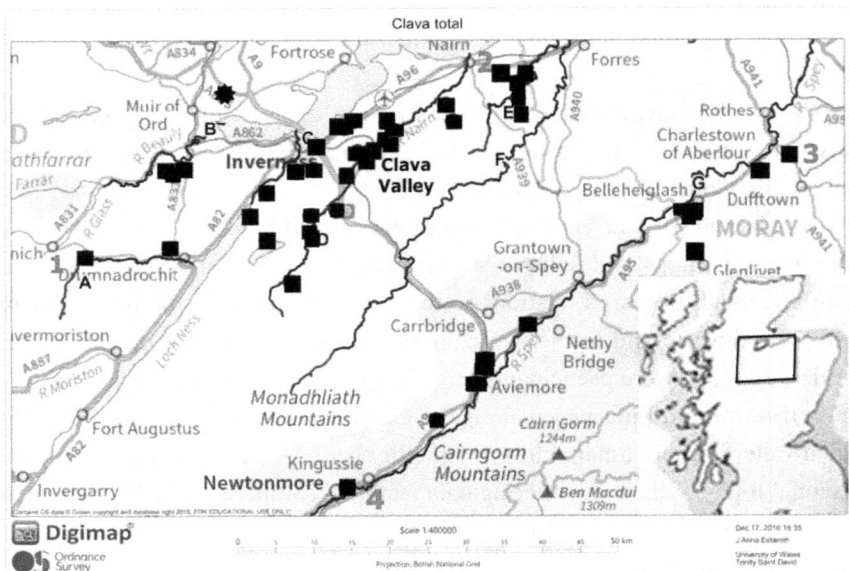

Map 2.1 Clava cairn distribution. © Crown Copyright. Digimap © Crown Copyright and Landmark Information Group Limited (2020). All rights reserved (2017).

uprights) and those surrounding the cairn base (peristalith orthostats) taper in size from smallest in the north-east to tallest in the south-west. This north-east/south-west orientation was recognized and described by Bradley, Henshall, and Ruggles.[18] The south-west emphasis suggests the builder's intentional utilization of the setting midwinter sun and midsummer full moon. A south-east orientation would have implied their rising and a northern emphasis would have indicated alternate seasons.

This is a landscape where the past is always present; thousands of years of human settlement leave tangible traces today, such as field systems, hut circles, and cairns. According to Jennifer Westwood and Sophia Kingshill, Clava cairns were 'said to mark the burial place of the family of the sixth century Pictish King Brude ... due to the digging up of a gold rod during some drainage operations near the site'.[19] Historically, King Brude converted to Christianity with St Columba, and the actual Pictish burial at Balnuaran, found by Bradley, is probably incidental.[20] Richard Hayman noted that Pictish kings were crowned at Grenish clava ring cairn and commented that this traditional conferring of regal authority, via ancient stone, continues unbroken today with the crowning of British monarchs over the Stone of Scone.[21] Bearing in mind that Grenish ring cairn received its power from the moon, via the mountains, it is that essence which was transferred to human monarchs. However, Stephen Driscoll argued that incorporating Grenish into their ceremonial landscape allowed the Picts to extend control over the area.[22] Therefore, the sacred meaning of the site was subsumed to serve Pictish political ends.

Another local tradition was recorded by Bain: at full moon the *Sithean* road, linking two ancient monuments, was traversed by the fairy procession and if humans encountered the ancestral *Sith* they would be transported at the termini to the *Sithean* realm.[23] That road still links Little Urchany clava ring cairn to Shian Hillock, a neolithic tumulus, which have different sol-lunar seasonal connections (midwinter sunset and midsummer full moon, respectively). Consequently, I theorized that cairns might have seasonal links and were perhaps designed to suit summer or winter rituals. This does not imply that cairn builders saw them as entrances and exits between worlds; these legends arose much later. It continues the theme of the passing of power, from moon to mountain, to cairn to humans, but in this case from humans to cairn and to mountain and celestial objects.

Kirk discussed how the *Sith* were best seen at twilight (British summer nights are permanently in twilight) and they always travelled at the change of the seasons, around the wheel of the year.[24] Although Kirk's ideas may seem fanciful, they touch upon something potentially inherently sacred, seasonal significance, and midsummer full moons. Robert Stewart, a biographer of Kirk, explained that Kirk was an Episcopalian minister who reconciled his Renaissance education with deeply felt religious teachings. Stewart argued that Kirk's seasonal changes meant midsummer, midwinter, the equinoxes, and those dates 'marked by the rising and setting of the Pleiades, celebrated in May and November'.[25] Balnuaran Central ring cairn has stones aligned with the solstices, equinoxes, Sirius, and the Pleiades. Kirk considered the *Sith* as being between Man and Angels and argued cogently for an interconnectedness between everything, 'Tis ane of their Tenets, that nothing perisheth, but (as the Sun and year) every Thing goes in a Circle, lesser or greater, and is renewed and refreshed in its Revolutions'.[26] This remarkably modern perspective implied a holistic approach to the universe. Kirk provided fairy lore to counter the growing atheism of his age. Regarding other-worldly beings Kirk said, 'All ages have offered some obscure testimonies of it, such as Pythagoras' Doctrine of transmigration; Socrates' Daemone that gave him precautions of future dangers; Plato's classing them as various vehiculated species of Spirit', and he included controversial ideas which he justified with biblical quotations.[27]

Conversely Keith Thomas saw 'fairy-beliefs as self-confirming' and their elusiveness enabled fraudsters to take advantage of the credulous.[28] The nineteenth century's prevailing religious attitudes became largely dismissive of second sight, condemning it as a Scottish phenomenon, although it resembles Greek concepts of *Mantike* or oracular divination. Kirk firmly believed in the *Sithean* otherworld, and his death on Doon Fairy-hill made it a place of modern pilgrimage. Belief in time-crossing double vision continues today. Shari Cohn's twentieth-century study of 130 families found 'an acceptance of the existence of second sight within the community'.[29]

Archaeology of Clava cairns

Balnuaran's three Early Bronze Age monuments are the most researched. Clava territory ranges from Corrimony passage grave in the west to Buchromb ring cairn in the east and from Mains of Moyness ring cairn in the north to Altlarie ring cairn in the south (Map 2.1). There is one disputed Clava-type cairn, north of the Moray Firth (Map 2.1). To the north and west Neolithic cairns of the Orkney-Cromarty variety were recorded by Henshall and to the east are Recumbent Stone Circles, which predated, paralleled, and potentially post-dated Clava cairn construction.[30] Scattered among the Clava cairns are many Late Bronze Age round cairns (c.1000 BCE), hut circles and field systems, plus undated henges, burnt mounds, tumuli, and crannogs. Cairns are sufficiently small that they could have been erected by an extended family group, unlike larger monuments such as Maeshowe or Stonehenge. Derek Simpson discovered a Neolithic building beneath the excavated cairn at Raigmore, potentially the builders' ancestral home.[31]

The majority of Clava cairns have not been radiocarbon-dated. Where recent excavations provided dating, they consistently indicated construction in the Early Bronze Age. Bradley reported Newton of Petty's radiocarbon dates being between 2340 and 2030 cal. BCE, but deduced that the main construction period at Balnuaran was c.2000 BCE with extensive reuse about a thousand years later.[32] Bradley's excavations at the three Early Bronze Age Balnuaran cairns confirmed that they were coetaneous; the cairns and circles were built together and all three interlinked.[33] There is no evidence that the cairns were initially constructed as tombs; all burial activities appear to be secondary usage and their initial purpose is unknown.

The Central Highland location meant that Early Bronze Age inhabitants could control the northern access to Loch Ness, an inland water route between east and west. To the south-west it connected with Ireland, the west coasts of England and Wales, through the Irish Sea and Kilmartin Glen. To the north-west it connected with the North Sea, Isles of Orkney and Shetland, Scandinavia, and the western European seaboard. Stuart Needham described Clava's location as pivotal in controlling early bronze trade routes, and the earliest British bronze items were found at sites in north-east Scotland.[34] While mountains are barriers to travel, rivers and lochs provide excellent transport. The materials were probably transported along both Loch Ness and River Spey, as the Hebridean sea route is notoriously dangerous.

Several factors combine to make Balnuaran unique, notably the large number of cup-marked stones and Balnuaran Central ring cairn's rays. Ruggles described Balnuaran's cairns as larger than most, incorporating coloured stonework.[35] Externally many kerbstones and passage stones that face the setting sun are pink, while internally red stones are favoured on the left with whiter stones on the right. Bradley suggested that cairn stones facing the rising sun tended to be white, pink, or grey and included minerals such as quartz to reflect light, while those caught by the setting sun were largely red and appeared to absorb light.[36] Thus light was at the core of Clava cairn construction. Bradley also noted that circle stones matched their kerb counterparts by colour and shape, plus quartz appears where midsummer sunrise hits the monuments.[37] Quartz makes stones sparkle and would have been dramatic when originally built and this positioning resembles the quartz facade at Newgrange in Ireland, which catches midwinter sunrise.[38] Most Clava cairns are not intervisible; their close proximity to one another in the Clava valley is exceptional. Bradley discovered a particular construction sequence, the use of large dressed stones in the south-west with rough small stones in the north-east, making the south-west emphasis even more marked, and suggested that the number twelve may have been important because the passage and the foundation course of the chamber consisted of twelve stones, whereas the peristalith orthostats tended to be forty-eight, a multiple of twelve.[39] It is unknown what number twelve meant to Early Bronze Age people, although worth exploring whether this occurs elsewhere.

Sacred narrative of Clava cairns

Claudia Moser and Cecilia Feldman described sacred spaces as derived from 'past and present interactions among humans, material implements, architecture, and landscape'.[40] The repetition of ritual reinforces a location's significance – attracting humans through pilgrimage and strengthening family/clan ties with the land. This is exemplified by the Pictish reclaiming of Grenish and the extensive *Sìth* legends. Ian Straughan said such (sacred) 'places happen not only through manipulation of the physical environment but through the weaving of narratives; they are at once hewn from stone and carved from story'.[41] Several narratives surrounding Clava cairns describe warnings against removing wood from nearby trees, turf from certain hills and stones from cairns, for fear of upsetting the *Sìth*. Local legends probably prevented excessive robbing of orthostats. Henshall suggested that the greatest loss of cairn material occurred relatively recently, during the nineteenth-century railway-building period.[42] Cairns were landmarks, often used as gathering places in preparation for battle, for Christian worship and for settling differences. Richard Oram described how Easter Kingussie cairn (since destroyed by flood) was utilized on the 10 October 1380 by Alexander Stewart, the Wolf of Badenoch, who convened his court to settle a legal dispute with Alexander Bur, the Bishop of Moray.[43] Apparently the stones conferred a higher authority than church or state (Alexander Stewart's brother was king). Perhaps it was the only safe neutral ground.

Balnuaran's celestial connections provide what Yi-Fu Tuan referred to as mythic space: a place connected with astronomy (sun, moon, and stars), cosmogony (pertaining to origins) and with human consciousness (how we experience it).[44]As the *Sìth* were considered ancestors, they epitomized the cosmogonic role of the cairns. Balnuaran's sacredness is exemplified by the continued use of the site for burial. In addition to Late Bronze Age and Iron Age burials, Milton of Clava South became a mediaeval Catholic Chapel with burial ground, probably used until the Reformation. Burials continued into the mid-nineteenth century as, according to George and Peter Anderson, local unbaptized children were still buried near this disused chapel.[45] Because unbaptized babies were barred from churchyards, such secret burials were common practice. Building a chapel from a cairn indicates a continued sense of a sacred location. In addition, during 1990s excavations, Bradley found modern visitor offerings such as coins and gemstones, which is comparable to the ancient tradition of votive offerings.[46] This implies that some people continue to venerate cairn sites today and that over four thousand years, humans have intermittently selected these sites to deposit their dead. Everything about Balnuaran indicates sacredness, from the quantity and quality of the cairns, their reuse, their interconnectedness, and their association with the *Sìth*, implying a celestial and otherworld connection. While undertaking fieldwork at Balnuaran my sense was that, nestled between the hills, Balnuaran is cut-off, separated from modern life, and even the shadows of the Victorian-planted trees (quite incorrectly thought appropriate for druid centres) add to this sense of otherworldiness. The entire valley seems to exude the agency of the hills. Thus, Stewart's comment that 'otherworlds were places of beauty, timelessness, light and power' not only applies to most Clava cairn locations but especially to Balnuaran.

There are two distinct types of Clava cairns, ring cairns and passage graves, and both are surrounded by free-standing stone circles. Ring cairns have no passage and their central spaces are open to the sky all year round, while passage graves are closed beehive-shaped cairns (Figure 2.1). Passage graves have lost their roofs, but were once dome-shaped equivalents of man-made caves. Chris Scarre recognized burial chambers as doorways to the otherworld, places for 'contact with otherworldly beings'.[47]The passage grave entrance was by crawling, suggesting an initiatory usage for rites of passage. In addition, acoustics alter considerably whenever other people are in the same chamber. Little sound penetrates the circular chambers, even today with their open roofs, so when they were fully enclosed the chamber's otherworldliness was reinforced by considerable sound isolation. Chris Fowler and Vicki Cummings considered the acoustics, rock art, and low lighting of chambered tombs, finding them appropriate places for 'altered states of consciousness and trance'.[48] Standing inside them they are decidedly liminal locations, with darkness generating an otherworldly connection. Cummings suggested three realms: the living realm, the upper realm of sky, birds, and spirits, and the lower realm of 'Underworld Rivers, caves and the dead'.[49] Passage graves appear to transect all three realms, thus making them suitable for rites of passage or private, secret, transformational rituals. Passage tombs were also considered as transitional places by Bronwen Price, who described them as caught between earth and sky, between 'present and ancestral realms or childhood and adulthood'.[50] Passage graves are exclusive and suit internal contemplation and connecting with the *Sìth*, while open-air ring cairns appear better adapted to inclusive open activities. From my experience, viewing the mountains from within ring cairns encourages a sense of expansiveness and connectedness. New moon nearest midwinter is the darkest phase of the year, while full moon nearest midsummer is the lightest period. My experience of the 2006 midsummer full moon at Calanais was warm, noisy, light, and communal, contrasting with the 2015 minor new moon at Balnuaran which was cold, quiet, dark, and solitary. Both were enriching, although different, experiences.

Bradley found that passage graves at Balnuaran were intentionally part-closed within fifty years of their construction, allowing light into the central chamber, but not humans.[51] The ring cairn centre was also infilled at some stage. This radically altered the ritual landscape. The most sacred areas where few could congregate (within the cairns) were off limits, but the areas between cairn and stone circle remained accessible for larger numbers of people. Bradley found evidence of fire in the forecourts of post-closure passage graves, independent of reuse, such as cremation activities.[52] By using bonfires to light up the dark cairn centre, prehistoric people may have deliberately echoed the action of the midwinter sun. During major limit years, the sun and full moon exchange their light-giving dominance. In winter, the sun is barely above the hilltop (parts of some valleys remain dark for months) and the full moon becomes the dominant light-giver, high in the sky. In summer the sun is the dominant light-giver, reaching high altitudes while the full moon barely rises over the horizon. For Clava cairn builders this seasonal juxtaposition of light and dark appeared important.

Methodology

Journeying along selected rivers within Clava territory allowed me to map the southerly hills and to understand what happened at midsummer full moon. Six of the seven selected rivers conformed to the prevailing geological south-west/ north-east orientation, with rivers flowing north-east into the Moray and Beauly Firths (Map 2.1). The east-west Ettrick was included because of Corrimony passage grave. Two short rivers lacking Clava cairns were deselected, although the lengthy Findhorn was chosen to explore this absence. Potentially Clava cairns dotted the coastal plains, but millennia of flooding have eliminated any evidence, so three coastal cairns were excluded. At every turn along the rivers, where the topography significantly altered, I took a series of measurements along the southern hilltops, to ascertain mountain heights and whether the midsummer full moon was visible. This generated one hundred road/riverside measurements indicating prevailing conditions, comparable with cairn sites. For example, at Clava valley, high hills make the midsummer full moon invisible, casting the valley into dark hill shadow. I used statistical analyses, Digimaps, the software Stellarium, and HeyWhatsThat.

I selected the least damaged cairns, situated along riverbanks, with reasonable access and surveyed thirty-eight cairns, twenty-five of which were Clava cairns. Some were excluded in advance, because dense forest surroundings impeded horizon measurements. Others had eroded altogether or were in fields containing standing crops. Repeated attempts at some sites were thwarted, when adverse weather conditions (snow or fog) obscured the horizon. The criteria for inclusion became proximity to a river and accessibility. Thus cairn inclusion was more organic than rigorous. I included thirteen non-Clava cairns because passing them was inevitable. In mountainous regions the choice of routes and cairn-building spaces is restricted to river proximity. For example, Little Urchany was included because it was along a shortcut between the Nairn and the Muckleburn, which later transpired to be the *Sìth* road.

I measured each cairn passage with a compass (measuring width), a clinometer (measuring height) and a GPS locator. Measurements were converted to true north and astronomical declination (celestial objects in relation to the earth) to ascertain accurate sol/lunar/stellar locations vis-à-vis the cairns and mountains. Two measurements were taken diagonally along the passages from the stone slabs marking the entrance to their opposite slabs at the opening to the chamber, in order to designate the shape and size of the horizon (or sky) visible from the chamber. This generated a window of visibility, which Fabio Silva defined as 'the region of the horizon, given the structure's corridor and entrance geometry, which can be seen from within its chamber'.[53] Similarly both sides of the largest circle orthostat were measured from the diagonally opposing sides of the largest peristalith orthostat, to see what section of sky was demarcated. By undertaking these cairn measurements, I was able to explore previous scholarly research, replicating some measurements and generating new on-site data in order to understanding how the shadow of the mountains might create sacred spaces in the Clava region.

I adopted a phenomenological approach. Christopher Tilley explained that phenomenology is the 'understanding and description of things as they are experienced by a subject'.[54] Clava cairns have engendered a sense of inspiration. For instance, Alexander Meldrum recommended visiting Balnuaran by moonlight to experience their eerie mystery and commented that a day visit 'can induce an almost uncanny atmosphere of the distant past'.[55] Conversely Bradley noted that they can evoke either frank bewilderment, as evidenced by a coach party mistaking the cairns for Culloden battle graves, or awe, indicated by individuals meditating and undertaking shamanic ceremonies.[56] Achieving a semi-meditative state at cairns allowed sounds to intensify: wind, rustling bushes, birdsong, racing rivers. Tilley recommended blending sensual experiences to enhance exploring the interchange between the body and the world.[57] My intention was to achieve a deep immersion into the landscape, hoping to discover insights into how it may have been utilized in the past. Not only did I listen, but I drew sketches to deepen my observation and fully engage my senses. Where possible I undertook repeated visits to cairns to expand my understanding.

I frequently experienced a temporal distortion at the Clava cairns or time-lived-differently; what appeared to be a short while turned out to be several hours. One might call this time dilation as opposed to time contraction. Bain might have described this as *Sìthean* altered time.[58] I devoted time to just being there, aware of alternative perceptions, such as that of birds and animals, for according to Tim Ingold, different creatures 'attend to the world in different ways'.[59] For example, on an overcast predawn near midsummer at Balnuaran, an oyster catcher accompanied me into the enclosure, flitting from stone to stone. With its mate they flew a dramatic dawn chorus display, swooping within arm's length, knee-high around me, and then soaring above the monuments and fields and repeating this several times. Remembering their song I still feel saturated by the experience. All three of us, the two birds and I, experienced Balnuaran differently that day; Ingold might have called them fellow participants.[60] This is what David Abram described as 'intersubjective phenomena – phenomena experienced by a multiplicity of sensing subjects'.[61]Despite the housing development built around Aviemore ring cairn, and Culbernie ring cairn being in a private garden, human habitation near cairns dwarfs in comparison with the extent of wildlife interactions. The ever-present hills dominate the senses, changing the auditory experience: winds and sounds flow like water, swirling, gusting, and buffeting along the valleys, at times enriched, dampened, funnelled, or focused.

Consideration of fieldwork outcomes

I surveyed seven rivers: Beauly, Ettrick, Ness, Nairn, Muckleburn, Findhorn, and Spey (Map 2.1). All, except the Ettrick, flow south-west to north-east, the same orientation as the cairns. Every location exhibited major limit phenomena, including ten coastal sites with normal lunar rising and setting. I measured 138 locations: thirty-eight cairns and one hundred river/roadside sites. The midsummer full moon was invisible at nearly half of road/riverside locations, due to high southerly hills. When visible, the moon exhibited various skimming-type images with chthonic qualities. The moon can emerge sideways out of a south-east hill, as though coming out of the earth, or rise normally then disappear sideways into a south-west hill as though entering the earth. This is visually distinct from normal rising and setting. Occasionally the gap between emerging and disappearing is sufficiently narrow that the moon appears dramatically cupped in the mountains' embrace. Mountains partially frame the moon. In some places a half-submerged moon travels along the horizon still integrated with the living hills, or the moon skims along the hills as it does at Calanais. Each cairn site reinforces the otherworldly connectedness between moon, mountains, and viewing people. As previously suggested, the flow of agency is from moon to mountain and from mountain to cairn and from cairn to people and potentially in reverse, from people to moon, via cairn and mountain. No Clava cairn site exhibited a normal rising and setting midsummer full moon. Each cairn was either in darkness or was a place from which to view these dramatic lunar variations. Lunar skimming, as at Calanais, was expected but these variations were not and are described in detail elsewhere.[62] These events would have been experienced by the builders as a vibrant, integral part of their cosmology or understanding of the world. In later millennia the moon's journey into and out of the otherworld would be described as similar to the abilities of the *Sìth*. It suggests that cairns were built in locations emphasizing the dramatic midsummer full moon experience and potentially different rituals occurred, depending on how the moon was perceived. These lunar events can occur in any mountainous region, although the earth's curvature makes them more likely at these latitudes.

While hills and hill shadow would be expected to dominate in a mountainous landscape, Clava cairn builders located most of their cairns in the fewer available visible moon sites in the west of their territory. For example, wide southerly vistas exist in the Beauly basin, north of the river, but all the cairns were built close to southerly hills, providing spectacular lunar viewing. The wide valley floors of the eastern rivers Muckleburn and Spey have many visible lunar locations, but fewer cairns, although cairn survival rates are an unknown factor. The twenty-five Clava cairns are distinctly different from non-cairn locations. Nine Clava cairns are situated where the midsummer full moon is invisible – seven in the Clava valley (including Balnuaran). The entire valley is in dark hill shadow while the midsummer full moon lights up the hilltops. This emphasizes the intense power of the site: during the darkest part of the year the (normally dark) passage graves are lit up by midwinter sunset, while during the lightest part of the year the (normally light) ring cairns are cast into darkness. This deliberate juxtaposition of light and dark reinforces Balnuaran's sacredness. Reversing seasonal light is an empowering experience, potentially altering the rituals suitable to this place.

In contrast the other sixteen cairns are positioned to provide an opportunity to experience distinctive lunar observations. Such locations are remarkably hard to find in a landscape with predominantly high southerly hills. Lunar visibility also depends upon river depth and width. Generally it occurs along wide rivers (such as the Spey) and lower stretches of rivers (the Muckleburn ambles across the coastal plain). Upriver and inland the moon was largely invisible. Except at Corrimony, Little Urchany and Clava valley, cairn locations favour the ability to view major limit phenomena. Generally light is favoured over dark. This dance of moon and earth would have been highly visible to prehistoric peoples and one can only speculate that it must have been significant for them, for it seemed particularly special to those of us attending the major limit event at Calanais in 2006.

The midsummer full moon often appears to roll along the horizon disappearing into the south-western hills, hinting at a pilgrimage way, not unlike the *Sìth* procession. Prehistoric people could time their arrival at cairn sites by travelling upriver in the direction of the vanishing moon. During the days prior to lunar fullness the moon gradually becomes lower in the sky, often emerging then vanishing into cairn-site hills. It implies that cairn builders were conscious of these dramatic lunar sights. These descriptions do not do justice to possible cairn-site experiences. For example, along the Nairn, hills prevent sight of the midsummer full moon for several kilometres, both upriver and downriver, except at Daviot ring cairn, where the moon emerges from the south-east escarpment to set into the largest orthostat. The cairn location appears designed to respond to the lunar skyscape and the hills are an integral part of the magic of the moment, acting as living mountains, as though the moon transfers their *Sithean*/otherworldly energy into the cairn.

Journeying through mountainous landscapes inevitably restricts available land resources. Cairns cluster at convenient stopping places such as Kiltarlity, Lagmore, Aviemore, and Newtonmore, where tributaries or hill trails link with other rivers. This suggests old pilgrimage pathways and trading routes, which later developed into the region's towns: this was both practical (the need to cross fords) and spiritual (where to view the moon meeting the earth). Ease of river access was probably significant. Findhorn's notorious flooding and irregular stretches of high river banks may explain its lack of Clava cairns. Paired cairns (Torrdaroch and Croftcroy) occur at easy river crossings suggesting they were halting places, where groups gathered and hospitality was available.

The Clava valley group remains different from most cairn sites. Although cairn clustering near tributaries is normal, such a large concentration, without a main tributary, is unique. Clava valley's river access links several cairns, hinting at ritualized journeys, potentially echoing the Avon journeys, described by Michael Parker-Pearson, which linked Durrington Walls with Stonehenge.[63] Cairn builders may have used boats for ritual purposes, for transporting stones or else water was integral to rituals. All cairns can be considered sacred through their reuse as burial sites; however, the interplay of dark and light in Clava valley is distinctive; this is where the sun and moon meet the earth and the landscape has agency (Figure 2.1).

Figure 2.1 (Left) Balnuaran of Clava's three Early Bronze Age cairns, an impression of intact cairns indicating alignments. Top right is south-west, river Nairn and the setting sun. S is due south. (Right) View from Balnuaran NE passage grave. The dotted curve is the midsummer full moon path, the unbroken line midwinter sunset and the broken line indicates the southern minor moonset. Diagram and photograph: Anna Estaroth.

Balnuaran's two passage graves' interiors are lit by the setting midwinter sun. Midsummer sunrise lights up the back of Balnuaran Northeast passage grave and Balnuaran Central ring cairn, which possibly explains it being offset (towards the west) from the other two cairns. All three cairns have their largest circle orthostat aligned with minor limit moonset (although Balnuaran Southwest's is broken). Two years before and after major limit, the midsummer full moon skims along the southern horizon, but during major limit years the midsummer full moon is invisible, because the southerly hill casts the valley into darkness, making the ring cairn's centre dark, when it is normally a place of light.

Of the twenty-five Clava cairns, three were too ruinous for clarity. Regarding the seven passage graves, Corrimony, Balnuaran Northeast, and Balnuaran Southwest align with midwinter sunset (lighting up the darkness), Kinchyle of Dores's and Milton of Clava North's passages align with southern major moonset, while Dalcross Mains's passage aligns with southern minor moonset. Upper Lagmore's passage was indeterminate. Some cairns were dual usage; for example, Kinchyle's passage and orthostat orientations are the exact opposite of Dalcross Mains's, hinting at a potential centrally controlled design.

Of the fifteen ring cairns four lack notable kerbstones or circle orthostats for orientation purposes. Balnuaran Central ring cairn is complex. It has connections with midsummer sunrise, midwinter sunset, equinoctial sunrise, midwinter sunrise, minor limits, Samhain sunset, the setting of Sirius, and the rising of the Pleiades, complying with Stewart's seasonal markers connected with the *Sìth* listed above. Four ring cairns are orientated on midwinter sunset – Culbernie, Delfour, Little Urchany, and Tullochgorum – suiting midwinter ceremonies connected with darkness and the minor limit, which Stewart associated with initiation and regeneration (rebirth).[64] The midwinter ring cairns are spread evenly across the region. Six ring cairns are orientated on the midsummer full moon. At Daviot and Tordarroch one can see an emergent moon; symbolically the moon comes out of the hill/*Sithean*/otherworld, perhaps embodying increasing light. At Aviemore and Bruiach one can view an emergent and disappearing moon; the moon exits one hill before entering another hill/*Sithean*/otherworld. This symbolizes a changing narrative of increasing light which vanishes, potentially requiring lunar revitalization. At Belladrum North one can see a partial moon indicating deep connections with the otherworld, while at Marionburgh one might view the moon vanish into south-westerly hills, symbolizing returning to darkness and perhaps drawing participants towards the otherworld. These locations suit ceremonies of light and revitalization (re-impregnation or fertility). The full moon's height would increase during the months following any prehistoric ceremonies, implying that human interventions were effective.

A subsidiary aim was to explore potential uses of contrasting cairn types. Comparing ring cairns and passage graves led to considering Fowler and Cummings' exploration of liminal locations, which reinforced otherworldly connections.[65] It generated theories about pairing; some cairns appear paired, such as Tordarroch ring (major limit) with Croftcroy passage (minor limit), suggesting they catered for different seasonal festival/ritual needs. Generally intervisibility is rare, but applies to cairn pairs. They could have been built by the same extended family group. Cairns were divided into those potentially suitable for winter festivals (midwinter sunset and minor limit) and those more suited to summer festivals (midsummer sunrise and major limit). Surviving cairns are evenly distributed between potential summer and winter festivals, providing easy access across the region. Contrasting styles (ring cairn versus passage grave) yielded no dichotomy of purpose, as both would have provided the same seasonal facilities to the community. This emphasis on seasonal light and dark appeared important, implying that contrasting cairn styles were significant for ritual, but cairn style made no detectable difference, as both types focus on winter or summer. How and why Clava peoples utilized different cairn styles remain a mystery.

Although the *Sìth* road legends are culturally anomalous (linking Neolithic and Early Bronze Age monuments) and stem from much later historical traditions, they are metaphorically correct in that they linked lunar (month) with solar (year) monuments, implying relative time. If time is a calendrical invention, based on the movement of the earth, sun, and moon, then the legends of second sight and alternative time in the *Sìthean* otherworld begin to make symbolic sense. My fieldwork evidence indicates that Clava cairns were places to view the earth, sun, and moon coming together, quite unlike other locations. Such seasonally interlinked cairns reinforce the notion that, in this region, the dance between the earth, sun, and moon is intrinsically tangible, visually stunning and phenomenologically otherworldly. If people of the twenty-first century are transported through this interplay of moonlight, mountains, water, and monuments, then it was perhaps similar in the past. As places which seem to touch the human psyche, they are shaped by their landscape, and became imbued with myth and sacredness; this is material religion as a continuing focus. Despite the modern unfamiliarity of lunar significance, Balnuaran still feels venerated, as the *Sìthean* myths attest.

While this study has largely focused on midsummer full moon and light, darkness proved equally significant. At midwinter darkness reigns for eighteen hours, while at midsummer darkness lasts a mere ninety minutes. The angle of the winter sun is so low on the horizon that it blinds people for several hours a day for months. At new moon nearest midwinter darkness reigns the longest. During major limit Clava valley is in darkness at midsummer full moon, whereas most other cairns are located where the light of the skimming midsummer full moon is visible. The agency of the moon and mountains appears to empower the cairns. Only low south-westerly hills can allow midwinter sunset to light up the dark passage graves, while high southerly hills cast shadow on the normally light ring cairn near midsummer at major limit. This celestial mountain-to-cairn combination is integral to generating sacred space, to which we humans have an almost visceral response.

Conclusions

This chapter explored the role of midsummer full moon along Central Highland Rivers and some riverside Clava cairns. Any sufficiently high mountain on earth can block out or frame the sun or moon, potentially demarcating sacred spaces in the landscape. Scotland's northerly latitude makes this more likely than elsewhere. The chapter therefore considered how prehistoric peoples may have responded in winter and summer, due to the exceptionally low sun and moon at these latitudes. My fieldwork found Balnuaran Central ring cairn had minor limit, but no major limit orientations. Balnuaran is in dark hill shadow during midsummer full moon, the moon is invisible behind the southerly hills, while everywhere else is bathed in moonlight.[66] As these hills also embody the *Sithean* domain, this lunar hill-shadow interplay connects Balnuaran with *Sithean* time.

The Balnuaran/Clava valley group differed from other Clava cairns, as the location provided the experience of lunar shadow at major limit rather than dramatic visual events. Darkness during the lightest part of the year seemed to have been chosen over light. Yet during the darkest part of the year Balnuaran's passage graves were lit up by the low midwinter sun. My research showed that the cairn builders designed structures which utilized the mountains and exceptionally low midwinter sun to cast light into the dark cave-like passage graves at Balnuaran, while simultaneously using the exceptionally low midsummer full moon's invisibility to cast shadow onto the normally well-lit central ring cairn. This interplay of light and shadow marks Clava valley as sacred. It is unique among Clava cairns, where much is made of lunar light at midsummer. Thus the mountains themselves appear to have an agency, transferring celestial light and dark into something that touches the lives of human beings, raising the spirit and giving a sense of meaningful connectedness.

At various times Clava cairns were considered as holes in the *Sithean* fabric of time, repositories of the ancestral dead, or locations to confer authority on kings. These are very human responses to their inherent sacredness, which arguably derives from their sol-lunar connections. The *Sithean* mythology implied a full moon connection and summer (twilight) which my research found applies at Clava cairns. People could see variations of dramatically visual midsummer full moon experiences, linking humans, cairns, mountains, and moon. The moon looks larger close to the horizon, especially when framed by otherworldly mountains. Sixteen cairns were designated winter or summer type, through their alignments. Mapping the cairns into potential summer and winter usage indicated that they spread evenly throughout the region with eight per season. This hints at a possible central control of cairn-building, implying a potential clan system of interrelated family groups who built across the region serving different, but shared, purposes. The most telling example is the reversed orientations of Kinchyle of Dores and Dalcross Mains passage graves, which are within 23 kilometres of one another.

My primary research objective found that midsummer full moon hill shadow was as significant as midwinter sunset light at Balnuaran. Both were imbued with otherworldly power, earmarking Clava valley's cairns as guardians of the timeless *Sithean* realm. My secondary objective compared horizons across many cairn locations and found that midsummer full moon darkness at Balnuaran was relatively abnormal. My tertiary objective suggested that cairns could have provided summer or winter ritual facilities, although no discernible functional explanation was found for different cairn styles: passage grave or ring cairn. Exploring the southern horizon across mountainous terrain in terms of the low midsummer full moon during major limit years led to my finding seven different lunar phenomena, implying potentially different rituals.

The mountains are integral in shaping how these phenomena are perceived and the dynamic interplay between the hills and sky, where lunar phenomena occurs, reinforced that sense of agency within the hills, potentially defining where Bronze Age peoples chose to build their cairns. It is the moon-mountain interplay that appears to be at the heart of the cairns' sacredness. By entering and leaving the hills in this unusual manner, the moon appears to travel into the otherworld, just as the *Sith* were thought to do at these locations. The cairns pinpointed significant sol/lunar phenomena for the builders; they were also considered throughout Scottish history as guardians of the *Sìthean* realm.[67] They still hold relevance today as sacred spaces.

The interplay of light and dark at Balnuaran highlights the significance of hill shadow. Thus the Clava cairn evidence suggests that a deep-seated core of human ideas about sacredness comes into play, when the heavens (sun and moon) appear to come down to earth. This is a dance involving sun, moon, and planet earth. Their combined interconnectedness imbues these mountains with an agency making them living mountains, across time and down through the millennia, from the Early Bronze Age to today.

Notes

1   Alexander MacGregor, *Highland Superstitions* (Stirling: Eneas MacKay, 1901), 12, 13.

2   George Bain, *History of Nairnshire* (Nairn: Telegraph Office, 1893 [1928]), 28.

3   Alexander MacKenzie, 'The Prophesies of the Brahan Seer, Coinneacg Odhar Fiosaiche', *Celtic Magazine* 2, no. 19 (1877): 258–63, at 262.

4   Robert Kirk, *Secret Commonwealth or, a Treatise displaying the chiefe curiosities as they are in use among diverse of the people of Scotland to this day*, special ed. (Llandogo: Old Stile Press, [1691] 2005), leaf 26.

5   Alan McKirdy, *Set in Stone the Geology and Landscapes of Scotland* (Edinburgh: Birlinn, 2015), 36, 68.

6   Richard Bradley, *The Significance of Monument: On the Shaping of Human Experience in Neolithic and Bronze Age Europe* (London: Routledge, 1998), 112.

7   Richard Bradley, 'The Dark Side of the Sky: The Orientations of Earlier Prehistoric Monuments in Britain and Ireland', in *The Archaeology of Darkness*, ed. Marion Dowd and Robert Hensey (Oxford: Oxbow Books, 2016), 51–61, at 56.

8   Gerald S. Hawkins, 'Callanish, A Scottish Stonehenge', *Science* New Series 147, no. 3654 (1965): 127–30, at 129.

9   Clive Ruggles, *Astronomy in Prehistoric Britain and Ireland* (New Haven, CT: Yale University Press, 1999), 136, 130, 246; Aubrey Burl, 'Dating the British Stone Circles: A Provisional Chronology for the Geometrical Designs of the Megalithic Sites Is Based on Evidence from Architecture, Carbon-14, and Artefacts', *American Scientist* 61, no. 2 (1973): 167–74, at 165.

10 Aubrey Burl, *A Guide to the Stone Circles of Britain, Ireland and Brittany* (New Haven, CT: Yale University Press, 1995), 129.

11 Ruggles, *Prehistoric*, 246.

12 J. Anna Estaroth, 'Clava Cairns, Midwinter Sunset and the Minor Lunar Limit', *Culture and Cosmos* 21, nos. 1 and 2 (2017): 51–71, at 70.

13 James Cornell, *The First Star-Gazers and Introduction to the Origins of Astronomy* (London: Athlone Press, 1981), 78.

14 Ruggles, *Prehistoric*, 151.

15 Colin Richards, Adrian Challands, and Kate Welham, 'Erecting Stone Circles in a Hebridean Landscape', in *Building the Great Stone Circles of the North*, ed. Colin Richards, 201–23 (Oxford: Windgather Press, 2013), 206.

16 Audrey Shore Henshall, *The Chambered Tombs of Scotland Volume 1* (Aberdeen: Edinburgh University Press, 1963), 17.

17 Henshall, *Chambered Tombs Volume 1, 22*, 25, 27, 358, 371, 372, 382, 383, 387, 388, 390, 398.

18 Richard Bradley, *The Good Stones: A New Investigation of the Clava Cairns* (Edinburgh: Society of Antiquaries of Scotland Monograph Series no. 17, 2000), 122–6; Audrey Shore Henshall, *The Chambered Tombs of Scotland Volume 2* (Aberdeen: Edinburgh University Press, 1972), 271; Ruggles, *Prehistoric*, 130.

19 Jennifer Westwood and Sophia Kingshill, *The Lore of Scotland: A guide to Scottish Legends* (London: Arrow Books, 2009), 423.

20 Bradley, *Good Stones*, 119.

21 Richard Hayman, *Riddles in Stone: Myths, Archaeology and the Ancient Britons* (London: Hambledon Press, 1997), 11.

22 Stephen T. Driscoll, 'Picts and Prehistory: Cultural Resource Management in Early Medieval Scotland', *World Archaeology* 30, no. 1 (June 1998): 142–158, at 148.

23 Bain, *History,* 27.

24 Kirk, *Secret Commonwealth*, 1.

25 Robert John Stewart, ed. *Robert Kirk, Walker between Worlds, a New Edition of the Secret Commonwealth of Elves, Fauns and Fairies* (Shaftsbury: Element Books, 1990), 80.

26 Kirk, *Secret Commonwealth*, 1, 27.

27 Stewart, *Walker between worlds*, 50.

28 Keith Thomas, *Religion and the Decline of Magic* (London: Penguin, [1971] 1991), 733

29 Shari A. Cohn, 'Second Sight and Family History: Pedigree and Segregation Analyses', *Journal of Scientific Exploration* 13, no. 3 (1999): 351–72, at 354.

30 Henshall, *Chambered Tombs Volume 2*, 276.

31 Derek Simpson, 'Excavation of a Kerbed Funerary Monument at Stoneyfield, Raigmore, Inverness, Highland 1972–3', *Proceedings of the Society of Antiquarians of Scotland* 126 (1996): 53–86, at 65.

32 Bradley, *Good Stones*, 157, 118–20.

33 Bradley, *Good Stones*, 27–31.

34 Stuart Needham, 'Migdale-Marnoch: Sunburst of Scottish Metallurgy', in *Scotland in Ancient Europe: The Neolithic and Early Bronze Age of Scotland in their European Context*, ed. Ian A.G. Shepherd and Gordon J. Barclay (Edinburgh: Society of Antiquaries of Scotland, 2004), 217–45, at 241.

35 Ruggles, *Prehistoric*, 246.

36 Bradley, *Good Stones*, 128.

37 Bradley, *Good Stones*, 27–31, 125.

38 Bradley, *Significance of Monuments*, 110.

39 Richard Bradley, *The Idea of Order: The Circular Archetype in Prehistoric Europe* (Oxford: Oxford University Press, 2012), 105.

40 Claudia Moser and Cecilia Feldman, Introduction, in *Locating the Sacred*, ed. Claudia Moser and Cecilia Feldman (Oxford: Oxbow Books, 2014), 1–11, at 1.

41 Ian B. Straughan, 'The Aptitude for Sacred Space', in *Locating the Sacred*, ed. Claudia Moser and Cecilia Feldman, 165–79 (Oxford: Oxbow Books, 2014), 174.

42 Henshall, *Chambered Tombs Volume 2*, 358.

43 Richard Oram, *Moray and Badenoch: A Historical Guide* (Edinburgh: Birlinn, 1996), 16.

44 Yi-Fu Tuan, *Space and Place: The Perspective of Experience* (Minneapolis: University of Minnesota Press, 1977), 131.

45 George and Peter Anderson, *Guide to the Highland and Islands of Scotland, Including Orkney and Zetland*, 3rd ed. (Edinburgh: G. Parker, 1851), 370.

46 Bradley, *Good Stones*, 231.

47 Chris Scarre, 'Mounded Tombs, Megalithic Art, and Funerary Ideology in Western Europe', in *Understanding the Neolithic of North-Western Europe*, ed. Mark Edmonds and Colin Richards (Glasgow: Cruithne Press, 1998), 161–87, at 183.

48 Chris Fowler and Vicki Cummings, 'Places of Transformation: Building Monuments from Water and Stone in the Neolithic of the Irish Sea', *Journal of the Royal Anthropological Institute* 9, no. 1 (2003): 1–20, at 15.

49 Vicki Cummings, *The Anthropology of Hunter-Gatherers: Key Themes for Archaeologists* (London: Bloomsbury Academic, 2013), 81.

50 Bronwen Price, 'Journeying into Different Realms: Travel, Pilgrimage and Rites of Passage at Graig Lwyd', in *Prehistoric Journeys*, ed. Vicki Cummings and Robert Johnston, 85–101 (Oxford: Oxbow Books, 2007), 96–7.

51 Richard Bradley, *Altering the Earth: The Origins of Monuments in Britain and Continental Europe*, The 1992 Rhind Lectures (Edinburgh: Society of Antiquities of Scotland Monograph Series No. 8, 1993), 93.

52 Richard Bradley, *The Moon and the Bonfire: An Investigation of Three Stone Circles in North-East Scotland* (Edinburgh: Society of Antiquaries of Scotland, 2005), 111.

53 Fabio Silva, '"A Tomb with a View": New Methods for Bridging the Gap between Land and Sky in Megalithic Archaeology', *Advances in Archaeological Practice* 2, no. 1 (2014): 24–37, at 27.

54 Christopher Tilley, *A Phenomenology of Landscape: Places, Paths and Monuments* (Oxford: Berg, 1994), 12.

55 Alexander Meldrum, *The Clava Cairns* (Inverness: Highland Herald, 1970), 1.

56 Bradley, *Good Stones*, xvii.

57 Christopher Tilley, *The Materiality of Stone Explorations in Landscape Phenomenology* (Oxford: Berg, 2004), 16, 18.

58 Bain, *History*, 27.

59 Tim Ingold, *The Perception of the Environment: Essays on Livelihood, Dwelling and Skill* (London: Routledge, 2000), 51.

60 Ingold, *Perception*, 51.

61 David Abram, *The Spell of the Sensuous – Perception and Language in a More Than Human World* (New York: Vintage Books, 1996), 38.

62 J. Anna Estaroth, 'The Clava Cairns of Scotland, the Midsummer Full Moon and the Major Lunar Limit', *Journal of Mediterranean Archaeoastronomy and Archaeometry* 18, no. 4 (2018): 149–55, at 152.

63 Michael Parker-Pearson, *Bronze Age Britain* (London: B. T. Batsford, 1993), 67.

64 Stewart, *Walker between Worlds*, 97.

65 Fowler and Cummings, *Places of Transformation*, 13.

66 Estaroth, 'Midwinter Sunset', 69.

67 Bradley, *Good Stones*, 122–6, xvii; MacGregor, *Highland Superstitions*, 15.

Bibliography

Abram, David. *The Spell of the Sensuous – Perception and Language in a More Than Human World*. New York: Vintage Books, 1996.

Anderson, George, and Peter Anderson. *Guide to the Highland and Islands of Scotland, Including Orkney and Zetland: Description of Their Scenery, Statistics, Antiquities and Natural History with Numerous Historical Notes and a Complete Map*, 3rd ed. Edinburgh: G. Parker, 1851.

Bain, George. *History of Nairnshire*. Nairn: Telegraph Office, [1893] 1928.

Bradley, Richard. *Altering the Earth: The Origins of Monuments in Britain and Continental Europe*, The 1992 Rhind Lectures. Edinburgh: Society of Antiquities of Scotland Monograph Series no. 8, 1993.

Bradley, Richard. *The Significance of Monument: On the Shaping of Human Experience in Neolithic and Bronze Age Europe*. London: Routledge, 1998.

Bradley, Richard. *The Good Stones: A New Investigation of the Clava Cairns*. Edinburgh: Society of Antiquaries of Scotland Monograph Series no. 17, 2000.

Bradley, Richard. *The Moon and the Bonfire: An Investigation of Three Stone Circles in North-East Scotland.* Edinburgh: Society of Antiquaries of Scotland, 2005.

Bradley, Richard. *The Idea of Order: The Circular Archetype in Prehistoric Europe.* Oxford: Oxford University Press, 2012.

Bradley, Richard. 'The Dark Side of the Sky: The Orientations of Earlier Prehistoric Monuments in Britain and Ireland'. In *The Archaeology of Darkness*, edited by Marion Dowd and Robert Hensey, 51–61. Oxford: Oxbow Books, 2016.

Burl, Aubrey. 'Dating the British Stone Circles: A Provisional Chronology for the Geometrical Designs of the Megalithic Sites Is Based on Evidence from Architecture, Carbon-14, and Artefacts'. *American Scientist* 61, no. 2 (1973): 167–74.

Burl, Aubrey. *A Guide to the Stone Circles of Britain, Ireland and Brittany.* New Haven, CT: Yale University Press, 1995.

Cohn, Shari A. 'Second Sight and Family History; Pedigree and Segregation Analyses'. *Journal of Scientific Exploration* 13, no. 3 (1999): 351–72.

Cummings, Vicki. *The Anthropology of Hunter-Gatherers: Key Themes for Archaeologists.* London: Bloomsbury Academic, 2013.

Driscoll, Stephen T. 'Picts and Prehistory: Cultural Resource Management in Early Medieval Scotland'. *World Archaeology* 30, no. 1 (June 1998): 142–58.

Estaroth, J. Anna. 'Clava Cairns, Midwinter Sunset and the Minor Lunar Limit'. *Marriage of Astronomy and Culture, a Special Issue of Culture and Cosmos* 21, nos. 1 and 2 (2017): 51–71.

Estaroth, J. Anna. 'The Clava Cairns of Scotland, the Midsummer Full Moon and the Major Lunar Limit'. *Journal of Mediterranean Archaeoastronomy and Archaeometry* 18, no. 4 (2018): 149–55.

Fowler, Chris, and Vicki Cummings. 'Places of Transformation: Building Monuments from Water and Stone in the Neolithic of the Irish Sea'. *Journal of the Royal Anthropological Institute* 9, no. 1 (2003): 1–20.

Hayman, Richard. *Riddles in Stone: Myths, Archaeology and the Ancient Britons.* London: Hambledon Press, 1997.

Hawkins, Gerald S. 'Callanish: A Scottish Stonehenge'. *Science* New Series 147, no. 3654 (1965): 127–30.

Henshall, Audrey Shore. *The Chambered Tombs of Scotland Volume 1.* Aberdeen: Edinburgh University Press, 1963.

Henshall, Audrey Shore. *The Chambered Tombs of Scotland Volume 2.* Aberdeen: Edinburgh University Press, 1972.

Ingold, Tim. *The Perception of the Environment: Essays on Livelihood, Dwelling and Skill.* London: Routledge, 2000.

Kirk, Robert. *Secret Commonwealth or, a Treatise displayeing the chiefe curiosities as they are in use among diverse of the people of Scotland to this day*, special ed. Llandogo: Old Stile Press, [1691] 2005.

MacGregor, Alexander. *Highland Superstitions.* Stirling: Eneas MacKay, 1901.

MacKenzie, Alexander. 'The Prophesies of the Brahan Seer, Coinneacg Odhar Fiosaiche'. *Celtic Magazine* 2, no. 19 (1877): 258–63.

McKirdy, Alan. *Set in Stone the Geology and Landscapes of Scotland*. Edinburgh: Birlinn, 2015.

Meldrum, E. Alexander. *The Clava Cairns*. Inverness: Highland Herald, 1970.

Moser, Claudia, and Cecilia Feldman. *Locating the Sacred*. Oxford: Oxbow Books, 2014.

Needham, Stuart. 'Migdale-Marnoch: Sunburst of Scottish Metallurgy'. In *Scotland in Ancient Europe: The Neolithic and Early Bronze Age of Scotland in Their European Context*, edited by Ian A. G. Shepherd and Gordon J. Barclay, 217–45. Edinburgh: Society of Antiquaries of Scotland, 2004.

Oram, Richard. *Moray and Badenoch: A Historical Guide*. Edinburgh: Birlinn, 1996.

Price, Bronwen. 'Journeying into Different Realms: Travel, Pilgrimage and Rites of Passage at Graig Lwyd'. In *Prehistoric Journeys*, edited by Vicki Cummings and Robert Johnston, 85–101. Oxford: Oxbow Books, 2007.

Richards, Colin, Adrian Challands, and Kate Welham. 'Erecting Stone Circles in a Hebridean Landscape'. In *Building the Great Stone Circles of the North*, edited by Colin Richards, 201–23. Oxford: Windgather Press, 2013.

Ruggles, Clive. *Astronomy in Prehistoric Britain and Ireland*. New Haven, CT: Harvard University Press, 1999.

Scarre, Chris. 'Mounded Tombs, Megalithic Art, and Funerary Ideology in Western Europe'. In *Understanding the Neolithic of North-Western Europe*, edited by Mark Edmonds and Colin Richards, 161–87. Glasgow: Cruithne Press, 1998.

Silva, Fabio. '"A Tomb with a View": New Methods for Bridging the Gap between Land and Sky in Megalithic Archaeology'. *Advances in Archaeological Practice* 2, no. 1 (2014): 24–37.

Simpson, Derek. 'Excavation of a Kerbed Funerary Monument at Stoneyfield, Raigmore, Inverness, Highland 1972–3'. *Proceedings of the Society of Antiquarians of Scotland* 126 (1996): 53–86.

Stewart, Robert John, ed. *Robert Kirk, Walker between Worlds, a New Edition of the Secret Commonwealth of Elves, Fauns and Fairies*. Shaftsbury: Element Books, 1990.

Straughan, Ian B. 'The Aptitude for Sacred Space'. In *Locating the Sacred*, edited by Claudia Moser and Cecilia Feldman, 165–79. Oxford: Oxbow Books, 2014.

Thomas, Keith. *Religion and the Decline of Magic*. London: Penguin, 1971 [1991].

Tilley, Christopher. *A Phenomenology of Landscape: Places, Paths and Monuments*. Oxford: Berg, 1994.

Tilley, Christopher. *The Materiality of Stone Explorations in Landscape Phenomenology*. Oxford: Berg, 2004.

Tuan, Yi-Fu. *Space and Place: The Perspective of Experience*. Minneapolis: University of Minnesota Press, 1977.

Westwood, Jennifer, and Sophia Kingshill. *The Lore of Scotland: A Guide to Scottish Legends*. London: Arrow Books, 2009.

Part Two

Medieval conversations

3

Time and place at Brentor: Exploring an encounter with a 'sacred mountain'

Jon Cannon

I can be relatively precise about the date of my first encounter with the rocky Devon hill called Brentor (NGR SX470804; Figure 3.1). It was in January 1974, and I was 11, recently moved to the English west country from London, and out exploring with my mother. As we drove down the road from Tavistock to Lydford, the site appeared on my right, a sudden eminence with a tiny church at the top (Figure 3.2, left). This moment had a powerful, instantaneous impact on me, and I have since described it as if someone took a giant key, put it in a keyhole in my heart that I didn't even know existed, and turned it. Indeed I have spent a lifetime trying to repeat, unpack, and understand the emotions of that moment, and have managed to carve a fragile living out of the concerns which arose from it: studying, writing, and communicating about places, in particular sacred places, especially medieval religious architecture in England.

I have often asked myself whether that encounter with Brentor could be called a religious experience. The church atop the hill is, as a Christian place of worship, a religious building. The emotions revealed that day took various courses thereafter, but one was a brief adolescent engagement with charismatic/ evangelical Christianity. In spite of this, I did not think of the experience as religious when it occurred. It certainly involved a series of emotions – aesthetic, spiritual, intellectual – all felt at once, and with equal intensity.

Certain kinds of place have continued to provoke such feelings. Often, these are places where the landscape has a strong character and where human beings have visibly responded to this natural setting by adding to it a work of religious architecture. Now, over forty years later, I describe my search for such experiences as a hunt for the Divine, by which I mean some kind of sentience

Figure 3.1 Brentor, Devon. General view, as seen looking south from the northern flanks of Dartmoor. Photo: Jon Cannon.

Figure 3.2 Brentor, Devon and St Michael's church from the south-west. Left: From the location of the author's first view of the site in 1974. Right: South flank of the church. The roofline of the first phase of the building is visible, as well as the south door, the tower, and the primary phase of the churchyard wall. Photos: Jon Cannon.

that unites and transcends all creation. I have come to see Brentor as a sacred place, if we can extend the term to mean a thing of the utmost significance, offering a glimpse beyond the quotidian.

In my personal mythology – the story I tell myself about my life – it occupies a central position. It is thus, perhaps, a personal version of the sacred mountains that are widespread in world religion. Even at the age of 11, though I would have used different words, I think it was clear that the power of this first glimpse resided in both the physical drama of Brentor's natural form and the charge of significance given to that form by the place of worship that occupies its highest point.

Brentor and the sacred mountain

Brentor, then, is for me a 'sacred mountain'. Nevertheless, the statement raises further questions. Is it sacred for anyone other than myself? Would it still have that status if this eye-catching natural feature did not have a church at the top of it? What was the nature of the conversation with Brentor that called me to my vocation?

No great body of religious tradition is attached to the rock. What there is will be discussed below. The site could thus be contrasted to those sacred mountains that are associated with a rich library of religious stories and ideas, but lack monumental architectural structures: one thinks of Uluṟu/Ayers rock, Olympus, and Ararat. In traditional Armenian culture, the very act of ascending Ararat was sacrilegious.[1] In such cases the mountain itself must have had the cultural charge, to which any resulting monuments are incidental. In Brentor's case, by contrast, the evidence for sacredness is physical, and man-made: St Michael's church. This is a medieval building, consecrated by Walter de Stapeldon, bishop of Exeter, on 4 December 1319.[2] It was built for a strongly sacramental form of Christianity. The altar at its east end was a place where, during the daily Mass, the Divine itself was believed to transform a physical object.[3] The resulting building is surely to some extent 'sacred'. Nevertheless, the portion of the earth's surface it occupies need not have been seen as sacred, too.

It is possible, however, that the tor was indeed significant before the church was placed on it. If the sole purpose of building the church was to create an enclosure in which priests could celebrate the Mass and (in the medieval period only at Easter) the local community could congregate and participate in this rite, then the choice of site is nonsensically inconvenient. People may live nearby, but they inhabit the valleys, not the frost-shattered tors; priests likewise. At Brentor, as with all buildings, the place was there before the building was located on it. It is thus *a priori* the case that the volcanic hill had something to do with the decision to site a church in this location, and that some religious motivation must have been behind the decision to build a church in this place, that Brentor was already felt to be in some sense a sacred mountain. The church becomes an expression of whatever emotions, ideas or beliefs were stimulated by the tor; it embodies pre-existing reactions to a natural landform.

Clearly, my first encounter with Brentor was a response to both architecture and place, to things both artificial and natural. The power of buildings and the power of landforms are akin: both are aspects of the human response to physical form. Architecture is artificial geology, and vice versa; a mountain and a church are subsets of a wider thing called 'place', which may be either 'natural', or 'artificial', or both. Not only that, but the two in combination can be particularly powerful. In this case, the tower of Brentor church, 32 feet (9.7 metres) higher than the natural high-point on which it sits (the elevation of which, 334 metres, raises it about 130 metres above the surrounding plateau), has effectively replaced and made immeasurably more powerful the peak of the tor itself.[4] This tendency can be seen in many other religious buildings which adorn mountaintops, perhaps especially in the Christian tradition. Examples – all also dedicated to St Michael – include Saint-Michel d'Aiguilhe (St Michael of the Needle) near Le Puy-en-Velay, Haute-Loire, France; Mont-St-Michel, Normandy; and St Michael's Mount, Cornwall. An important cross-fertilization between mountains and religious buildings might thus exist. Both, after all, are architectonic forms, powerful, eye-catching, and high.

This chapter will explore the relationship between the tor and the church, taking into account the wider evidence for human engagement with the landscape. Comparators from other traditions and locations will also be discussed. However, the discussion is ultimately only an attempt to come to terms with, and help to understand, the power of my first encounter with Brentor, which preceded such knowledge. I thus aim to bring personal experience to bear on the phenomenology of landscape itself, especially remarkable hills, as a way of exploring the possible causes of the particular conversation this 'mountain' had with me in January 1974. Here, I am following Christopher Tilley and others in emphasizing the contextuality of perceptions of place, and of the primacy of the human individual as the medium through which it is perceived.[5] The word 'conversation' used by the editors of this volume is also relevant: this first encounter was not a conversation at all, in that it was entirely one-sided, but I have spent much of my life since replying to what was 'said' to me that day.

As a result, much of the present chapter aims to unpack the phenomenological 'narrative' that Ingold, extending and reinterpreting Heideggerian ideas, described as the dynamic 'dwelling perspective' of this specific place.[6] I will describe much that is empirical about the Brentor landscape, in order to explore the ways in which it would have been perceived over time, including how successive human alterations to the landscape might have shaped its later perception and development. But my experience of the tor at a young age involved no such knowledge.

I thus ultimately want to raise questions of fundamental importance to the human understanding of places, especially sacred places, and their power. These questions are rooted not in my empirical knowledge of Brentor, but in my subjective experience of it as a child. While I do not here propose any answers to them, these questions raise the important matter of where the human perception of sacredness in a place – in this case, specifically a 'sacred mountain' – comes from. My experience on the tor has much in common with Mircea Eliade's famous 'hierophany', but I am not sure the 11-year-old me would have recognized it as an experience of the 'divine'. Even looking back, the experience was more a powerful glimpse of the possibility of such an entity than an actual manifestation of it.[7] However, Brentor is a good example of what Thomas Tweed called a 'differentiated space', a space set apart by increased intensities of sensual experience or imaginative association.[8] Many authors – Tweed and Tilley among them – have commented on the power such places have to shape human actions. I will take the qualities that differentiate the tor in chronological order, starting with its geology, proceeding to the layers of activity visible on the tor but predating construction of the church, then discussing the church itself. I will conclude with some aspects of this palimpsest-like layering of evidence which are either undated or very recent indeed. Throughout, we should bear in mind that Brentor is a location that almost differentiated itself, stimulating a reaction in spite of being effectively free of preceding knowledge, yet which had the power to define and embody this writer's lifelong vocation.

Geology and landform

Landscapes start as geology. Such accounts are, in effect, 'origin myths' supplied by science: that is, they are facts. But they are also stories, narratives which enrich appreciation of a site. They also act as a reminder that even rocks are testaments to dynamic processes, often incomprehensibly slow and ancient, but sometimes brief and intense. All this is certainly true of Brentor, the view from the top of which is spectacular. Less than 2 kilometres to the east, the upland mass of Dartmoor spreads out, its highest point reaching 621 metres. Bodmin moor lines the horizon 30 kilometres to the west. Between them stretches a hilly plateau which rarely climbs above 200 metres, and is bisected by the north-south Tamar valley; that river's estuary at Plymouth Sound is visible in the southern distance. Brentor is the most conspicuous landmark between the two moors. Its geological story is as distinctive as its form.

The main plateau between the moors, like much of the finger-like peninsula that is south-west England, consists of Devonian and early Carboniferous sedimentary rocks, made of materials gradually laid down on a sea floor about 419–358 million years ago (ma). These rocks were transformed in the course of the Carboniferous and early Permian periods, as a result of a tectonic event known as the Variscan orogeny. Early in this process, lava erupted in pulses onto the sea floor in various parts of south-west England. Brentor, and significant stretches of the plateau to its west, was one result; it is the remnant of a seamount, a small underwater volcano, which probably erupted around 346–329 ma. Its rocks are basaltic, created by the rapid cooling of the lava on exposure to the ocean.[9] Some of the surrounding lava fields, meanwhile, are the source of the locally popular greenish-grey Hurdwick building stone.

A more large-scale development took place as the Variscan events were drawing to a close, from about 300 ma. The rocks I have discussed were by now positioned deep underground. As a side-effect of the tension being applied to the crust, a vast mass of magma known as a batholith welled up from below, putting the surrounding rocks under enormous pressure. They were contorted and cooked; one result was the creation of the metal deposits for which west Devon and Cornwall are famous.[10] The much harder rocks that make up Brentor, however, managed to retain something of the form of a small volcano. For example, the pillow lavas visible at the tor's peak have the reddish tinge produced by proximity to oxygen, suggesting both that the surface of the sea was not far away when the volcano was active and possibly that the top of the tor is not much lower now than it was then.[11] Certainly the tor's steep eastern and southern slopes have a cone-like form, whereas to the north and west the tor presents a cliff of frost-shattered basaltic crags, topped by two peaks (Figure 3.2, left). The highest and largest of these – that to the south – has the church on it (Figure 3.2, right). These crags are largely the result of ice age freeze-and-thaw effects, the most recent of which finished about eleven thousand years ago.

The wider landscape has taken its current form more slowly, as the covering layer of rocks was gradually removed. Eventually, parts of the top of the buried granite batholith were exposed at the surface, forming the high country of Dartmoor and Bodmin moor, as was Brentor itself. These granites and basalts are acidic and support only a thin covering of soil. The contorted sedimentary rocks that stretch between them are softer and have eroded more quickly; they thus form a lower plateau, with rich earths that today form a well-settled grazing country.[12] The basalts of Brentor, in conclusion, are as distinctive and dramatic in origin as the landform itself: older than the granites, younger than the sedimentary plateau, and – unlike either – born in the throes of a volcanic eruption. Such accounts indicate the distinctive nature of Brentor's origins. They may have been preceded by other stories, whose veracity seemed equally certain to those who told them. Whether in the form of scientific knowledge, literary associations, myths, or religious beliefs, such stories embody an invisible layer, called by some a mythosphere or noosphere, that help explain what people have done in a sacred place.[13] I will unpack further layers of Brentor's mythosphere in the account that follows.

Geology and holy mountains

As a result of its unique geology, Brentor has a distinctive form, and stands in isolation from other areas of high ground. Many such landforms have attracted human attention. Not all such attention has been religious; often, highly visible and defensible hills have been strongholds, centres of political power. Tilley has pointed out the significance of politics in such sites.[14] Indeed one might consider all such eye-catching landforms as 'naturally significant places' – places which are likely to attract human reaction – and then consider sacred mountains to be merely a subdivision of this category. Many other kinds of landform – caves, sources of water, and so on – may also be 'naturally significant', but here the focus is on unusual hills and mountains, the naturally significant high place.

Such patterns will be true of many such places. They are also likely to have certain geological characteristics in common. Isolated hills are most likely to result from one of a limited number of processes, including:

- Mountains formed in recent orogenic or mountain-building episodes, resulting in high, dramatic, little-eroded peaks such as the Alps or the Andes. Olympus is a sacred mountain of this type.
- Mountains made of particularly ancient and hard rocks, highly resistant to erosion and often brought to the surface as a result of later tectonic activity along a geological fault. The Malvern hills, Worcestershire, and Taishan, China, are examples of this.
- Mountains made of sedimentary rocks that have been subjected to unusual erosional processes, such as the karstic limestone hillscapes of Guangxi

province, China, and central Anatolia. Both have yielded many small sacred mountains.

- Mountains formed in volcanic events, which may create conical cones, or leave behind dramatic plugs of rocks which originally formed deep within the volcano. Such mountains may become especially significant where the volcano is still active, as with Mt Fuji, Japan, and Mt Merapi, Java.[15]

The cultural significance of such landforms goes far beyond their dramatic visual qualities. Mountains are necessarily closer to the heavens than other places. They are often the sources of rivers. Where the geology permits, they may contain caves. Any observer of the sky will see that they attract clouds, and conclude they control the weather itself. Such a combination of features – mountains as points of access to the underworld, sources of fresh water, controllers of the weather, and also the places in which special rocks such as obsidian could be found – was, for example, the key to Aztec cosmology.[16] At Brentor, there is a spring near Holyeat farm on the tor's southern slopes, which in 1522 was described as being in a 'close' and dedicated to St Michael, a figure to whom this chapter will return.[17]

Before the church

Brentor is a classic example of a 'naturally significant high place'. A study of its history reveals evidence for a series of human responses over time. The oldest man-made aspect of the tor is not the church, but a steep-sided earthwork 216 metres long (A on plan), extending about three-quarters of the way around its northern and eastern sides (Map 3.1A). This is most impressive on the tor's north-western corner, where it is 5 metres high externally. This corner clearly mattered to its builders, who placed here a monumental hornwork or entrance complex, funnelling visitors down a corridor 10 metres long towards a narrow, west-facing gateway (Map 3.1B).

This is a hillfort, probably built towards the end of the first millennium BCE. It is part of an apparent ring of hillforts surrounding Dartmoor, all of them distinctive, as Phil Newman has pointed out, for being surrounded by a single bank and having a monumental entrance.[18] The site may not have been permanently settled; none of the other, less substantial earthworks on the tor look like those of an Iron Age settlement. Hillforts are understood as having been centres of power, on occasion inhabited and even town-like in nature, but often simply acting as nodal places for trading, refuge, and potential defence, and perhaps as focuses for ceremonial acts.[19]

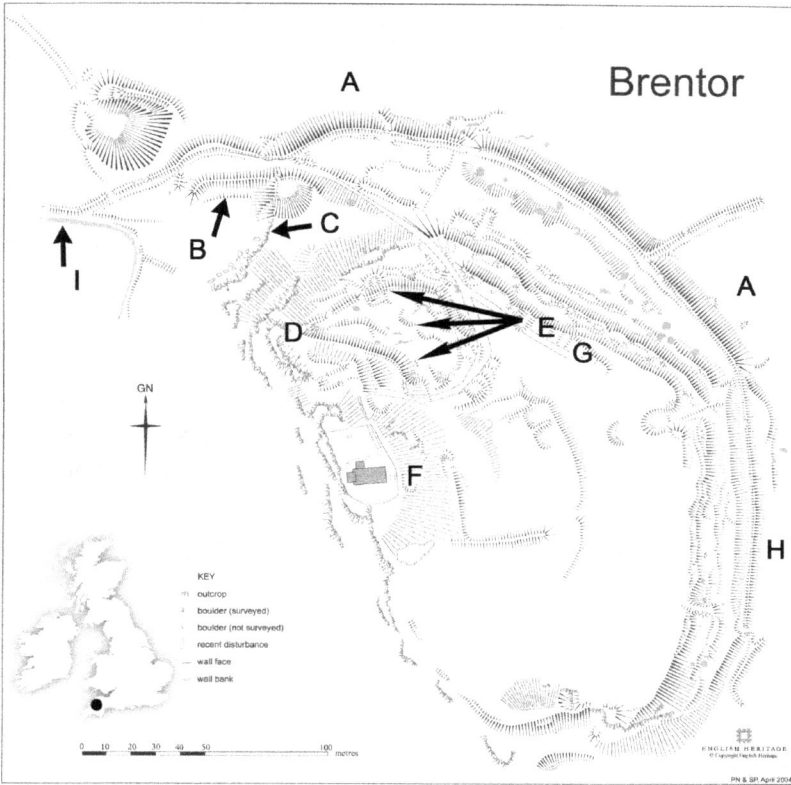

Figure 3 1:1000 earthwork survey of Brentor.

Map 3.1 Brentor, plan. Map: © Historic England Archive; UK inset map © maproom. net.

The Brentor hillfort is unusual for enclosing the bottom rather than the top of the tor. Though practicality may be one reason for this, hillforts of this period do sometimes occupy very steep and narrow hilltops – the Mither Tap O'Bennachie in Aberdeenshire and Tre'r Ceiri in Gwynned are two examples. At Brentor it was more important to enclose a reasonably large space than to maximize the visibility from a distance of the hillfort itself. As one neared the site, however, the hillfort would have become unmistakable. The earthwork would have been steeper and higher than at present, and topped with a timber stockade, an intimidating presence as one approached from the north and the west and was funnelled between the jaws of the hornwork. Tilley has discussed the significance of paths and routes. I would add to this an assertion of the significance of their punctuating points, of entrances and thresholds.[20] Certainly this one – and there are further more recent 'gateways' to come – seems to have been the most important element in the monument, the banks of which reduce in height away from the north-west corner until they come to an abrupt end, now reduced to 2 metres high, on its shallow southern slopes, an area that earthworks of purely defensive function might have sought to prioritize. This arrangement is odd, and it is part of a pattern: several Iron Age hillforts on the fringes of Dartmoor are unfinished, and, according to Newman, in all of them the most impressive portion faces away from the moor, contains the entrance, and was completed first.[21] Some historical development may be the reason for the apparent abandonment of these projects; but it may also be that nothing else was felt to be necessary, that it mattered more that these sites looked like a hillfort than that they could be used as one. By any interpretation it seems that an awesome and defensive-looking approach was the overriding priority in the creation of these sites.

This is also impressive for its responsiveness to the lie of the land. A short stretch of the earthwork links the gateway to the crag that forms the northern peak of the tor (Map 3.1C); it runs along a steep existing scarp, and dies into it in a manner that may always have made it hard to distinguish the natural from the artificial. Newman suggested that the main rampart may also follow a now-hidden scarp slope, enabling it to remain several metres high on the exterior while being just 1 metre high on the inside.[22]

Something of the thrill of this approach can be experienced today. The visitors' car park, gate, and footpath are aligned on and follow its route; to take this path is to be forced towards the tor's dramatic northern peak (Figure 3.3 and Map 3.1D); to then become aware of the scale of the highest part of the earthwork ring; and then to be forced into the funnelled form of the hornwork itself. Remove the church from the picture and the visual significance of the northern peak increases greatly. This architectonic sculpting of the tor's lower flanks is clearly designed to create the most dramatic and awe-inspiring approach possible.

Once through the hornwork one is on gently rising ground. The rockiest landforms fall away, though the slope that climbs towards the northern peak remains a steep one; the natural route forwards involves contouring around it, entering an ever-broader space as one goes. All this must replicate the Iron Age experience, but the nature of any intended progress beyond this point is unknown. The church, of course, was not there. More to the point, no evidence exists for how the area enclosed by the earthwork was used. All that can be

Figure 3.3 Brentor, Devon and St Michael's church from the north-west. Left: View from the entrance path. Right: North side of the church, as seen from the northern peak of the tor. The porch and the proposed second phase of the churchyard are visible. Photos: Jon Cannon.

said is that the tor presented itself as an artificially enclosed landform, but was in fact not one; that in spite of this it had a climactic main entrance through which access was controlled; that the enclosing structure went out of its way to maximize the drama of the natural rockform; and that all of this was most powerful when the tor was approached from the north-west (Figure 3.3, left). At Iron Age Brentor, natural and artificial power were combined.

The first known monumental human intervention in the landscape of Brentor, then, was an enclosing structure rather than a crowning one; it served to dramatize and control approaches to the hilltop. It was either left unfinished or was to some extent symbolic in nature. There is no sign that the hilltop itself was a focus for monuments; if any part of it was emphasized it is the northernmost of the two peaks, which is bare. The earthwork enclosure evokes secular power, but seems to have a strong cultural dimension, too, though it would be an overstatement to call it a religious structure. This Iron Age hillfort contributes to the present discussion in various ways. First, it bears fruitful comparison with other such forms at sites that are emphatically sacred mountains. It can be seen as marking out the outer limits of a significant space, a very common feature in, for example, Hindu, Egyptian, and Classical Greek temples. In the latter tradition it is known as a *temonos*.[23] There can be practical reasons for this: it is hard to build an elaborate work of architecture on top of a mountain. There can also be religious ones. By providing an impressive enclosure, a prelude or a foil at the foot of a sacred mountain, one is setting it aside – and also amplifying the otherness of the mountain top itself. Sacred mountains may lack buildings simply because they are felt to be too sacred to be built on. The monument at the base only serves to emphasize the significance of the untouched peak. Perhaps, too, such monuments serve to control access, and provide a manageable setting for rites associated with the mountain. At several such sites the largest religious building is located at the foot of the mountain near the edge of this enclosure, as at Dion, at the foot of Olympus, or the Dai Miao, at the foot of Taishan, China.[24]

Such observations potentially relate as much to the political function of a site as to any religious one. Naturally significant high places can seem almost designed to make effective strongholds, at once defensible and visible; here, aesthetics is never far away, whether one is talking about Harlech castle, Gwynedd, on its Snowdonian crag, or Clifford's tower, York, on its prominent motte. However, as many cultures have seen political power, for example when invested in a king, as divinely ordained, the distinction between the way in which a site makes political authority visible and its status as a sacred place may not be a clear one. The sacrifices on Taishan, which emphasized the emperor's unique role as the fulcrum between the heaven and earth, are an example of this potential elision of the political and the religious.

There are other, shallower earthworks on the tor, their significance not agreed. Some of these will be associated with medieval and later sheep fairs and quarries. One group, however, does not easily sit with this interpretation. This occupies the saddle between the north peak and the south one (Map 3.1E), and includes an attempt to monumentalize or enclose the northern lip of this steep ground, which overlooks the area inside the Iron Age gateway. An earthwork runs along this ridge, and then makes a hairpin bend at the foot of the northern peak, before running back across the saddle, where it is less visible from below. The saddle contains an arrangement of other, shallower traces, which include at least two large and orthogonal arrangements of mounds. These suggest buildings, one about 15 metres long and 6.5 metres wide.[25] The relationship between these and the hairpin 'enclosure' is obtuse, but Tom Greeves has argued that some of this represents an early medieval religious site.[26] Certainly the most substantial of the 'buildings' sits precisely on the saddle, though it is outside the hairpin enclosure, and is oriented roughly east-west. Certainly, too, early medieval Christian sites in nearby Cornwall are known for reoccupying Iron Age hillforts.[27] St Michael, dedicatee of the current church, is likewise associated with early medieval reoccupations of prehistoric sites in Devon and Cornwall.[28] These shallow earthworks suggest tantalizing possibilities, but without excavation their true nature cannot be known.

It is more firmly possible to ascribe to this early medieval period the first piece of documented mythosphere related to the tor: its name. Tilley has emphasized the significance of place names to understanding landscape.[29] While the name is not recorded before the mid-twelfth century, Charles K. Burton and Gerald L. Mathews have observed that it is surely pre-Conquest, like almost all Old English (OE) place names.[30] Both *brant* and *toor* are of Germanic/OE origin, so must post-date the eighth-century expansion of the Anglo-Saxon kingdom of Wessex into the previously British territories of this area. A *Torr* is a rocky outcrop or peak; *brant* indicates steep.[31] An early and attractive tradition that it meant 'burnt' is now discredited.[32] The related proposal that the hill has acted as a beacon is unsupported by any evidence.[33] These place names are a further reminder of the shifting nature of the layers of human place-making at Brentor. To sum these up, the Iron Age earthworks attempt an enclosure of the natural feature as a whole, and play up the drama of approach from the north-west; there are undated structures between the two peaks; and finally, St Michael's church was constructed on Brentor's highest point.

The church of St Michael

Today, the visitor approaches the church (Figures 3.2, right; 3.3, right; Map 3.1F) by arcing around the northern side of the tor and climbing steeply towards the north-facing churchyard gate. Here one is confronted by a man-made structure for which documentary evidence exists. The 1319 consecration comes comparatively late in this story, which starts in the first half of the twelfth century. According to H. P. R. Finberg, in a document from Tavistock Abbey dated 1155–62, local magnate Robert Giffard's son stated that his father built St Michael's church on the rock of Brentor at his own expense, and gave both church and rock to Tavistock Abbey, along with thirty acres of land in the manor of Lamerton.[34] The church was thus founded a generation before the late 1150s. In documents of the 1190s it is called 'sancti Michaelis de Rocta' and 'sancti Michaelis de Rupe', strengthening the argument that the tor was a fundamental part of the identity of the building.[35] A document of 1224–45 described its intended function: Tavistock Abbey supplied a priest, whose job was to celebrate daily offices in the name of Giffards living and dead, and of the parishioners.[36]

So Giffard's foundation was to be both a parish church and a venue for commemorative masses, intended to aid the passage through purgatory of the souls of Giffard, his descendants, and the parishioners. Of these two functions, the parochial dimension may have been associated with Giffard's gift of lands. These resulted in the creation of a new manor, Holeyeat [*sic*], which united the estates of Tavistock Abbey into a single contiguous territory.[37] The small parish was probably sparsely settled; as late as the 1790s it was described as only having eighteen houses in it. (The only nucleated settlement for several miles, North Brentor, is largely an industrial-era creation.[38]) Given this and the church's inaccessible location, the purgatorial function appears to be the dominant one, especially given the significance of its dedication to St Michael.

The connection between St Michael with high places is well-attested.[39] The archangel was the principal intermediary between earth and heaven – and his powers were particularly important in medieval commemorative spirituality; for example, as the key figure in the anticipated Judgement, St Michael played a crucial role in funeral rites.[40] As the victor over the devil, he was also associated with former pagan sites.[41] St Michael, in short, was the glue between Giffard's motivation, the building of the church, and the role played by the tor itself, perhaps including its encircling ring of Iron Age embankments.

The church is an east-west oblong 37 feet 6 inches (11.43 metres) wide and 14 feet 9 inches (4.50 metres) broad.[42] It has a single window in each wall. Identical north and south doors sit opposite each other in the western part of the building. The north door opens onto a substantial porch; there is a thirty-two-foot western tower (Figures 3.2 and 3.3).[43] There are few enrichments; the dominant impression rests on the simple geometries of the horizontal church, the squarish porch, and the vertical tower. The church is made out of pieces of the local landscape: the basalts of the tor itself, removed from quarries that are still visible on its south-east flank, with dressings in local Hurdwick greenstone.

As one approaches the tor, the defining aesthetic experience is one of contrast: the tor, a complex interplay of frost-shattered rock exposures; the church, a simple shift of one orthogonal form against another (Figures 3.2 and 3.3). 'Artificial' and 'natural' features in the landscape are emphatically separated, while the church transforms the flattish, if crag-edged, profile of the hill's highest point into a dramatic and emphatic peak. The form of the church gives a deceptive impression of simplicity. Every flank of the building features the building breaks suggestive of a complex structural history, and only one part of the structure, the lower 2.4 metres or so of the nave south wall, seems likely to be a remnant of Robert Giffard's church (Figure 3.2, right). A window just to the east of this is round-headed, suggesting heightening and extension within a few decades of completion. This first church – in size, it was barely a chapel – was thus certainly lower and probably significantly shorter than the current building. As no trace of this phase is visible on the north side it may have been narrower, too. It is unlikely to have had a porch or a tower, both of which are unusual in smaller churches of this date; the west wall would as a result have been further from the cliff edge than it is today. Even its expanded, later twelfth-century form would have played a much less demonstrative role in the landscape than it does now.

Given the scale of this building, and its probable lack of a tower, the natural forms of the tor would have dominated any approach for twelfth-century viewers. The power of the hill would have been emphasized over that of the building on its peak, which nevertheless provided a new kind of visual focus and an obvious ultimate destination. The first church thus sat in the landscape in a way comparable to the Chinese tradition, where mountaintop temples are set low, complementing rather than transforming the natural power of the site: at Taoist Taishan, the temples of the Blue Dawn (*Bìxiá Cí*), Confucius, and the Jade Emperor Peak (*Yù Huáng Dǐng*) are set low on the upper ridge; at Buddhist Wutaishan, there is only a small temple on each of five sacred peaks.

Only a few further documents throw light on the history of the building before the Reformation, though, significantly for the tor as a whole, Finberg established that a Michaelmas sheep fair was founded on the hill in 1231; the footings of booths related to it may survive (Map 3.1G).[44] The fair was moved to Tavistock in 1550.[45] Burton and Matthews noted that it may have been associated with a stone cross whose base, recorded at the foot of the tor in 1836, was said to have been linked to one Amice de Wyke.[46] The fair may also have caused the belated extension of the Iron Age earthworks around the remaining southern portion of the tor, in the form of a stone-reinforced field boundary (Map 3.1H); perhaps the hillfort formed a kind of *temonos* to the fair.[47] Worth just 6s. 8d. in 1536, the fair was likely to have only been locally significant. [48] Nevertheless, given the increased number of visitors to the tor over the period of feast of St Michael, and the special liturgical emphasis that one can assume was a feature of worship in the church at this time, this must have been a particularly busy period at Brentor. One might even ask whether it was during this annual event that the respective significance of church, *temonos*/earthwork, and hilltop reached its greatest intensity.

In 1285 the parishioners agreed to pay 3s. a year towards repair of the fabric and the ornaments of the church, followed in 1319 by the rededication of the building.[49] This has to be squared with the remaining art-historical and archaeological evidence for the building. The architectural detailing remains very simple, but the emphatic Early English lancet of the nave north window would be happiest in the first half of the thirteenth century, the roll-moulded roof corbel brackets are also thirteenth-century in character, and the mouldings of the north and south doors are happier in the Decorated era of the earlier fourteenth century. Applying Occam's Razor to the whole, and allowing for considerable leeway given the simplicity of the forms and the potential conservatism of the masons, the body of the church could have reached its present form at some point in the *c.*1285–1319 date range suggested by the documents, though the reality may have been more episodic. It is impossible to say whether the many building breaks, especially marked on the north corner of the chancel and as running down the north wall of the nave, are the result of difficulties in the course of construction, or later repairs.

Again, at this point there is no evidence for a tower or a porch, nor any reason to expect them to exist. The west wall, which reached its current extent at this point if not earlier (its site in the later twelfth-century is unclear), was a good 4 metres from the steep west-facing cliff of the peak. The building thus remained less obtrusive than it is today. Instead, it is the arrangement of space in the building itself that stands out. For example, the north and south doors have hood moulds; both were intended to face the open air. It is unusual for such doors to be of identical design. They suggest processional use, for example on Palm Sunday, was at least as much a priority as access.[50] Inside the church, the north and south windows have a single step to their east, marking the entrance to the chancel, which would have been separated from the nave by a rood screen. The step predates the Victorian restoration and the two windows are well-placed to light the area immediately west of any screen located on it, suggesting the divide is in its original location.[51] Nothing survives of this screen, or the images that would have filled the building; the granite font is the only medieval fitting. The most valuable items at Brentor, as assessed under Edward VI, were two bells, later recast.[52]

The changes attributable to *c.*1285–1319 thus arguably made more visible one of the chief qualities of the building's design: its orientation. The twin doors emphasized north-south procession; the main axis, now very emphatic, sacramental events, focused to the east. The focus is not only on time, in the form of the liturgical year – the daily mass, Palm Sunday processions – but also on place, in the form of the cardinal directions, which embody the spatial arrangement of the universe. (Editors' note: The tor has a true azimuth of 85° which is 5° north of east.) Émile Durkheim himself compared the properties of time and place, and Claudia Moser and Cecelia Feldman have emphasized how 'to practise ritual is to be emplaced'.[53] Jaś Elsner has asserted that the marking of landscapes and the making of buildings are an important element in such ritual processes.[54] Certainly, as a result of the changes this small church in a high place visibly tied liturgical performance to cosmology. It stood as a universalizing, ordering contrast to the chaotic power of the rock beneath. Its power as a visible intermediary between heaven and earth was enhanced.

The construction of the tower was a late development, and a step change for the church's presence in the landscape (Figures 3.2 and 3.3). The square spandrels of its belfry windows and the handling of its battlements are Perpendicular in style, and very like those of other local churches of the fifteenth and earlier sixteenth centuries. Effectively a new peak to the hill, located alarmingly close to the precipice of the tor, it is this structure that made St Michael's a diminutive cousin to such dramatic hilltop churches as Mont-St-Michel and Saint-Michel d'Aiguilhe. It is the only part of the church that seeks to dominate the tor visually. It might be added that such visibly tall structures are frequent in ambitious religious buildings, and often deliberately evoke mountains, from the *sikhara* or 'mountain peak' spire of a Hindu temple, to the Mesopotamian ziggurat, to the Buddhist stupa.[55] One might add church towers and minarets to this discussion, and propose an architectural category of 'artificially significant tall building' to match that of the 'naturally significant high place'.

Dramatic changes will have affected Brentor church in the decades after the 1539 dissolution of Tavistock Abbey. The sacramental and commemorative aspects of the church's function would have ceased, and the building refitted for Protestant worship. Maintenance of its parochial function depended heavily on clergy based at Lamerton or Tavistock. In 1795 a stable was built at the foot of the tor for the use of the vicar of Tavistock.[56] The building's site remained relevant, however; in 1791, R. Polwhele recorded Matthew 16.18, 'Upon this rock will I build my church, and the gates of hell shall not prevail against it', as being written on a 'little tablet' on the south wall of the nave. It had been whitewashed over before 1865.[57] Textual wall plaques such as this are typical of the seventeenth century. The evocation of the solidly patristic St Peter rather than the suspiciously mythological St Michael marks a distinct shift in the mythosphere surrounding the church. The bells, recast in 1909, include one said to have an original medieval inscription *gallus vocor ego, solus per omne solo* ('I am called the cock, and I alone sound above all'). The message seems to evoke the church's location in a high place; it may again have Petrine associations.[58] Such texts offer an insight into how a sacred building can be re-interpreted, even within a single faith tradition, attaching new elements to its mythosphere. In 1889/90 the building was restored by the Dukes of Bedford, who had been given many of Tavistock Abbey's lands at the Dissolution. Works were extensive and included the roof, which is said to be a copy of a medieval original, and all the internal fittings apart from the font.[59]

This leaves one element of the building unaccounted for, and it is its principal entranceway: the porch (Figure 3.3, right). It was there in 1791, but its outer portal is made of large pieces of (mostly) straight-sided stonework. Several of these, which have mouldings of broadly fifteenth-century character, have been recut to form a rough arch shape. [60] It seems certain that this stonework has been reused from elsewhere in the church, perhaps the medieval east window, which may thus have been Perpendicular in date. The window present in 1865 was not the original, and was replaced in turn in 1889/90.[61] It seems that the porch is post-medieval, but pre-dates the Victorian restoration. It is important to this discussion because it is the only aspect of the architecture that prioritizes access from a single direction – in this case the north-west – or indeed lay access at all.

Before investigating the significance of this further, other features of the church which date between the Dissolution and the Victorian restoration need to be factored in. In terms of fittings and tombs, all are works of the late seventeenth century, a period when many churches were enriched following the end of Puritanism. Change ringing was effectively a seventeenth-century invention, and it may not be a coincidence that extra bells were added in 1668.[62] There is also a primitive, slate-carved sundial dated 1694 and inscribed with the initials 'WB'[63] and a tomb slab with the same monogram to Walter (d. 1677) and Alice (d. 1681) Batten of Brinsabach, just below Brentor. Many other wall plaques and gravestones have since joined this monument, especially from the nineteenth century onwards, making burial and commemoration in a modern, post-Reformation form a visibly defining aspect of the site's function.

The churchyard in which these monuments are set is one of the most monumental works on the tor (Figures 3.2, right; 3.3, right; Map 3.1F). Three sides of the peak of the hill have been enclosed with a drystone wall (the western side is a cliff), and substantial amounts of earth moved to raise a burial ground within them. 'Doubtless they rest there as securely as in sumptuous St Peters [*sic*], until the day of doom', Tristram Risdon commented in 1811.[64] At most times it would have been this enclosure, rather than the Iron Age earthworks, which functioned as the site's *temenos*. The period around Michaelmas, at least before the Reformation, is here proposed as an exception to this. One could also view the sequence hillfort/graveyard/church, and within the church, porch/nave/chancel, as embodying the onion-skin layers of significance seen in many sacred spaces, in which space is arranged in a hierarchy moving from the mundane, to the holy, to the sacred. Such sequences have been reviewed for the medieval period by Sarah Hamilton and Andrew Spicer.[65]

The churchyard appears to be a two-phase structure. The roughly circular form of its southern side may be original, but the orthogonal shape of the north side suggests it is an extension (Figures 3.2, right; 3.3, right; Map 3.1F). The change may be Victorian, given that in 1791 the churchyard's dimensions were given as 90 feet (27.4 metres) long by 60 feet (18.3 metres) broad, rather than the present 22 metres × 33 metres.[66] The 5-metre discrepancy in (east-west) length between the earlier and the later measurement may be ascribed to human error, given the difficulty of accurate measurement on the site. But that relating to (north-south) breadth is enormous. However rough the 1791 measurements were, it thus seems likely that the site more or less doubled in size at some point after 1791.

It is the porch and the churchyard which direct visitors up the steep northern approach to the church, and they are late additions to the landscape (Figure 3.3). That the southern approach has declined in importance is indicated by the removal of a gateway on the south side of the churchyard wall, where a gatepost with iron fixings survives. Parishioners may once have taken a spiral path, contouring round the hill and entering from the south. Or they may have used either door, depending on their direction of approach. It is possible that these nineteenth-century changes reinstated the focus of access from the north-west which is such a notable feature of the Iron Age enclosure. However most visitors at all periods are likely to have approached from the north-west, the location of the historic core of the parish; both the present, turnpiked road (Map 3.1), and the earlier route shown on a sixteenth-century map now held at the Devon Record Office, also pass to the west.[67] Anyone approaching from the south-east would have had a gradual sense of arrival, in which the church and the peak were viewed from shifting angles. The north-western approach, by contrast, emphasizes arduousness of approach and the drama of the site (Figure 3.3, left). The increased emphasis on it is probably a reflection of the Romantic approach to landscape pioneered by William Gilpin, combined with the many changes in the parish at this time; indeed a more convenient church was built at North Brentor in 1856.[68]

The emphasis on doors and gates at all periods – the Iron Age hornwork, the medieval north and south doors, and the post-medieval porch and churchyard – emphasizes how thresholds and routes are among most significant aspects of the human 'engineering' of sacred places. At Taishan in China and Delphi in Greece, for example, such routes became the focus for monumental staircases and walkways lined with minor temples/treasuries and other devotional foci.[69]

The creation of an emphatic northern focus now becomes a distinctive and possibly post-Reformation intervention. The medieval arrangement, as previously explored, had prioritized an oriented structure designed for sacramental rituals – a building visibly focused on the cosmological and the ineffable. This was now replaced by an arrangement which emphasized more earthly concerns: lay access, a picturesque approach, a monumental entrance, more space for burial. Throughout, it is worth reflecting that from the first half of the twelfth century until 1856, when a chapel of ease was built in North Brentor, the inhabitants of the parish climbed an exposed 334-metre crag in order to participate in acts of worship and mark rites of passage. It also remains possible that for over two thousand years the vast majority of visitors to the tor have approached it from the north-west.[70]

Modern myths

A series of traditions are associated with Brentor which further cement the powerful relationship of architectural and geological form at the site. They are best approached as a relatively recent layer in the mental stratigraphy of Brentor, and the last and most tantalizing aspect of its story. However, the first two are effectively undatable. In one, the church was founded by a merchant who was lost at sea and guided into Plymouth Sound by the sight of Brentor, rising above an obscured coast. In the other, retold in various ways in different sources, the devil himself opposes the construction of the church and takes it upon himself to make a nightly relocation of the building works from the bottom of the tor to the top. St Michael appears, pelts him with stones, and he flees.[71] Intriguingly, this story means that the devil did not want to destroy the building, and was successful in determining its location.

These stories form a slender but significant outline of a mythology for Brentor. The first is a reminder that Plymouth Sound is visible from the hilltop. The second evokes on many levels the strangeness of the location of the church, the rocky nature of its setting, and the very visible layering of human activity there. They are also the least stratigraphically helpful of all the human culture associated with the hill. Both are *topoi*, stories very close to those told of other churches in unusual locations. Both may be retrospective responses to the remarkable nature of the church's site. Most importantly, neither is attested before the 1830s, seven hundred years after the decision was made to build the church. As myths they are marvellous; as history, close to useless.

That can also be said of the most recent development in the mythosphere of Brentor, the proposal that there is a 'St Michael's line', a ley line or path of energy connecting sites, often hilltop sites associated with St Michael and St George, and running from St Michael's Mount to the Suffolk coast, with a particular concentration between St Michael's Mount and Ogbourne St George, Wiltshire, which – in a remarkable coincidence – is the village where I now live. This is a very recent idea, whose point of origin and authors are known.[72] It has created a new mythology around the tor, linking it to other places in the landscape of southern Britain. Few historians give credence to the idea of ley lines, but they are an important part of the belief system that some present-day visitors bring to the site.[73] This modern myth has served to resacralize the landscape, while adding a new layer to its mythosphere.

Conclusion: Place and time

At Brentor, a stone church was built on top of an extinct sea volcano surrounded by an unfinished hillfort on the edge of Dartmoor. Every stage of this story has a complex stratigraphy, one that is fundamental to the aesthetics of the site. Yet this knowledge is the result of years of looking at Brentor, combined with a review of existing literature, art history, archaeology, and geology at the site. None of it was known to me in 1974. Neither is any ordinary visitor necessarily aware of it. The source of Brentor's power is thus unclear. But the issue of stratigraphy may be relevant to understanding it. At such sites, all the layers in the landscape are apprehended as present all-at-once. A series of phenomena, unfolding in linear time and full of themes relevant to sacred mountains and their architecture in other times and places, are brought together with density and power. Perhaps this is one of the most significant qualities of such places, that they are perceived as being outside time, eternal and unchanging, while in fact embodying a vast range of interventions made over long periods of time.

Humanity has thus had a 'conversation' with Brentor that has enriched and marked its landscape over a period of some three thousand years. The physical remains of that conversation, combined with whatever aspects of the mythosphere that a visitor is aware of, play a fundamental role in enhancing and enriching the sense of specialness that the tor has, contributing to its status as an example of Tweed's 'differentiated space'. Nevertheless, and equally importantly, most modern viewers will simply take from the natural form of the tor, the various man-made humps and bumps to be seen on it, and the church and churchyard itself, a hazy sense of 'oldness'. The impressions made in 'conversation' with the landscape over a very long period are, for visitors, flattened and compressed, part of a single experience of the place's otherness.

Brentor is not a sacred mountain of the same order as Taishan or Ararat, Olympus or Wutaishan. It is a small but dramatic hill with a simple church at its peak. Yet the level of importance that its powerful combination of forms has had in my own life cannot be overstated. The word 'sacred' is the only one appropriate. My childhood 'conversation' with Brentor occurred before I knew anything about St Michael or the Reformation, hillforts or purgatory, geology or ley lines. There was no mythosphere to lean upon, but there may have been triggers for me from children's fantasy literature, such as Alan Garner, C. S. Lewis, and J. R. R. Tolkein; and while a child from a mixed Nonconformist/ Jewish but entirely secular background might possibly have been indifferent to churches at that point, he would certainly have known that the building was one. Whether this was conscious to me at the time or not, Brentor embodied, for me, the power of place in its purest form.

Archival sources

Devon Archives, W1258M/0/D/79.
National Heritage List for England, 1104836.
Ordnance Survey. *Launceston & Holsworthy*, Explorer 112. Southampton: Ordnance Survey, 2011.

Notes

I am most grateful to Darrelyn Gunzburg and Bernadette Brady, whose incisive and constructive editing has transformed this chapter.

1   Thomas Stackhouse, *A History of the Holy Bible* (Glasgow: Blackie, 1836), 93; Ken Dowden, Zeus (Abingdon: Routledge, 2003), 58.

2   F. C. Hingeston-Randolph, *The Register of Bishop Walter Stapeldon* (London: Bell, 1892), xxxiii, 137, 556.

3   Matthew 26, 26–28.

4   Ordnance Survey, *Launceston & Holsworthy*, Explorer 112.
    (Southampton: Ordnance Survey, 2011); James Hine, 'St Michael's, Brent Tor', *Transactions of the Devonshire Association* I, Pt. V (1866): 116–21. Imperial measurements are only cited where they are given as such in the source.

5 Christopher Tilley, *A Phenomenology of Landscape* (Oxford: Berg, 1994), 11–15.

6 Tim Ingold, *Being Alive: Essays on Movement, Knowledge and Description* (London: Routledge, 2011), 9–13.

7 Mircea Eliade, *The Sacred and the Profane: The Nature of Religion*, trans. Willard R. Trask (Orlando: Harcourt, 1987), 11–12.

8 Thomas A. Tweed, 'Space', in *Key Terms in Material Religion*, ed. S. Brent Plate (London: Bloomsbury Academic, 2015), 225–6, at 225.

9 P. A. Floyd, C. S. Exley, and M. T. Styles, *Igneous Rocks of South-West England* (London: Chapman and Hall/Joint Nature Conservation Committee, 1993), 129.

10 Arlène Hunter and Glynda Easterbrook, *The Geological History of the British Isles* (Milton Keynes: Open University, 2009), 81–2.

11 Floyd et al., *Igneous Rocks*, 129.

12 John Whittow, *Geology and Scenery in Britain* (London: Chapman and Hall, 1992), 22–36.

13 David Miles, *The Tale of the Axe: How the Neolithic Revolution Transformed Britain* (London: Thames and Hudson, 2016); Teilhard de Chardin, *The Vision of the Past* (London: Collins, [1923] 1966), 71, 230, 261.

14 Tilley, *Phenomenology of Landscape*, 26–7.

15 Jan Fontein, 'The Path to Enlightenment', in *Borobudur: Majestic Mysterious Magnificent*, ed. John N. Miksic, Noerhadi Magetsari, Jan Fontein, and Timbul Haryono (Borobudur, Prambanan and Ratu Boko: Persero, Taman Wisata Candi, 2010), 111–12.

16 Nicholas J. Saunders, 'Deity and Place in Aztec Religion', in *Sacred Sites, Sacred Places*, ed. David L Carmichael, Jane Hubert, Brian Reeves and Audhild Schanche (London: Routledge, 1994), 172–83, at 176.

17 Charles K. Burton and Gerald L. Matthews, *The Church of St Michael, Brentor* (Church Guide, 1981), 6; Devon Archives, W1258M/0/D/79.

18 Phil Newman, *Brentor: An Earthwork Site on Western Dartmoor, Devon*, English Heritage Research Report 136/2003 (Swindon: English Heritage 2003), 8–10, 12, 13.

19 D. W. Harding, *Iron Age Hillforts in Britain and Beyond* (Oxford: Oxford University Press, 2012), 271.

20 Tilley, *Phenomenology of Landscape*, 30–1.

21 Newman, *Brentor*, 12, 13.

22 Newman, *Brentor*, 12.

23 Walter Burkert, *Greek Religion*, trans. J. Raffan (Oxford: Blackwell, 1985), 84–7; Richard H. Wilkinson, *The Complete Temples of Ancient Egypt* (London: Thames and Hudson, 2000), 56–7.

24 Brian R. Dott, *Identity Reflections: Pilgrimages to Mount Tai in Late Imperial China*, Harvard East Asian Monographs 244 (Harvard: Harvard University Press 2004), 240–2.

25 Newman, *Brentor*, 8–10, 11, 14–15.

26 Tom Greeves, 'Was Brentor a Dark Age Centre?', *Dartmoor Magazine* 71 (2003): 8–10.

27 Newman, *Brentor*, 15.

28 Graham Jones, *Saints in the Landscape* (Stroud: Tempus, 2007), 77, 80.

29 Tilley, *Phenomenology of Landscape*, 18, 33.

30 Burton and Matthews, *Church of St Michael*, 3.

31 *Key to English Place-Names* (Nottingham: Institute for Name Studies), http://kepn. nottingham.ac.uk/map/place/Devon/Brentor (accessed 4 October 2018).

32 Hine, *Brent Tor*, 116.

33 Tristram Risdon, *The Chorographical Survey of the County of Devon* (Plymouth: Rees and Curtis, 1811), 218; Hine, 'Brent Tor', 116.

34 H. P. R Finberg, *Tavistock Abbey: A study in the Social and Economic History of Devon* (Cambridge: Cambridge University Press, 1951), 16.

35 W. D. Dugdale, *Monasticon Anglicanum* (London: Longman 1819), II: 498, VIII (abbot Herbert, active in 1193, died *c.*1200), 490, IX (pope Celestine III, 1191–8).

36 Burton and Matthews, *Church of St Michael*, 6; Dugdale, *Monasticon*, 498, VIII.

37 Finberg, *Tavistock Abbey*, 16; Dugdale, *Monasticon*, 498.

38 R. Polwhele, *The History of the County of Devonshire* (London: Cadell, Johnson and Dilly, 1797), II: 443, additional note of 1791.

39 Jones, *Saints*, 70; Richard Morris, *Churches in the Landscape* (London: Dent, 1989), 52–6.

40 Paul Everson and Paul Barnwell, *Summoning St Michael: Early Romanesque Towers in Lincolnshire* (Oxford: Oxbow, 2006), 82–9.

41 Jones, *Saints*, 79–80.

42 Hine, *Brent Tor*, 119.

43 Hine, *Brent Tor*, 120.

44 Finberg, *Tavistock Abbey*, 198.

45 Finberg, *Tavistock Abbey*, 267, 274.

46 Burton and Matthews, *Church of St Michael*, 14; Mrs Bray and the Rev. E. A. Bray, *A Description of the Part of Devonshire Bordering on the Tamar and the Tavy* (London: Albermale 1836), I: 252.

47 Newman, *Brentor*, 5, 11.

48 Finberg, *Tavistock Abbey*, 199.

49 Burton and Matthews, *Church of St Michael*, 6.

50 Eamon Duffy, *The Stripping of the Altars: Traditional Religion in England, 1400– 1580* (New Haven, CT: Yale University Press, 1992), 22–5.

51 Hine, 'Brent Tor', 119.

52 Burton and Matthews, *Church of St Michael*, 9.

53 Émile Durkheim, *The Elementary Forms of the Religious Life* (New York: Free Press [1912], 1995), 8–10; Claudia Moser and Cecelia Feldman, 'Introduction', in *Locating the Sacred: Theoretical Approaches to the Emplacement of Religion*, ed. Claudia Moser and Cecelia Feldman (Oxford: Oxbow, 2014), 1.

54 Jaś Elsner, 'Material Culture of Ritual: State of the Question', in *Architecture and the Sacred: Ritual, and Experience from Classical Greece to Byzantium*, ed. Bonna D. Wescoat and Robert G. Ousterhout (Cambridge: Cambridge University Press, 2012), 2–4; and see the editors' 'Afterword', 378.

55 Stella Kramrisch, *The Hindu Temple* (Calcutta: University of Calcutta, 1946), 161; Henri Frankfort, *The Art and Architecture of the Ancient Orient* (Harmondsworth: Penguin, 1970), 20–2; Gilles Béguin, *Buddhist Art: An Historical and Cultural Journey* (Bangkok: River Books, 2009), 27–30; Martin Brauen, *The Mandala: Sacred Circle in Tibetan Buddhism* (London: Serindia 1997), 26–31, 68–74.

56 Burton and Matthews, *Church of St Michael*, 12.

57 Polwhele, *Devonshire*, 443; Hine, 'Brent Tor', 118.

58 Burton and Matthews, *Church of St Michael*, 9.

59 Nikolaus Pevsner and Bridget Cherry, *The Buildings of England: Devon* (Harmondsworth: Penguin, 1991), 210; National Heritage List for England, 1104836.

60 The porch is mentioned in Polwhele, *Devonshire*, 443, and again in 1865: Hine, 'Brent Tor', 121.

61 Hine, 'Brent Tor', 119.

62 'St Michael de Rupe' (Brentor: Brentor Community Trust), http://www. brentorvillage.org/?page_id=411 (accessed 21 November 2018).

63 Jeannie Crowley, 'Sundials in South Devon', *Transactions of the Devonshire Association* XCIII (1961): 266–84, at 267–9.

64 Risdon, *Chorographical Survey*, 218.

65 Sarah Hamilton and Andrew Spicer, 'Defining the Holy: The Delineation of Sacred Space', in *Defining the Holy: Sacred Space in Medieval and Early Modern Europe*, ed. Andrew Spicer and Sarah Hamilton (Aldershot: Ashgate 2005), 1–26, at 6–9, 12.

66 Polwhele. *Devonshire*, 443.

67 Devon Record Office, 189 M Add.

68 William Gilpin, *Observations on the River Wye* (London: R. Blamire, 1782).

69 Dott, *Identity Reflections*, 27; Michael Scott, *Delphi and Olympia: The Spatial Politics of Panhellenism in the Archaic and Classical Periods* (Cambridge: Cambridge

University Press, 2010), 42, 48–9, 64–5, 78–80, 104–8, 115–16. Like Brentor, the current arrangement at Delphi is a very late one: 24, n. 91.

70 Pevsner and Cherry, *Devon*, 210.

71 Bray and Bray, *A Description*, 251–5.

72 Alfred Watkins, *The Old Straight Track: Its Mounds, Beacons, Moats, Sites, and Mark Stones* (London: Methuen, 1925); John Michell, *The View over Atlantis* (London: Abacus, 1969), 61–7; Hamish Miller and Paul Broadhurst, *Summoning St Michael* (Launceston: Pendragon, 1989).

73 Tom Williamson and Liz Bellamy, *Ley Lines in Question* (Littlehampton: Littlehampton Book Services, 1983).

Bibliography

Béguin. G. *Buddhist Art: An Historical and Cultural Journey.* Bangkok: River Books, 2009.

Brauen, M. *The Mandala: Sacred Circle in Tibetan Buddhism.* London: Serindia, 1997.

Bray, Mrs, and Bray, Rev. E. A. *A Description of the Part of Devonshire Bordering on the Tamar and the Tavy.* London: Albemarle, 1836.

Burkert, W. *Greek Religion*, translated by J. Raffan. Oxford: Blackwell, 1985.

Burton, C. K., and G. L. Matthews. *The Church of St Michael, Brentor.* Church guide, 1981.

Crowley, J. 'Sundials in South Devon'. *Transactions of the Devonshire Association* 93 (1961): 266–84.

De Chardin, T. *The Vision of the Past.* London: Collins, [1923] 1966.

Dott, B. R. *Identity Reflections: Pilgrimages to Mount Tai in Late Imperial China*, Harvard East Asian Monographs 244. Harvard: Harvard University Press, 2004.

Dowden, K. *Zeus.* Abingdon: Routledge, 2003.

Duffy, E. *The Stripping of the Altars: Traditional Religion in England, 1400–1580.* New Haven, CT: Yale, 1992.

Dugdale, W. D. *Monasticon Anglicanum.* London: Longman, 1819.

Durkheim, Émile. *The Elementary Forms of the Religious Life*, translated by Karen E. Fields. New York: Free Press, [1912] 1995.

Eliade, M. *The Sacred and the Profane: The Nature of Religion*, translated by Willard R. Trask. Orlando: Harcourt, 1987.

Elsner, Jaś. 'Material Culture of Ritual: State of the Question'. In *Architecture and the Sacred: Ritual, and Experience from Classical Greece to Byzantium*, edited by Bonna D. Wescoat and Robert G. Ousterhou, 1–26. Cambridge: Cambridge University Press, 2012.

Everson, P., and P. Barnwell. *Summoning St Michael: Early Romanesque Towers in Lincolnshire.* Oxford: Oxbow, 2006.

Finberg, H. P. R. *Tavistock Abbey: A Study in the Social and Economic History of Devon*. Cambridge: Cambridge University Press, 1951.

Floyd, P. A., C. S. Exley, and M. T. Styles. *Igneous Rocks of South-West England*. London: Chapman and Hall/Joint Nature Conservation Committee, 1993.

Fontein, Jan. 'The Path to Enlightenment'. In *Borobudur: Majestic Mysterious Magnificent*, edited by John N. Miksic, Noerhadi Magetsari, Jan Fontein and Timbul Haryono, 111–12. Borobudur, Prambanan and Ratu Boko: Persero, Taman Wisata Candi, 2010.

Frankfort, H. *The Art and Architecture of the Ancient Orient*. Harmondsworth: Penguin, 1970.

Gilpin, W. *Observations on the River Wye*. London: R. Blamire, 1782.

Greeves, T. 'Was Brentor a Dark Age Centre?' *Dartmoor Magazine* 71 (2003): 8–10.

Hamilton, Sarah, and Andrew Spicer, 'Defining the Holy: The Delineation of Sacred Space'. In *Defining the Holy: Sacred Space in Medieval and Early Modern Europe*, edited by Andrew Spicer and Sarah Hamilton, 1–26. Aldershot: Ashgate, 2005.

Harding, D. W. *Iron Age Hillforts in Britain and Beyond*. Oxford: Oxford University Press, 2012.

Hine, J. 'St Michael's, Brent Tor'. *Transactions of the Devonshire Association* I, Pt. V (1866): 116–21.

Hingeston-Randolph, F. C. *The Register of Bishop Walter Stapeldon*. London: Bell, 1892.

Hunter, A., and G. Easterbrook. *The Geological History of the British Isles*. Milton Keynes: Open University, 2009.

Ingold, T. *Being Alive: Essays on Movement, Knowledge and Description*. London: Routledge, 2011.

Jones, G. *Saints in the Landscape*. Stroud: Tempus, 2007.

Key to English Place-Names. Nottingham: Institute for Name Studies, http://kepn. nottingham.ac.uk/map/place/Devon/Brentor.

Kramrisch, S. *The Hindu Temple*. Calcutta: University of Calcutta, 1946.

Michell, J. *The View over Atlantis*. London: Abacus, 1969.

Miles, D. *The Tale of the Axe: How the Neolithic Revolution Transformed Britain*. London: Thames and Hudson, 2016.

Miller, H., and P. Broadhurst. *Summoning St Michael*. Launceston: Pendragon, 1981.

Morris, R. *Churches in the Landscape*. London: Dent, 1989.

Moser, Claudia, and Cecelia Feldman. 'Introduction'. In *Locating the Sacred: Theoretical Approaches to the Emplacement of Religion*, edited by Claudia Moser and Cecelia Feldman, 1–12. Oxford: Oxbow, 2014.

Newman, P. *Brentor: An Earthwork Site on Western Dartmoor, Devon*, English Heritage Research Report 136/2003. Swindon: English Heritage, 2003.

Pevsner, Nikolaus, and Bridget Cherry. *The Buildings of England: Devon*, Harmondsworth: Penguin, 1991.

Polwhele, R. *The History of the County of Devonshire*. London: Cadell, Johnson and Dilly, 1797.

Risdon, T. *The Chorographical Survey of the County of Devon*. Plymouth: Rees and Curtis, 1811.

'St Michael de Rupe' (Brentor: Brentor Community Trust), http://www.brentorvillage.org/?page_id=411.

Saunders, N. J. 'Deity and Place in Aztec Religion'. In *Sacred Sites, Sacred Places*, edited by David L Carmichael, Jane Hubert, Brian Reeves and Audhild Schanche, 172–83. London: Routledge, 1994.

Saunders, N. J. *Ancient Americas: Maya, Aztec, Inca and Beyond*. Stroud: Sutton, 2004.

Scott, M. *Delphi and Olympia: The Spatial Politics of Panhellenism in the Archaic and Classical Periods*. Cambridge: Cambridge University Press, 2010.

Stackhouse, T. *A History of the Holy Bible*. Glasgow: Blackie, 1836.

Tilley, Christopher. *A Phenomenology of Landscape*. Oxford: Berg, 1994.

Tweed, T. A. 'Space'. In *Key Terms in Material Religion*, edited by S. Brent Plate, 223–30. London: Bloomsbury Academic, 2015.

Wei-Cheng, L. *Building a Sacred Mountain: The Buddhist Architecture of China's Mount Wutai*. Seattle: University of Washington Press, 2014.

Whittow, J. *Geology and Scenery in Britain*. London: Chapman and Hall, 1992.

Wilkinson, R. H. *The Complete Temples of Ancient Egypt*. London: Thames and Hudson, 2000.

4

Building paradise on the Hill of Hell in Assisi: Mountain as reliquary

Darrelyn Gunzburg

The town of Assisi in Umbria, Italy, located on a sloping and precipitous mountain ridge halfway up the dome-shaped, wood-covered sides of Mount Subasio, has long been known as the birthplace of Franciscanism. Today the Basilica that houses the human remains of St Francis (*c.*1181/2–1226), the founder and leader of the Friars Minor, draws pilgrims and visitors alike, either to worship or admire the beauty of the architecture and fresco schemes. This influx of people makes Assisi one of Italy's prime tourist attractions. It wasn't always so. The journey to its transformation is also an exploration of the creation of a sacred and religious landscape via one man, St Francis of Assisi, one of a handful of historical figures associated with a town and a mountain.[1]

This chapter thus investigates a unique human conversation with a mountain and how mountainous land that a community considered wild and barbaric can be changed by what they buried in it. It also explores what is believed about human remains that are buried, and how burials in such terrain affect a people's activities around the mountain and thus change the dynamics between human and mountain. It centres around the events that occurred following the death of St Francis and the desire by the Franciscan brothers to create a lasting monument to his memory via his human remains. St Francis was considered to be a phenomenon of his time and his life was full of paradox. A small, dark, nuggety man, born to a wealthy cloth merchant, he was educated as a youth and dreamed of being a knight, yet in adulthood he lived a life of poverty, dressed only in tunic, rope belt, and sandals.[2] Although actively engaged with towns, St Francis sought inner peace in a hermitage, Eremo delle Carceri, 4 kilometres from Assisi, built on a rocky outcrop in a steep forest gorge 791 metres above sea level, and higher up the steep slopes of Mount Subasio. His other sanctuary was at La Verna, on Mount Penna, an isolated mountain of 1,283 metres situated 113 kilometres north-west of Assisi in the centre of the Tuscan Apennines above the valley of the Casentino in central Italy. He traversed a wide section of the Apennines and the places that he made his retreats created what Tim Ingold would call 'a node in a matrix of trails'.[3] Living through the century that saw the rise of universities, he rejected scholarship and books. As economic wealth increased and the first ducats, florins, and gold crowns were minted, he had a deep loathing for money and the greed and avarice that it carried.[4] He found inspiration in the natural world and he actively encouraged peace in a time full of turbulence and strife. He was instrumental in changing one of the major courses of philosophical religious thinking. In death, his final resting place – the extreme western flank of the town of Assisi, Italy – positioned the location as a pilgrimage site. As a result of this man and the afterlife of his body, a multitude of people drawn to his way of thinking have engaged in various conversations with this mountainous location. This chapter considers those 'conversations' through the themes of bodies, burials, and bones, and how mountain landscapes shape and are shaped by the people who live among them and whose stories become mythically entwined with place and landscape.

Place, map, landscape

Place, according to E. V. Walter, is 'a location of experience; the container of shapes, powers, feelings, and meanings'.[5] Far from being neutral, a place is one that is imbued with meaning. That framing is further inflected by Christopher Tilley, who noted that the meanings that people placed upon or into a location created an attachment to it.[6] Attachment was achieved in several ways. Through regular encounter, continued and consistent movement to and from, through and within a place, natural objects or topographical features generated familiarity and became entwined into story, which further embedded those memories and experiences. Furthermore, place had a way of acting upon a person through what was remembered, the incidents that occurred there or the journeys undertaken through it. Place became, as it were, a receptacle for where events happened. Naming also invested a place with meaning. 'Place names', Tilley wrote, 'are of such vital significance because they act so as to transform the sheerly physical and geographical into something that is historically and socially experienced' and thus 'in a fundamental way names create landscape'.[7] This becomes noticeable from observing twenty-first-century maps. Blank spaces on a map are places that hold no memories or experiences for the map-maker, hence although they exist geographically, they have not been identified by name. Furthermore, while any place on conventional maps can be designated by longitude and latitude, the reality is that places are relational. As Walter observed, 'We learn *where* it [a place] is in another sense by its relation to established places.' It is uncommon to say 'in 23.4162° N and 25.6628° E' or 'near 48.8566° and N, 2.3522° E', for unless a person works with map coordinates, such terminology is meaningless. The former coordinates, however, become meaningful when changed to the phrase 'in the Sahara Desert', which implies qualities of hot and dry, wind and sand, nomads and camels; the latter coordinates when identified as 'near Paris' raise images of the 2019 fire in the roof of the cathedral of Notre-Dame, the late nineteenth-century ironwork of the Eiffel Tower, waiters serving café crème on the Île Saint-Louis, the energy and stimulus of the Marais, the wide boulevards, and the many bridges.[8] Alfred Korzybski argued, 'A map is not the territory it represents, but, if correct, it has a similar structure to the territory, which accounts for its usefulness.'[9] A contemporary map of places can therefore help in planning a journey and, by naming the sites, buildings, or monuments found along the way, identify objects that create that place. They offer nothing in terms of the people or the life forms that one may encounter.

Medieval maps gave greater certainty to place because, as Michel de Certeau pointed out, they were stories that exemplified and illustrated journeys and included striking and unforgettable experiences.[10] Ancient maps offered a similar benefit. The *Classic of the Mountains and Rivers*, a book from ancient China, *c*.600 BCE, said to be the oldest travellers' guide in the world, is a book of mythic geography. Walter, taking inspiration from the work of Joseph Needham, pointed out how the *Classic* described the Nine Cauldrons of Hsia, 'metal surfaces covered with pictures that represented the nine provinces of the country'.[11] It was written to give people guidance on how to recognize good and evil spirits in the physical features of the land, enabling cross-country journeys to be undertaken without fear by showing travellers where to tread safely and how to avoid giving offence to the landscape spirits through inadvertent intrusion into territory that was not safe.[12] Walter recognized that, while what was being portrayed may have appeared, to a twenty-first-century reader, to be fantastical, the descriptions in the book nevertheless illustrated the spirits of places and the places of spirits. Spirits that lived in the landscape described the qualities experienced by the traveller, thus these maps captured how people felt regarding those places. Such maps emerged from reading landscapes as living territories and offered travellers ways to exist in them and how to journey through them. While this chapter is not about mapping per se, in Assisi, it is possible to appreciate the development of such qualitative landscape mapping through the life and afterlife of St Francis and his connection with Mount Subasio.

Assisi, inferno, wild

Assisi is located above the plains on a sloping and precipitous ridge halfway up the dome-shaped, wood-covered slopes of Mount Subasio, Umbria, part of the Apennine mountains extending the length of peninsular Italy (Figure 4.1). When St Francis was alive, the area beyond the town was considered to be wild and barbaric. It was known as the *Collo dell'Inferno*, or 'Hill of Hell', due to it being

Figure 4.1 View from the south looking towards the Basilica di San Francesco and the *Collo dell'Inferno*, the town of Assisi, and Mount Subasio. Photo: D. Gunzburg.

a place for the torture and execution of the condemned.[13] It could, however, simply have been an aberration of the word *inferius* meaning 'lower', as the location was situated further down the rocky outcrop from Assisi overlooking the Tiber valley towards Perugia (Figure 4.2).[14]

The term 'wild' and its connotations are worth pursuing, however. Robert Macfarlane initially identified wild as 'somewhere boreal, wintry, vast, isolated, elemental, demanding of the traveller in its asperities'.[15] In his haptic exploration of wild places, however, Macfarlane came to realize that, rather than somewhere distant and remote, without a past and unnoticed, the wildness of natural life was everywhere, the power and strength of a presence that was energetic, and chaotic, in a state of becoming.[16] He applied the term to the life that inhabited a place, the weed and tree root both finding ways to gain upward thrust through pavement and tarmac to air and sustenance. He saw it as a dynamic experience, one that was not limited or obstructed, but pushing skyward and moving forward.

In medieval Italy, towns and city states perched precariously along narrow ridges, ringed with defensive walls and gates. Towns in Italy today still maintain their hazardous hold on the land, yet in the medieval world, the land beyond a medieval city wall was held to be wild and dangerous, a place for bandits and criminals, lepers and the poor. Wild places beyond city gates acquired another quality through their connection to the human experience of Jesus of Nazareth, who had been crucified at Golgotha, 'the place of the skull' (Mt. 27.33; Mk 15.22; Lk. 23.33; and Jn 19.17), and died as a criminal beyond the city wall of Jerusalem (Heb. 13.12) visible to all passers-by (Mt. 27.39 and Mk 15.29). Jesus was the exemplar that St Francis followed, so much so that he became known as *Franciscus alter Christus*.[17] According to Silvestro Nessi, in 1277, Fra Raniero d'Arezzo (d. 1304), a contemporary of the companions of St Francis, heard them say that St Francis had explicitly requested to be buried on the Hill of Hell, following the way of Jesus. When the companions of St Francis pointed out the disreputable status of the *Collo dell'Inferno*, he had replied: 'If the place is now called the Hill of Hell, it will be called the Gate of Heaven and the Entrance of Paradise.'[18] The story may be apocryphal; Antonio Cadei has suggested that Pope Gregory IX (1145–1241) intentionally named it thus to evoke an old legend.[19] Nevertheless, the story has now become locked into this landscape and, as Walter and Tilley would term it, woven into meaning.

St Francis was, however, already accustomed to wild places. The hermitage at Eremo delle Carceri, where St Francis came to pray and contemplate, still contains the stone bed where he slept. It originally consisted of a series of caves and an oratory built on a rocky outcrop in a steep forest gorge 791 metres above sea level. The sanctuary at La Verna was also used as a retreat for contemplation by St Francis. It was given to him in 1213 by Count Orlando Cattani of Chiusi of La Verna, who used the words 'molto solitario e selvatico' ('much isolated and wild') to describe the place.[20] These places were in keeping with St Francis's belief that to live in the world was to live an ecological life, in joy and harmony with the natural surroundings. He strove to implement a life underscored by an ecological perspective, one that recognized the divine presence in all creatures, based in joy rather than sadness (*accedia*).[21] He described this joy in *The Canticle of Brother Sun*: 'Praised be you, my Lord, with all your creatures', and he expressed his habitat both as qualities and as familiars, members of his family who worked together harmoniously and, in so doing, sustained life: 'Sir Brother Sun,/Who is the day and through whom You give us light,/ And he is beautiful and radiant with great splendour; and bears a likeness of You, Most High One'; Sister Moon and the stars – 'clear and precious and beautiful'; Brother Wind and the air and weather that was 'cloudy and serene'; Sister Water, 'useful and humble and precious and chaste'; Brother Fire, who lit the night and who was 'beautiful and playful and robust and strong'; Sister Mother Earth, who 'sustains and governs us,/ and who produces various fruit with coloured flowers and herbs'; and finally Sister Bodily Death 'from whom no one living can escape'.[22] Macfarlane identified a similar joy in the plethora of senses that assailed him as he walked the old ways of Britain in 2012 in search of the stories created by ancient paths – the temperature of the air, the dynamic display of natural light, the quality of surfaces, the smells, and 'the uncountable other transitory phenomena and atmospheres that together comprise the *bristling* presence of a particular place at a particular moment'.[23] Being in a landscape, for Macfarlane, was to be immersed in a present of qualities, perspectives, and substances:

> I prefer to think of the word as a noun containing a hidden verb: landscape scapes, it is dynamic and commotion causing, it sculpts and shapes us not only over the course of our lives but also instant by instant, incident by incident.[24]

On 30 March 1228, the owner of the Hill of Hell, Simone da Pucciarello, who was, according to tradition, a faithful companion of St Francis from his youth, donated a plot of this wild land beyond the gates of Assisi to enable a burial site to be constructed. Since Franciscans were prohibited from owning any property, Pope Gregory IX, in the name of the Holy See, took on the patronage and ownership of both church and convent. On 17 July 1228, one day after St Francis was canonized and less than two years after his death, Pope Gregory laid the first stone.[25] Despite St Francis declaring that the tiny church of the Porziuncula, a

Figure 4.2 View of the Basilica di San Francesco today, taken from Mount Subasio looking towards the west and the plains. Photo: D. Gunzburg.

mile south of the walls of Assisi, was to be the head and mother church of the Roman Catholic Order of Friars Minor, Pope Gregory decided otherwise, and on 22 April 1230 he awarded that role to the Basilica that was yet to be built.[26] On 25 May 1230, on the eve of Pentecost, the body of St Francis was translated from the church of San Giorgio to the previously wild and barbaric place beyond the city walls of Assisi (Figure 4.2).

Bones and saints

While the proper place of cemeteries in the Roman world was beyond the walls of cities, by the end of the sixth century the landscape of cemeteries had undergone a ground change and, catalysed by the graves of saints, reframed the centres of religious life. They became places where tomb and altar were joined, glorified by the architecture and art that created the sites and made accessible to the whole community via symbolic rites.[27] By offering access in this way burials became much more than customs surrounding the care of the dead and graves became much more than monuments tended by the family on whom rested the incumbent agreement of ritual and closure around bodily separation. The graves of the saints were where the community came to meet the saint as intercessor, thus creating a place where the community could be in dialogue with him or her. This joining of earth with heaven thought to occur at the gravesite occurred through a phenomenon Peter Brown termed *praesentia*, the physical presence of the holy.[28] The belief that at the grave one could meet this presence was exemplified by the inscription on the tomb of Saint Martin of Tours (316 or 336–8 November 397):

> Hic conditus est sanctae memoriae Martinus episcopus
> Cuius anima in manu Dei est, sed hic totus est
> Praesens manifestus omni gratia virtutum.
>
> Here lies Martin the bishop, of holy memory
> whose soul is in the hands of God; but he is fully here,
> present and made plain in miracles of every kind (trans. Brown).[29]

Once this idea took hold in the Patristic period, it resisted change until well after the Reformation.[30] Although there are saints whose bodies on exhumation have been found to be incorrupt, such as St Zita (*c.*1218–72), St Rita of Cascia (1381–1457), and St Virginia Centurione (1587–1651), among others, for the most part, bones are what are left in the tomb. Bones below the ground, as was the case with St Francis, are different. Although the aim of this chapter is not to encompass the full extent and significance of the life of St Francis, nor the meaning of his body after death, nevertheless, a summary of these events will place the reception of that life in context.

St Francis – hagiography, biography, context

The events of that life are well known, despite the loss of valuable primary source documents, such as the first 'Rule' that St Francis wrote in *c.*1209, and several of St Francis's personal letters, combined with the fact that St Francis himself did not write his own story. This has made it difficult to piece together an accurate Franciscan historiography. In addition, due to the proliferation of biographies, the general chapter of the Franciscan Order of 1260 requested Saint Bonaventure to write the official hagiography – the *Legenda major*. This was approved by the Order in 1263, followed by a resolve in 1266 to obliterate all earlier biographies. Other works have since emerged, such as Thomas of Celano's first biography (*Vita prima*).[31]

St Francis was born *c*.1181/1182 in Assisi to Pietro di Bernardone, a prosperous cloth merchant, and Pica de Bourlemont, a French noblewoman from Provence. As stated earlier, his original ambition was to find glory as a knight. Over the course of a handful of years, visited by dreams, and an illness which gave him time to think about the commensality of body and mind, gradually a conversion took place. There were several catalysing moments in St Francis's life that shaped him and brought him closer to the life he envisaged for himself, a life that sought to protect and defend core values despite the material changes he saw around him. They created what Jacques Le Goff has identified as a man who acted as 'an eddy in the rising tide of material comfort'.[32] This new materiality of change was one that had been incrementing since the year 1000 when, over a period of years, population increase in north and central Italy generated towns. Initially these were villages accreted around church and castle; gradually the focus on military and administrative concerns shifted to an economic, political, and cultural emphasis. Towns became the focus for new work processes and new economic exchange. Merchant bankers took over the handling of money from monasteries, and Jews and a growing number of Christian merchants became consumer lenders, also known as usurers. As Le Goff has summarized, 'Economic and social inequality was based no longer on birth and family, but on possessions and property, ownership of land and buildings in town, of rents and rates in the form of money'.[33] Craftsmen and merchants (*arti*) combined with political organizations (*comuni*) to change the fabric and make-up of urban centres.

The first symbolic rejection of St Francis's dream of becoming a knight occurred on his way to war in Apulia in 1205 when he met an impoverished knight in meagre clothing and gave him his coat. The second occurred in 1206 when he observed the rundown church of San Damiano and, in an act of seeming irrationality, sold his father's stock of cloth, along with the horse that carried the cloth to market, to raise money for the repairs. His father being understandably enraged at this action, St Francis sought protection with the bishop of Assisi. Then, in front of his father and the priest, he removed all his clothes in a gesture that emblematized cutting ties with his past. Subsequently, while praying in San Damiano, the Romanesque rood cross spoke to him, urging him to repair God's ruined house. Taking this as a literal injunction, St Francis picked up a trowel and taught himself masonry. The completion of his irrevocable change came in 1209 at the age of 26 or 27, during a sermon at the Porziuncula when he heard the words of Matthew 10 anew. In response, he discarded his shoes and staff, tied his tunic with a rope, and began his life as mendicant preacher. Although he often sought solitude and space at La Verna and Eremo delle Carceri, he also chose to engage with the living, and thus took the Order on a different direction to that of the monasteries, which operated as a separative existence. In 1224, at La Verna, when meditating on a vision of a man with six wings with open arms and joined feet, fixed to a cross, he received the stigmata, becoming the first Christian to do so (Figure 4.3). He was a man who always suffered with poor health and in the intervening two years until his death he endured blinding headaches and impoverished eyesight.

Figure 4.3 Giovanni Bellini (*c.*1424/35–1516), *St. Francis in the Desert, c.*1476–8, oil on panel, 49 1/16 × 55 7/8 inches (124.6 × 142 cm). Image: Copyright The Frick Collection.

When he was close to death, his wish to return to the Porziuncula was jeopardized by the fact that the closest road passed by Perugia. His companions were deeply concerned that he might be kidnapped by the Perugians, and his burial bring them profit from pilgrimage.[34] Saintly bodies were also stolen for the relics they could yield through bodily division. Organs such as the heart were prized. Bodies could also be boiled to remove the flesh so that bones could be distributed, such as occurred with Saint Louis XI of France (1214–1270) and Saint Thomas Aquinas (1225–1274).[35] With his death imminent, his companions were determined that his body would not be used for profit and would be kept whole. A safer, more circuitous route back was taken and his death in the Porziuncula occurred on 3 October 1226. In accordance with his wishes, he was laid out naked on the floor and his body covered with dust and ashes. The funeral was held the following day and his body was buried at the church of San Giorgio, now a chapel in the basilica of Santa Chiara, in the town of Assisi.

Evidence from a variety of *post-mortem* miracle scenes painted on early *Vita* panels depict St Francis's coffin as wooden, rectangular, and raised off the ground by four legs.[36] The literature is, however, silent as to where in San Giorgio he was buried. In the decomposition that follows death, nature is highly expedient. Decay of the body occurs in stages and in the process, the body moves from corpse to cadaver to skeleton. In the first twenty-four hours autolysis occurs. The body looks fresh, yet internal organs begin to break down. After two or three days when active bacteria distend the body with odorous gases, it begins to decompose. In order to facilitate drainage of liquids from the decomposing body to avoid sanitary and health problems, a hole would be drilled into the base of the coffin. Black putrefaction develops when the corpse turns black and shrinks from escaping gases. This is followed by fermentation when the body begins to dehydrate and releases strong odours. In a state of dry decay, all the moisture of the body disappears, and decomposition is significantly reduced. The corpse has now become a cadaver.[37] It takes a long time to form bones, however.

Found in translation

From the day of translation on 25 May 1230 onwards, controversy surrounded the exact whereabouts of the tomb of St Francis and in the confusion that followed, deliberate or otherwise, the ensuing motif of 'the secret tomb' gained traction within the Order's collective memory. Over nearly six hundred years of time, stories of the tomb and the search to locate the shrine's exact placement compounded; these have been comprehensively reviewed by Donal Cooper.[38] Two failed searches occurred, one in 1755 and a second in 1802–3. In the interim, doubt was even cast by the Observant branch of the Order over whether the tomb actually existed.[39] Fifteen years after the second unsuccessful search, Pope Pius VII (b. 1742 and head of the Catholic Church and ruler of the Papal States from 14 March 1800 to his death in 1823) sanctioned an expedition led by the Papal Commissioner for Antiquities, Carlo Fea. This one was successful. On 12 December 1818, after fifty-two nights of digging, workmen reached an iron grating beneath which was a stone coffin and skeleton. Cooper has rightly noted the debt modern scholarship owed to Fea for his meticulous notes and careful plan and cross-section drawings of the area beneath the high altar of the Lower Church and these notes indicate the great care that was taken to conceal the body from view.[40]

Bartolomeo da Pisa in his *De Conformitate vitae Beati Francisci ad vitam Domini Iesu* (1385–90) emphasized the link between the tomb of St Francis and the tomb of Christ: 'As Christ's tomb was sealed and watched by guards, so St Francis's tomb has been sealed, to prevent his body ever being visible to anyone.'[41] Cooper has further observed that, while St Francis's burial below the high altar was an outmoded style for thirteenth-century Italian shrines, such a placement may have reflected Early Christian martyr burials, as noted in Revelation 6:9, and thought appropriate for St. Francis's standing as head of the new Order.[42] This below-ground burial was also motivated by the fear of theft. Whatever the reason, this is what Fea found.

To create the burial place, a small chamber measuring approximately 380 square centimetres, although made smaller by rubble in-fill, was carved into the mountain side. St Francis was placed into a simple stone sarcophagus, probably of Early Christian origin, around which was placed a wrought iron cage or arca, on top of which a free slab of travertine limestone served as a lid. Leaving a small gap above the sarcophagus, two enormous slabs of travertine limestone were then cemented together one on top of each other and set into the walls of the cavity, and placed onto three iron bars, to hold their weight separate from the sarcophagus below them. The burial chamber was surrounded by rock on all four sides, but a small cavity was created above the cemented travertine slabs. Once the chamber was sealed, the only indication that established the location of the now-hidden tomb was the position of the high altar of the Lower Church. Thus for pilgrims, the altar served as a physical synecdoche for the saint, and became the place where the community gathered to meet him and to be in conversation with him.

Although buried into rock, which suggests a degree of permanence and immovability, the tomb as a point of stillness also became a pivot point for thinking about the life of St Francis, what he represented, and his journeys across and through this mountainous landscape. For as Walter observed, 'Human experience makes a place, but a place lives in its own way. Its form of experience occupies persons – the place locates experience in people.'[43] The tomb was set into a 'wild' place on the side of the mountain with plains below and wooded landscape around, thus the place amplified the encounter. The impact of St Francis's death was that it drew followers to pay homage to the places that shaped him: the hermitage at Eremo delle Carceri, the sanctuary at La Verna, the forest and mountainous area of Greccio where St Francis celebrated the crib at Bethlehem, the tiny church of the Porziuncula, and the church of San Damiano where the rood spoke to him. Ingold has described the complex of interwoven trails which people produce to create their life a 'meshwork'. Ingold in turn borrowed the term from Henri Lefebvre who defined 'meshwork' as 'the reticular patterns left by animals, both wild and domestic, and by people (in and around the houses of village or small town, as in the town's immediate environs)'.[44] The itinerant preaching that was to become St Francis's way of life created such a meshwork of habitation, weaving his life with this living mountainous landscape around Assisi. In traversing the landscape to reach the places that had shaped him via such a meshwork, pilgrims opened themselves to the possibility of the landscape 'scaping' them as it had St Francis.

The mountain as reliquary

In their exploration of the properties that exist essentially or permanently in bone, Cara Krmpotich, Joost Fontein, and John Harries asked not what it is that people do with bones but rather 'what do bones do to people?'[45] As noted previously, the bones of a saint sanctify place. Thus, the raised tomb as a place for holding the relic of the saint becomes venerated. As the place where the tomb is situated draws people to it, so this becomes an established pilgrimage site. The raised tomb envisioned in 1233 for St Dominic in Bologna was the style that became influential for thirteenth-century shrines of saints.[46]

Once the body is in the ground, however, the soil itself becomes a living receptacle for the decomposing body. Meaning becomes interred into bones, into soil, into place. Robert Pogue Harrison has suggested that humans bury their dead 'to humanize the ground on which they build their worlds and found their histories'.[47] The body of a saint changes the trajectory of this thinking slightly. Human yet more-than-human in their holiness and closeness to God, once buried in the ground, the bones of saints acted as conduits for change. Harrison rested on Giambattista Vico's (1668–1744) etymologizing of *humanitas* ('humanity'), *humando* ('burying'), and *humus* ('earth' or 'soil'). Carrying this further, in the case of a saint, bone, rock, and soil join together as transformative agents and all that a monument on the burial ground can do is point to what we, as humans, place into the ground to keep it safe and retain its memory. As long as the tomb of St Francis was hidden underground, body, bones, soil, and place created a different perspective, one that at least until 1818 was unique, for the sacred relic was invisible, totally hidden. It was, as Antonio Cadei observed, 'replaced by a space that represents it rather than containing it'.[48] The high altar placed over it in the Lower Church, pointed to it, but as few people had seen it directly, a degree of trust was required. Corroboration of such trust can be seen in Cooper's research where, working from the insights of Niccolò Papini, OFM Conv., he observed an entry from the Sacro Convento's archive dated 23 June 1380. The entry established that Pietro di Giovanni had been present at a Mass in honour of St Francis as part of his fulfilment of a pilgrimage by proxy, and that he had 'placed his hand on the altar beneath which lies the body of the Most Holy Father Francis, in the presence of a number of trustworthy friars from this convent'.[49] As Cooper noted, 'Pietro di Giovanni touched the altar *mensa* as he might the Saint's tomb.' The high altar-tomb reversal also meant that it could produce miracles. In 1308 Francesco Bartoli described how a female pilgrim was cured when she placed her hand on the *mensa*: 'posita manu sua super altari in quo Corpus beati Francisci conditum requiescit.'[50]

In addition, a small iron grate set into the uppermost step of the altar platform facing the nave allowed the pilgrim kneeling on the steps of the high altar a shadowy view of the vaulted chamber below. In this they were required to have faith that the chamber contained the body and which, as noted above, the 1881 excavations revealed that it did indeed do so, but clearly much deeper than anticipated. Since it was lit by oil lamps this space was known as the *buca delle lampade*.[51] Kneeling at the high altar, experiencing the contrast of glowing altar lamps in the dim light, the pilgrim would have been encouraged to reflect on the stories of St Francis's life in the place of his death, a sensory experience encompassing not only the visual but also the aural sounds of prayer, weeping, sighing, breathing, and the smell of incense and burning candle. It became the location of experience to which Walter referred and imbued with the attachment discussed by Tilley. The place became the receptacle for the events that had occurred there, bound to the bones, but encouraging pilgrimage across the mountainous area to the places that were meaningful to St Francis: the Porziuncula, Eremo delle Carceri, Mount La Verna, the church of San Damiano, and Greccio, among others. The point of stillness at the high altar encouraged the faithful to think widely about the connection between the sensory –what was seen and felt – the *vita* – what was known, understood, and propagated by the church about the life of St Francis – and the materiality of the place – tomb, Basilica, town, and the mountains that created the meshwork of his life. In this regard, Mount Subasio changed from wild (*Collo dell'Inferno*) to buried (tomb/ Lower Church high altar/Basilica) to container, and by becoming a vessel that held a precious relic, the mountain became a reliquary.

In discussing body-part reliquaries, Cynthia Hahn recognized how subject-object reversal applied to the container and the contained, that the reliquary facilitated the power of the relic and, at the same time, gave it potency and thus, over time, the status of one supplanted the other. The reason for this was understandable since, as Hahn went on to observe, 'Unadorned relic bones are inexpressive, anonymous, perhaps even repugnant. Without proper identification and a cultural matrix – what medieval sources call a proper veneration – relics remain inert.'[52] Ultimately, Hahn argued, the reliquary functioned as a sign. The precipitous ridge of Mount Subasio could be said to have taken on a similar role – when St Francis died, the mountain became a living reliquary. Not only did it hold and contain the bones of the saint, it directed focus to the environment within which it sat (Figures 4.1 and 4.4).

When the redesigned crypt was opened in the 1824, pilgrims had previously unprecedented access to the sarcophagus. The newly cleared space created to form the crypt gave pilgrims the opportunity to process around it (Figure 4.5). Such access was fittingly summed up by Cooper: 'The modern pilgrim to Assisi experiences the tomb of St. Francis in a manner wholly unrelated to its medieval origins.'[53] Place, Walter observed, located experiences in people and seeing the tomb offered a different dialogue between story and stone, between the myth and the man, and an ongoing conversation based on visuality anchored the material presence of St Francis to the mountain more fully.

There is one more point to be added to this discussion regarding this conversation with this mountain. In *Underland*, Macfarlane offered a view of stone in deep time. Deep time he defined as that kept by 'stone, ice, stalactites, seabed sediments and the drift of tectonic plates.'[54] Deep time stretched so far backwards and forwards in epochs and aeons that it was almost unfathomable for the human mind to grasp. Yet in deep time, the view of rock and stone changed.

Figure 4.4 The entrance to the Lower Church, Basilica di San Francesco. Photo: D. Gunzburg.

'We tend to imagine stone as inert matter, obdurate in its fixity', Macfarlane wrote. 'But here in the rift it feels instead like a liquid briefly paused in its flow. Seen in deep time, stone folds as strata, gouts as lava, floats as plates, shifts as shingle. Over aeons, rock absorbs, transforms, levitates from seabed to summit.'[55] Stone thus has its own pace. The Apennine mountain range, of which Mount Subasio is part, developed when the African and Eurasian tectonic plates crushed against each other between one hundred million years and two million years ago.[56] The limestone rock that formed the mountain range was the repository from remote shallow seas that were in existence three hundred million years ago.[57] The events that occurred at the beginning of the thirteenth century in Assisi culminated in the tomb of St Francis being hewn into the substrate. The nineteenth-century search for the sarcophagus took fifty-two days of digging through the rock. It

Figure 4.5 Crypt of St Francis, Basilica di San Francesco, Assisi. Photo: Martin Schmidt, https://martinschmidtinasia.wordpress.com/.

took four more years to hew the chamber of the crypt. Faith placed body and bones into deep time and anchored the sanctified space with and around St Francis. This in turn began an ecological conversation with the mountain.

Conclusion

This chapter has taken as its beginning point of exploration the fact that St Francis of Assisi is one of a handful of historical figures associated with a town and a mountain. Born in the region, he maintained a connection to it his whole life. Although his preaching took him through central and northern Italy, his pivot point of regeneration and recuperation was in the church of the Porziuncula,

4 kilometres south of the walls of Assisi. The meshwork he created gave him anchor points or nodes at the hermitage at Eremo delle Carceri 4 kilometres south-east of Assisi, and at La Verna, 113 kilometres north-west of Assisi. Fear of theft around his body's translation and burial beneath the high altar of the Lower Church meant that throughout the medieval period it was never visible. An issue equally alive, as Cooper has noted, is thus a lack of major relics, predicated on the insistence by the Order that 'the tomb contained the Saint's whole and undivided body'.[58] More than any other saint, the coalescing of body and bone with earth and stone focused a conversation with place, mountainous land that humans considered wild and barbaric and which was changed to sacred and holy by what the community buried in it.

St Francis is famously known for preaching to the birds; those were not the only conversations he had with the natural world. This chapter has considered those 'conversations' through the themes of bodies, burials, and bones, and how mountain landscapes shape and are shaped by the people who live among them and whose stories become mythically entwined with place and landscape. In its physical state the mountainous environs that shaped St Francis, his ideas and his thinking, also created the conditions for his conversion of faith. Thus it could be said that place shaped the man. In turn, the town and its environs responded to his death and experienced a conversion of place, thus the man shaped the place. At the heart of this sequential shaping was the mountainous landscape of Assisi. It was this landscape that, as noted earlier, amplified St Francis's belief that to live in the world was to live an ecological life, in joy and harmony with the natural surroundings.

This Franciscan conversation began in the twelfth century and over the last eight hundred years has been one that has occurred in slow time, drawing people in a continuous flow to the Basilica di San Francesco in Assisi and once there, engaging them in the landscape St Francis's life. Through the mountain, this slow conversation continues to take place, make place, and create place.

Notes

1   Andre Vauchez, *Francis of Assisi: The Life and Afterlife of a Medieval Saint*, trans. Michael F. Cusato (New Haven, CT: Yale University Press, 2012), 3.

2   Jacques Le Goff, *Saint Francis of Assisi*, trans. Christine Rhone (London: Routledge, 2004), 54–5.

3   Tim Ingold, 'Ways of Mind-Walking: Reading, Writing, Painting', *Visual Studies* 25, no. 1 (2010): 15–23, at 16.

4 Le Goff, *Saint Francis of Assisi*, 61.

5 Eugene Victor Walter, *Placeways: A Theory of the Human Environment* (Chapel Hill: University of North Carolina Press, 1988), 215.

6 Christopher Tilley, *A Phenomenology of Landscape* (Oxford: Berg, 1994), 18.

7 Tilley, *Phenomenology of Landscape*, 18–19.

8 Walter, *Placeways*, 118.

9 Alfred Korzybski, *Science and Sanity: An Introduction to Non-Aristotelian Systems and General Semantics*, 5th ed. (Brooklyn, NY: Institute of General Semantics, [1933] 1994), 58.

10 Michel de Certeau, *The Practice of Everyday Life*, trans. S. Rendell (Berkeley: University of California Press, 1984), 120–1.

11 Walter, *Placeways*, 118.

12 Walter, *Placeways*, 118–19; Joseph Needham, *Science and Civilisation in China. Vol. 3, Mathemativs and the Sciences of the Heavens and the Earth* (Cambridge: Cambridge University Press, 1970), 503.

13 Carla Pietramellara et al., *Il Sacro Convento Di Assisi* (Roma: Laterza, 1988), 6, 11, 65.

14 Antonio Cadei, 'The Architecture of the Basilica', in *Saint Francis: Patriarchal Basilica in Assisi; Artistic Testimony, Evangelical Message*, ed. Roberto Caravaggi (Milan: Gruppo Editoriale Fabbri, 1991), 43–76, at 72.

15 Robert Macfarlane, *The Wild Places* (London: Granta, 2007), 7.

16 Macfarlane, *Wild Places*, 316.

17 H. W. van Os, 'St. Francis of Assisi as a Second Christ in Early Italian Painting', *Simiolus: Netherlands Quarterly for the History of Art* 7, no. 3 (1974): 115–32, at 115.

18 Ms. Vat. 4354, c. 108. 'Si locus ille modo vocabatur Colli Inferni erit quando vocabitur porta coeli et janua paradisi.' Silvestro Nessi, *La Basilica Di S. Francesco in Assisi E La Sua Documentazione Storica*, vol. 5, Il Miracolo Di Assisi (Assisi: Casa Editrice Francescana, 1994), 20.

19 Cadei, 'Architecture of the Basilica', 72.

20 La Verna Santuario Francescano, https://www.laverna.it/santuario/storia/ (accessed 23 September 2019).

21 Le Goff, *Saint Francis of Assisi*, 61.

22 Jacques Dalarun, *The Canticle of Brother Sun: Francis of Assisi Reconciled*, trans. Philipe Yates (New York: Franciscan Institute, 2016), 2–3.

23 Robert Macfarlane, *The Old Ways: A Journey on Foot* (London: Hamish Hamilton, 2012), 255.

24 Macfarlane, *Old Ways*, 255.

25 Nicola Giandomenico and Paolo Rocchi, *Basilica Patriarcale Di San Francesco in Assisi: Il Cantiere Dei Restauri* (Milano: Electa, 1999), 6.

26 Michael Robson, *The Franciscans in the Middle Ages* (Woodbridge: Boydell Press, 2009), 44–5.

27 Peter Brown, *The Cult of the Saints: Its Rise and Function in Latin Christianity*, Haskell Lectures on History of Religions. New Series, No. 2 (Chicago: University of Chicago Press, 1981), 9.

28 Brown, *Cult of the Saints*, 88.

29 Cited in Brown, *Cult of the Saints*, 4.

30 John Crook, *The Architectural Setting of the Cult of Saints in the Early Christian West, C.300–1200* (Oxford: Clarendon Press, 2000), 17.

31 See Le Goff, *Saint Francis of Assisi*, in particular pp. 13–22 for a fuller account of the sources that account for Francis's life.

32 Le Goff, *Saint Francis of Assisi*, 61.

33 Le Goff, *Saint Francis of Assisi*, 3.

34 Linda Bird Francke, *On the Road with Francis of Assisi: A Timeless Journey through Umbria and Tuscany, and Beyond* (New York: Random House, 2005), 226.

35 E. Richard Gold, *Body Parts: Property Rights and the Ownership of Human Biological Materials* (Washington, DC: Georgetown University Press, 1996), 131.

36 Donal Cooper, '"In Loco Tutissimo Et Firmissimo": The Tomb of St. Francis in History, Legend and Art', in *The Art of the Franciscan Order in Italy*, ed. William R. Cook, The Medieval Franciscans (Leiden: Brill, 2005): 1–38, at 5, and Figure 1.

37 Christopher Daniell, *Death and Burial in Medieval England, 1066–1550* (London: Routledge, 1997), 120–1.

38 Cooper, 'In Loco Tutissimo Et Firmissimo'.

39 Cooper, 'In Loco Tutissimo Et Firmissimo', 12, n.37.

40 Cooper, 'In Loco Tutissimo Et Firmissimo', 12–13. See also Figure 3: Plan of the 1818 excavation of St Francis's tomb, and Figure 4: Cross-section of the 1818 excavation of St Francis's tomb.

41 Cited in Cooper, 'In Loco Tutissimo Et Firmissimo', 9.

42 Cooper, 'In Loco Tutissimo Et Firmissimo', 34 and n.124.

43 Walter, *Placeways*, 131.

44 Tim Ingold, *Lines, a Brief History* (London: Routledge, 2007), 80.

45 Cara Krmpotich, Joost Fontein, and John Harries, 'The Substance of Bones: The Emotive Materiality and Affective Presence of Human Remains', *Journal of Material Culture* 15, no. 4 (2010): 371–84, at 373.

46 Joanna Cannon, *Religious Poverty, Visual Riches: Art in the Dominican Churches of Central Italy in the Thirteenth and Fourteenth Centuries* (New Haven, CT: Yale University Press, 2013), 92.

47 Robert Pogue Harrison, *The Dominion of the Dead* (Chicago, IL: University of Chicago Press, 2003), xi.

48 Cadei, 'Architecture of the Basilica', 62.

49 Cooper, 'In Loco Tutissimo Et Firmissimo', 22 and n.82.

50 Cooper, 'In Loco Tutissimo Et Firmissimo', 22.

51 Cooper, 'In Loco Tutissimo Et Firmissimo', 19–21, and Figure 9: High altar of the Lower Church with surrounding pergola, engraving from Francesco Antonio Maria Righini, OFM Conv., *Provinciale Ordinis Fratrum Minorum S. Francisci Conventualium* (Rome: Ex Typographia Joannis Zempel, 1771).

52 Cynthia Hahn, 'The Voices of the Saints: Speaking Reliquaries', *Gesta* 36, no. 1 (1997): 20–31, at 28.

53 Cooper, 'In Loco Tutissimo Et Firmissimo', 2.

54 Robert Macfarlane, *Underland: A Deep Time Journey* (London: Hamish Hamilton, 2019), 15.

55 Macfarlane, *Underland*, 37.

56 Gian Battista Vai and I. Peter Martini, *Anatomy of an Orogen: The Apennines and Adjacent Mediterranean Basins* (Dordrecht: Springer Science+Business Dordrecht, 2001), 15.

57 Vai and Martini, *Anatomy of an Orogen*, 267.

58 Cooper, 'In Loco Tutissimo Et Firmissimo', 34.

Bibliography

Brown, Peter. *The Cult of the Saints: Its Rise and Function in Latin Christianity*. Haskell Lectures on History of Religions. New Series, No. 2. Chicago: University of Chicago Press, 1981.

Cadei, Antonio. 'The Architecture of the Basilica.' In *Saint Francis: Patriarchal Basilica in Assisi; Artistic Testimony, Evangelical Message*, edited by Roberto Caravaggi, 43–76. Milan: Gruppo Editoriale Fabbri, 1991.

Cannon, Joanna. *Religious Poverty, Visual Riches: Art in the Dominican Churches of Central Italy in the Thirteenth and Fourteenth Centuries*. New Haven, CT: Yale University Press, 2013.

Certeau, Michel de. *The Practice of Everyday Life*, translated by S. Rendell. Berkeley: University of California Press, 1984.

Cooper, Donal. '"In Loco Tutissimo Et Firmissimo": The Tomb of St. Francis in History, Legend and Art'. In *The Art of the Franciscan Order in Italy*, edited by William R. Cook. The Medieval Franciscans, 1–38. Leiden: Brill, 2005.

Crook, John. *The Architectural Setting of the Cult of Saints in the Early Christian West, C.300–1200*. Oxford: Clarendon Press, 2000.

Dalarun, Jacques. *The Canticle of Brother Sun: Francis of Assisi Reconciled*, translated by Philipe Yates. New York: Franciscan Institute, 2016.

Daniell, Christopher. *Death and Burial in Medieval England, 1066–1550*. London: Routledge, 1997.

Francke, Linda Bird. *On the Road with Francis of Assisi: A Timeless Journey through Umbria and Tuscany, and Beyond.* New York: Random House, 2005.

Gold, E. Richard. *Body Parts: Property Rights and the Ownership of Human Biological Materials.* Washington, DC: Georgetown University Press, 1996.

Hahn, Cynthia. 'The Voices of the Saints: Speaking Reliquaries'. *Gesta* 36, no. 1 (1997): 20–31.

Harrison, Robert Pogue. *The Dominion of the Dead.* Chicago, IL: University of Chicago Press, 2003.

Ingold, Tim. *Lines, a Brief History.* London: Routledge, 2007.

Ingold, Tim. 'Ways of Mind-Walking: Reading, Writing, Painting'. *Visual Studies* 25, no. 1 (2010): 15–23.

Korzybski, Alfred. *Science and Sanity: An Introduction to Non-Aristotelian Systems and General Semantics,* 5th ed. Brooklyn, NY: Institute of General Semantics, [1933] 1994.

Krmpotich, Cara, Joost Fontein, and John Harries. 'The Substance of Bones: The Emotive Materiality and Affective Presence of Human Remains'. *Journal of Material Culture* 15, no. 4 (2010): 371–84.

La Verna Santuario Francescano, https://www.laverna.it/santuario/storia/ (accessed 23 September 2019).

Le Goff, Jacques. *Saint Francis of Assisi,* translated by Christine Rhone. London: Routledge, 2004.

Macfarlane, Robert. *The Wild Places.* London: Granta, 2007.

Macfarlane, Robert. *The Old Ways: A Journey on Foot.* London: Hamish Hamilton, 2012.

Macfarlane, Robert. *Underland: A Deep Time Journey.* London: Hamish Hamilton, 2019.

Needham, Joseph. *Science and Civilisation in China. Vol. 3, Mathemativs and the Sciences of the Heavens and the Earth.* Cambridge: Cambridge University Press, 1970.

Robson, Michael. *The Franciscans in the Middle Ages.* Woodbridge: Boydell Press, 2009.

Tilley, Christopher. *A Phenomenology of Landscape.* Oxford: Berg, 1994.

Vai, Gian Battista, and I. Peter Martini. *Anatomy of an Orogen: The Apennines and Adjacent Mediterranean Basins.* Dordrecht: Springer Science+Business Dordrecht, 2001.

van Os, H. W. 'St. Francis of Assisi as a Second Christ in Early Italian Painting'. *Simiolus: Netherlands Quarterly for the History of Art* 7, no. 3 (1974): 115–32.

Vauchez, Andre. *Francis of Assisi: The Life and Afterlife of a Medieval Saint,* translated by Michael F. Cusato. New Haven, CT: Yale University Press, 2012.

Walter, Eugene Victor. *Placeways: A Theory of the Human Environment.* Chapel Hill: University of North Carolina Press, 1988.

Part Three

Animistic conversations

5

Mountains as sources of power in seen and unseen worlds

Fiona Bowie

Introduction

The notion of the sacred is tied up with concepts of energy and power, human and other-than-human activity, and mediation between worlds. Some mountains have long been considered particularly sacred and active, both by the people who live around them and by those who visit them. The ethnographic record speaks of a two-way relationship between 'other-than-human entities' and living people, who are in constant dialogue with one another. To ignore this dialogue and only consider the views of living human observers and actors is to only tell half the story of these sacred mountains. The types of 'other-than-human entities' identified are numerous (a term coined by Irving Hallowell), and each mountain has what might be described as a key energy signal associated with it that is related to the sum of the spirit activity in each place (a notion put forward by the theosophist Annie Besant and elaborated in the writings of Cynthia Sandys). The aim of taking the perspective of other-than-human actors seriously is to avoid both narrowly culturally constructivist and naively romanticist interpretations of sacred space and to allow different voices to inform the narrative. Whatever the ontological reality of spirits these narratives have a central role in the way these mountains are perceived and experienced.

Sacred natural sites and the idea of the holy

Mountains and high places are frequently regarded as sources of power by the peoples living around them. There is evidence of rock cults and sacred mountains from prehistoric times to the present, as documented by Robert Hertz in his study of St Besse in Italy's Graian Alps, exhibiting continuity over time in the reverence given to particular landmarks.[1] Sacred mountains can be regarded as a subset of revered natural places, which include water, trees, and weather phenomena. Almost any natural feature, as well as humanly constructed monuments and buildings, can acquire or manifest a reputation for holiness. Mountains generally have a number of microclimates associated with changes in altitude, with forest zones and water sources in the form of glaciers, rivers, or springs. The veneration of different spirits or recognition of different sources of power is associated with these different climactic zones. In this chapter I address the phenomenon of powers associated with sacred natural sites using examples of two very well-known mountains. The first is Mount Everest (Sagarmatha/ Chomolungma), in the Himalaya, which is just one of a number of similarly sacred peaks along the Chinese/Nepalese border. The second is Mount Fuji in Japan. I draw on conventional ethnographic information in my discussions, as well the channelled writings of an English non-professional medium, Lady Cynthia Sandys.[2] I use the latter communications as a counterpoint to more conventional ethnographic data. Taken at face value their post-mortem experiences add an additional perspective to the notion of sacred power associated with these particular mountains. A view from beyond the earth planes, as expressed by discarnate beings through the mediumship of Sandys, links the local topography with notions of cosmic forces and energies that are otherwise invisible to most informants, even if they are also affected by them, and in some cases can affect and manipulate them. Such a perspective brings to the fore Tim Ingold's notion of people and landscapes involved in a process of mutual becoming and indwelling in what he calls a temporal 'taskscape'.[3]

A study such as this inevitably raises questions concerning the nature of the sacred, as well as the use of the term 'sacred natural sites', adopted by the World Conservation Union (WCU). While their focus is on the conservation of both biodiversity and cultural diversity in various regions of the world, WCU ethnographic reports are a useful starting point for an exploration of mountains as sources of power. The WCU defines sacred natural sites as 'natural areas of special spiritual significance to peoples and communities' which 'include natural areas recognized as sacred by indigenous and traditional peoples, as well as natural areas recognized by institutionalized religions or faiths as places for worship and remembrance'.[4] The word 'sacred' is variously given as originating from an obsolete Latin verb *sacren* 'to make holy', Old French *saceres*, 'to consecrate, dedicate', or Latin *saceres*, 'to set apart, immortalize, dedicate'. It is often seen as synonymous with 'holy', from the Old English *halig*, relating both the notion of being dedicated or set apart, and wholeness. A sacred mountain or sacred natural place is therefore one which is set apart from other places in some way. The etymology of the terms 'sacred' and 'holy', with the notion of being made holy, anointed, or dedicated, suggests that a mountain or other natural feature of the landscape acquires this designation as a result of human intention and ritual activity. Émile Durkheim (1858–1917) defined religion as 'a unified system of beliefs and practices relative to *sacred things*, that is to say, things set apart and forbidden'.[5] The realm of the sacred, for Durkheim, was always set in opposition to ordinary or profane life and space. This language is echoed in more recent descriptions of the sacred, such as Bas Verschuuren's description of sacred natural sites as often representing 'the highest human aspirations and spiritual values of any given culture', or Paola Demattè's discussion of sacred mountains and rivers on China's northern frontier.[6] Demattè observed that in this region,

> No matter what the structure of belief or its complexity, or whether the believers were roaming nomads who relied on the natural environment for sustenance, traveling merchants who sought respite from it, or urban dwellers who longed for lost nature, particular places *acquired sacredness or sacred value* because of their positions, structures, and cumulative histories (my italics).[7]

Some writers reject or wish to modify this anthropocentric view of the sacred, adopting the notion of numinosity (from the Latin *numin*, 'divine will') in contradistinction to the Durkheimian notion of the sacred as a human construct. For the German Lutheran theologian Rudolf Otto (1869–1937) the *experience* of the holy was what mattered. For Otto the numinous was 'wholly other' and not reducible to anything other than itself, it evoked the awe, power, majesty, and unapproachability of God, as well as feelings of dependence. Despite the terror it could induce, numinosity was also attractive or fascinating.[8] Mircea Eliade (1907–86) adopted the language of sacred and profane, and Otto's focus on experience and the irreducibility of religion and the numinous. He added to this the idea that the basis of religion was a 'hierophany' or manifestation of the sacred, which is re-enacted through ritual and performance. Despite the popularity of many of Eliade's ideas, his essentialization of the sacred as something that inheres to a place, at the expense of social and political or other contextual factors, his focus on pure forms of ancient religion (an ideal *homo religiosus*) from which modern forms are said to have become debased, and his theological rather than ethnographic approach to the sacred, make his ideas problematic for many anthropologists and scholars of religion.[9]

Denis Byrne also adopted the language of numinosity, introducing the term 'spiritscapes' in his discussion of sacred natural sites. Byrne claimed that

> those people who hold these places to be sacred believe them to be occupied or constituted by spirits or deities which have certain powers, for instance the miraculous power to cure illness or bring rain. Such powers are commonly described as supernatural or magical, but the term 'numinous', indicating the presence of a divinity, seems more appropriate.[10]

For Byrne, as for Rudolf Otto, the site itself possessed agency. Fear of the power of a sacred site can help protect it, through prohibitions on cutting down trees for example, whether the power was seen as emanating from a deity or nature spirits. Byrne did not comment on the ontological reality of spirits or the numinous, but stressed its universality, observing that 'rather than being a peculiarity of religion in certain regions, what these places (or what 'the numinous') represents is a characteristic way in which humans everywhere at different times have engaged spiritually with their topographic surroundings'.[11] It is hard to deny that mountains in particular seem to evoke a sense of awe, fascination, and dread (Otto's *mysterium tremendum et fascinans*) that is not confined to any one culture or religion.

Robert Macfarlane quoted a Buddhist scholar, Lama Govinda, on the power of attraction asserted by the peaks of the Himalaya: 'People are drawn to them from near and far, as if by the force of some invisible magnet; and they will undergo untold hardships and privations in their inexplicable urge to approach ... the centre of this sacred power.'[12] In his book entitled *The Old Ways*, Macfarlane described a trip to Minya Kinka, 'The White Snow Peak of the Kingdom of Minyak' on the Burma-China-Tibet-India border, with a Tibetologist friend, Jon Miceler. The mountain peak is the focus of a number of pilgrimage routes, some dating back more than seven hundred years. As they approached the mountain Jon was reminded of the Sanskrit word, *darshan*, which he glossed as a face-to-face encounter with the sacred on earth, a physical manifestation of the holy. This struck Macfarlane as appropriate and 'a good alternative to the *wow!* that I usually emitted on seeing a striking mountain'.[13] On climbing Minya Konka, Miceler and Macfarlane eventually reached a Buddhist monastery perched on the side of a ravine. Macfarlane commented, 'I hadn't ever before reached a mountain landscape so wholly sacralised, in which almost every human mark was either an expression of devotion or a marker of hierophany.'[14] Whether a sense of the sacred is inherent in the landscape, or lies in its effects on human beings, it is apparent that rocks and mountains have been regarded as places of power and as a source of danger and blessing since prehistoric times.[15]

Mount Everest – Sagarmatha – Chomolungma

The mountain known in the West as Peak 15 or Mount Everest, after the surveyor general of India George Everest, is more respectfully referred to as Sagarmatha in Nepalese ('Forehead' or 'Goddess of the Sky', 'Peak of Heaven') and Chomolungma or Jomolungma ('Goddess Mother of the World', 'Snow Mother of the World', or 'Goddess of the Valley') in Tibetan (Figure 5.1). It lies on the border between Nepal and Tibet (China) in the Sagarmatha National Park. This is a demarcated protected area, together with the so-called Buffer Zone consisting of the regions of Khumbu and Pharak. The Khumbu region below the peak is known for its dramatic river valleys carved out by the melting glaciers, whose sides are covered with forests of pine, birch, and fir, which rise to the tree line at around 4,100 metres above sea level. The mountain is only one of a great number of peaks in the Himalaya rising to over 6,000 metres in height, which can be regarded as a single 'sacredscape' for the peoples of the region.

Figure 5.1 Sunset over Mount Everest (Sagarmatha/Chomolungma) (middle), Nuptse and Changtse while descending Mt Kala Patthar (5,644 metres) to Gorakshep, Khumjang, Nepal. Photo: howlingred, Unsplash.

The mountain is closely associated with the Sherpa people of Eastern Nepal who have specialized as mountain guides for the thousands of visitors who visit the region each year. Sherpa villages are mainly to be found on the barer upper slopes of the Khumbu, with its alpine vegetation, with some smaller summer hamlets above the tree line. Jeremy Spoon has written extensively on the place-based spiritual values of the Khumbu Sherpa, who live inside the protected area. They practice a form of Tibetan Nyingma Buddhism, which incorporates an earlier religion of the region known as Bon, and various animistic folk traditions. From Buddhism the Sherpa have adopted the notions of sin, merit, and reincarnation, but they also view the world as 'a place occupied by a diversity of supernatural beings, including deities, spirits and ghosts'.[16] In a useful summary of this animistic side of Sherpa religion, Spoon wrote,

> Under the appropriate conditions, the deities and spirits protect the land, the people and their faith. In order to receive protection, the Sherpa regularly perform rituals and make offerings to please the deities and to ask for their forgiveness. Worship of these entities occurs in monasteries, homes or open spaces.[17]

Spoon's main interest is the relationship between Sherpa spiritual values and conservation of the natural environment. The Khumbu Sherpa recognize two categories of sacred landscape, *beyul* or hidden valleys and *yul-lha* or sacred mountains. The former are associated with Buddhism, as the *beyul* were identified by Buddhist lamas as places for retreat and silence. The *yul-lha* or sacred mountains, on the other hand, are associated with animistic beliefs that link supernatural beings to particular parts of the landscape. Inside the *beyul* there are taboos on killing animals, cutting live trees, and polluting water sources, as well as angering the spirits through cheating or immoral behaviour. It is following the taboos associated with a *beyul* that makes these places sacred and powerful. These taboos also enhance conservation, as due to the restrictions in place there is a greater diversity of plant and animal life within the *beyul* protected areas than outside them.

Yul-lha refers not only to the sacred mountains but is also a generic term for a range of nature spirits and deities. From a Buddhist perspective they were demons, subdued by Guru Rinpoche, the eighth-century monk credited with bringing Buddhism to the region, and by subsequent Buddhist monks and lamas (priests or teachers). They are now bound to offer protection from avalanches, floods, and plane crashes. According to Spoon, 'Each deity has its own associates or khor in the form of wildlife, livestock and other mythical creatures. People respect these associates and do not harm them.'[18] Guru Rinpoche appointed a deity known as Khumbu Yul-Lha or Khumbila, literally 'Khumbu country god', to protect the area. The Sherpa worship these deities by burning incense from aromatic plants, and by placing white flags over their houses on specific days of the year and during an annual ceremony. Numerous other mountains also embody protector deities who are important to different clans and settlements. The deity of Mount Everest is a goddess known as Jomo Miyo Lang Sangma, who is seen as a provider of wealth (*norbu*). Before the growth of tourism, her wealth was manifest as plentiful harvests and abundant pastures. With the advent and rapid growth of tourism her status has increased in the region and her gifts include the wealth to be made from paid employment in the tourist industry. Climbing to the summit of sacred mountains inhabited by protector deities is generally forbidden, although there is a Buddhist tradition of circumambulation. In the case of Mount Everest this prohibition has been lifted for tourist purposes, but Khumbila remains off limits.

The forest zones below the peaks are also regarded as sacred, and similarly reflect the Buddhist, Bon, and animistic religious heritage of the region. Some forests are considered sacred because of the spirits that reside there, while others are protected groves associated with powerful lama or with monasteries. Spoon explained that 'Lama protected forests originated when a powerful lama sanctified or cursed a forest patch, where trees must not be felled by using cutting implements. Monastery forests are typically groves that surround or are nearby village monasteries.'[19] A further category of deities or spirits are the *Lu*, associated with individual natural features such as trees, rocks, and water sources, or taking the role of house guardians living in a specially constructed shrine in the home. According to Spoon,

> Lu can bestow wealth and long life to a family, but can also cause hardship, often in the form of physical ailments that can only be treated by a shaman. Women take care of Lu using knowledge passed down from female to female. Lu are upset by pollution, cutting trees, breaking boulders and digging land. These values thus influence environmental decision-making, such as taboos on polluting water sources and protecting various tree species.[20]

Sherry Ortner discussed another type of spirit in the Sherpa cosmology known collectively as *pem-nerpa*. The *pem* are witches and the *nerpa* ghosts, and along with the *lu*, the locality spirits, are a major source of illness. While in Buddhist ideology all spirits might be classed as demons, Sherpa shamanism distinguishes between these spirits and demons, who are more generalized forces, thought to have existed before the human race came into being and still around, ready to eat people. They are motivated by drives such as greed or aggression. According to Ortner, 'As the demons have come from nowhere, being uncreated existents, so their motivating drives are "natural", essential and self-generated'.[21] *Pem*, on the other hand, 'are forces embodied in living members of the community' and are activated through envy. They operate through links of kinship and neighbourhood.[22] *Nerpa* are the ghosts of deceased individuals who are personally remembered. They are what are sometimes referred to in Western contexts as 'earthbounds', spirits who died in accidents or who 'have failed to end their social relationships satisfactorily, and remain attached to and dependent on their former world'.[23] Like earthbound spirits described in Spiritualist traditions in the West they can be identified as particular, known, individuals, in need of help to leave the 'earth plane'. Like lost spirits anywhere they are described as being miserable, 'homeless, hungry, and thirsty, wandering about striking people with illness as a way of expressing their need for food and drink'.[24] Ortner draws out the differences between the relationality of the *pem* and *nerpa*, who are able to express their needs and describe their plight through the shamans in a community setting, often evoking pity and sympathy from villagers, and the more abstract and psychologised drives of demons. According to Ortner, 'The demons in the monastic context seem intended to represent, evoke, and contribute to the formation of an altered sort of personhood, socially decontextualized, mobile and uncommitted in terms of social relationships'.[25] This reflects the highly individualized life of the monk or nun within Tibetan Buddhism, for whom spiritual development is the responsibility of the individual rather than the community, and depends on leaving behind the ties and demands of lay village life.

Another aspect of Sherpa religion described by Ortner is the popularity of reincarnated lamas or *tulku*. A tulku is 'a mortal human body permanently possessed, as the shaman is occasionally possessed, by a god (or in some cases by a nearly divine soul on its way to godhood). The figure of the reincarnate lama in Tibetan Buddhism is a literalized version of the Mahayana notion of the bodhisattva renouncing nirvana to save all sentient beings'.[26] The tulku is seen as 'a very unique and individually powerful and charismatic person'.[27] As will be seen below this is another manifestation of sacred power that is echoed in Sandys's *Awakening Letters*, which speak of the Himalayan people's relationship to earth spirits, power centres, both positive and negative, as well as to great teachers.

The question that arises is what, if anything, can the mediumistic communications of Sandys add to these ethnographic accounts of spirits and supernatural forces associated with Mount Everest/Chomolangma. What is of interest is the way in which they provide an independent account of many of the different types of energy and supernatural beings described in local traditions, bridging the more impersonal forces of Buddhism and the local and personalized spirits of animistic traditions. They are personal narratives in the way that Macfarlane's travel writings are, the difference being that the narrators are no longer in their physical bodies. One thing that is clear from Sandys' communications is that there is no sudden change in personality, knowledge, or interest when people die. There is a gradual process of learning and adaptation as discarnate individuals become accustomed to a new etheric body, free of gravity, able to move by the power of intention or thought. Her interlocutors are by definition still close to the earth plane, or they would not be able to communicate through Sandys's mediumship. They are not suddenly omniscient and are beginners in the etheric and astral worlds, exploring the ways in which different planes of existence interact and influence one another. There is no eternal rest, rather a curiosity and zest for life and a desire to work and explore the possibilities of life on the etheric plane. Rosamond Lehmann's deceased daughter Sally, for example, might well have been describing the nature spirits or *lu* when she wrote, 'I never get used to the wonder of entering the solid earth and walking about in both earth and water as if they non-existed. They are both teeming with life and energy, and the spirit of each is entirely separate and individualized.'[28]

A persistent theme in these channelled writings is the notion of power centres, such as Glastonbury and Iona in Great Britain, Chartres Cathedral in France, and various mountain ranges, including the Himalaya and Mount Fuji. Sandys's daughter Patricia described working with Florence Nightingale (Flo), her first cousin thrice removed, in collecting healing energies or vibrations for her:

> Flo sends us off to collect vibrations for this and that. They aren't always drawn from the atmosphere. They are all born in the ether, but their growth and development takes them into the animal and vegetable kingdoms. The last time I was sent off on one of these expeditions was to Central Asia, to the power centres which you have been told about. They range all over the Himalayas [*sic*] into Tibet, and into China, Turkestan and Afghanistan and so on. The range is immense, touching Persia, Arabia, and Southern Mongolia.[29]

Patricia's particular task was to collect flower essences for healing. The descriptions of the beauty and vibrancy of nature as seen by Patricia from her perspective in the etheric realm mirrors the heightened accounts familiar to those who have 'peak experiences' in which all the senses are enhanced and the world comes alive. Patricia wrote,

> The complexity and the beauty of those mountains leaves me gasping ... and the snow! I had no understanding of snow ... Snow is the concentrated essence of all the rays. When it falls, we all know a strange sense of release, and I-don't-care-what-happens feeling. Imagine the snow falling in the valleys of the Himalayas [*sic*], where the tiny plants are already drenched in the powerful mountain rays which come from goodness knows where, and then imagine the flowers as I found them, and the pure joy I had in even touching them. Of course they carry immense energy ... As I picked each flower, the etheric force surrounding it seemed to suck away the physical and leave a much stronger prototype in my hand.[30]

Patricia described how each member of the group had their own allotted task. Some collected the energy from stones or vibrations from among the glacier peaks. Others found the healing rays they were looking for in the birds or clouds that hung around the high mountain peaks.

In the first volume of the *Awakening Letters* there are a series of communications from Sandys's brother Joe, who had travelled widely while alive as a diplomat. After death he revisited many of the places he had once lived, while also engaging in the energy work associated with sacred power places. Joe spoke of his work with Gandhi in the Himalaya, and he continued this theme when he wrote,

> I told you about our journey through the mountains of Asia when we gathered the vibs [vibrations] from the mountain peaks and brought them to bear in a concentrated way upon the peasantry in the appropriate valley, blending them with the physical vibs of the people ... They live here with, by, and in close touch with the great earth spirits, and so to them the vision of a great Teacher was not unknown. It had often happened in their history, and even in their own personal experience. So, with the power, we began a careful direction to construct the moulds into which higher spirits might become visible and audible. I was enormously interested to see how this could be done. So far I have myself seen some of the great initiates, but only for brief moments, my work has been with men whom I've known and admired ... most of all Gandhi; and now through him were learning to concentrate the rays into a mass of light and colour; and when this had been done to an intense degree I suddenly saw and felt that the light was pregnant with *life*. A being of transcendent beauty was absorbing and gathering in all the tendrils of light into one body of celestial form. I was so intensely excited that I could have cried for joy.[31]

On another occasion Joe took the opportunity to climb Everest with Gandhi, and watched him draw colour and scent from the flowers along the way. He noted, 'Each mountain top possessed its own earth spirit. Gandhi saluted them each in turn, asking for their help, not only for our climb, but for his work among the animals and peoples of India.'[32] The Sherpa sense of respect for the power of the mountains, with their taboos on ascending the peaks and knowledge of their guardian deities, was echoed by Joe, when stated that

> the great Spirit of the Mountain does not welcome humanity except in a very advanced form. I learned this from Gandhi who explained that he could not let me climb alone. I should have lost my way and returned without seeing any of the peaks; they would have withdrawn and shrouded themselves in mist; but his coming dispelled all the unfriendly aspects, so that I was made to feel at one with all nature. Nature can do this everywhere, but here in the Himalayas [*sic*] the withdrawal can be vicious. These heights have been kept sacred to admit only certain vibs. The Sherpa who made the summit with Hunt knew this; he belonged to the country and together with their superb courage they were granted success.[33]

Joe's impression when standing on the peak was that 'the beauty and the strength of all the surrounding peaks seemed to flow into this great power centre of Everest.'[34] Gandhi appeared to him as a transfigured being 'far in advance of my comprehension'. Joe ended this letter with a powerful affirmation of the enormous power and supernatural presence of the mountain. He described a 'bearable rapture' descending upon him and 'saw a figure of light so transcendent that I was blinded and could only sense the semi-transparent wonder of this marvellous Presence'.[35]

Not all mountains were described as sources of divine power and inspiration. According to Joe there were also those invested with negative energy. He wrote, 'There are some in central Asia from which stem enormous roots of negative force. Where there is white magic you will nearly always find the equivalent in some form directed against the God Power.'[36] He described an experience in China when he stood on the summit of a peak, ready to open his energy centres to draw in power to redistribute where it was needed in the world, when he noticed that the mountain was emitting horrible black smoke. He thought he was looking at a volcanic eruption but then remembered that he was seeing the etheric rather than the physical mountain. He received a long-distance message from his niece Patricia, who was known to the family as Pat, that he should close the centres of his aura and brace himself against the darker powers. In an instant Pat and Douglas (his son in his last earth life) were beside him, leaving Joe 'feeling rather like a naughty boy who'd gone to the larder without leave'.[37] There ensued a cosmic battle. Joe described how Pat threw a strong blue ray around the three of them as they stood on the pinnacle of the mountain, and told them to emit all the white power that they could muster. Pat explained to Joe that she and Douglas were there not only to save him but also the mountain, as, 'Here, for centuries, have been imprisoned the entities of those who have done much evil; but they have mostly expiated their sins and are ripe for release. That is why you came here, led unconsciously by their need'.[38] The three of them were then enveloped in dark smoke which Joe felt was suffocating them. When he thought that they could hold out no longer Douglas and Pat 'emitted a ray of dazzling white light, which was instantly reflected by numerous other peaks and points of light all over the vast expanse of mountains before and beneath us'.[39] Joe then witnessed an extraordinary contest of light and darkness that took place within as well as around him, accompanied by a deafening noise. Eventually,

> with the light came *calm*, and as we three stood together I sensed that the battle had been won and the mountain cleansed of these horrible vibrations for ever …
> It had been a soul-rending experience, and one which they say must be repeated over and over again before the earth is cleansed and able to absorb the white light completely.[40]

The idea that human actions and spiritual forces are reflected in atmospheric events as well as being located in particular places is very common and widespread. One has only to look at much of the work produced by war artists, often depicting sea battles, to note that the human drama is often eclipsed by the greater battle taking place on a metaphysical level, reflected in the skies. Despite the Christian linguistic frameworks used by Pat to describe this cosmic battle, it is possible in these letters to discern numerous links with the ethnographic descriptions of the area, as well as to more universal religious themes.

Mount Fuji, Japan

As Japan's tallest single peak, Mount Fuji, or Fujiyama (in Japanese often referred to respectfully as Fujisan), stands as a symbol of mountain worship as a whole (Figure 5.2). The age of the mountain is unclear, but the present peak is composed of three successive volcanoes, known as Kimitake, Ko Fuji ('Old Fuji'), and Shin Fuji ('New Fuji'). With a base of around 50 kilometres in diameter, and a summit of 3,776 metres, Mount Fuji dominates the landscape for miles around. The origin of the mountain's name is uncertain, but it could be derived from an Ainu term meaning 'fire mountain'. The Chinese ideograms (*kanji*) for Fuji denote fortune or prosperity.[41] According to the authors of a recent study of Mount Fuji's role as a sacred natural site,

> The history of Mount Fuji as a spiritual place originates in the universal primitive form of mountain worship that is common throughout Japan. Over time, traditional mountain worship merged with introduced religions and evolved into a unique form of worship particular to Mount Fuji.[42]

For many Japanese people, and in particular the syncretic Fujikō sect, the mountain has a personality or soul, and is the dwelling place of Shinto gods.[43] The mountain was registered as a cultural World Heritage site in 2013 and is a designated national park, attracting tens of thousands of visitors a year. The water sources around the foot of the mountain are indispensable for local farmers and the peak has been an inspiration for generations of artists. As is the case in the Himalaya, the diverse natural environments of the mountain form part of its religious worship, as well as providing important ecological habitats.

There are many parallels between pre-Buddhist Himalayan traditions and the animistic Shinto religion of Japan, with its reverence for natural phenomena.

Figure 5.2 Mount Fuji and Sayama Lake. Photo: Pixabay.

Shinto pays attention to the spirits who dwell in mountains, rivers, oceans, trees, boulders, stones, and other natural features of the environment. Toshihiko Ono, Tetsuro Hongo, Kiyotatsu Yamamoto, and Noaya Fuitura explored the links between the means of production and worship of a particular deity. For hunters the mountain deity was a hunting deity, for miners it was a deity of minerals, for foresters, a deity linked to timber, and so on. For those who lived from agriculture there was an exchange between the mountain deity and the spirits who controlled farm labour and harvests, with the mountain deity descending from the peaks to exchange places with the local agricultural spirits at certain times. Mountains were also thought of as holy sites inhabited by ancestral spirits. With the advent of rice agriculture these ancestor spirits would travel back and forth between the mountains and the fields, giving rise to a number of festivals, customs, rituals, and shrines. There are also gods of the rice paddies who, like ancestor spirits, act as both protectors of the rice, ensuring its proper growth, and protectors of the family or clan.[44]

There is a respectful separation around Mount Fuji between the *okuyama* or 'deep mountain', which is the abode of the mountain deity, and the *satoyama* or 'village mountain', the grassy and arable areas between the farmland and mountain foothills. The villagers can enter the *satoyama* to forage, but avoid regular travel to the higher sacred zones. Shrines to the mountain god are mainly situated in this marginal zone between the high mountain and the areas of human habitation. While organized religions introduced buildings such as the *shinden* ('deity hall') and *haiden* ('worship hall'), the oldest shrines demarcate the entry to the divine zone by a gate rather than a building for worship. Another type of shrine is the *yohaisho*, a place to bow towards the object of worship, such as Mount Fuji, at the top of a stone staircase. There was an evolution in Japan from the earliest forms of mountain worship, which paid respect to the deity at a distance from a *yohaisho*, to the practice of climbing the mountain.

Practitioners of *Shugendo*, a syncretic Buddhist-Shinto sect which emphasizes enlightenment 'through becoming one with nature and Shinto deities', climb mountains such as Mount Fuji as a religious practice. Mount Fuji is an active volcano and multiple eruptions and lava flows gave rise to a fire-extinguishing faith and the establishment of shrines along lakes and rivers 'symbolizing their role as sacred spaces for prayer for the extinguishment of fire'.[45] The last confirmed eruption on Mount Fuji was in 1707, and following the cessation of activity the shugendo practice of climbing the mountain as a religious observance became increasingly popular. Only those who had purified themselves could enter the Buddha zone above the treeline. 'Religious activity was clearly demarcated by means of spiritual purification and effected by the mystic, divine quality of the trees and forests.'[46] The sanctity of the mountain with its deity and worship of nature spirits combined in the respect for trees in Shinto practice. As Ono commented, 'When the trees of a forest are several centuries old … they are no longer just a magnificent sight, but emit an aura of the sanctity of nature, communicating an almost overpowering spiritual presence.'[47]

For Buddhists there was an evolution of Mount Fuji's volcano deity, Asama no Kami, into Sengen bodhisattva, an avatar of Mahavairochana, the main Buddha ('Enlightened One') of Pure Land Buddhism. Climbing the mountain was like going to the Pure Land for rebirth and practitioners would wear white robes, the colour associated with death. Just as the hidden valleys of the Himalaya remained a key area of sanctity, protected by certain taboos, so the forest zone retained its importance as a sacred zone on Mount Fuji.

For Shinto practitioners the whole of Mount Fuji was seen as 'a protective deity rising in the centre of Japan' and the forest and mountain as a whole regarded as the deity's dwelling place. Its tutelary or guardian spirits 'were seen as deities protecting the nation, the shrine or temple, the village, and the local area.'[48] Mount Fuji remains a popular pilgrimage destination and there are a series of pilgrimage routes marked by numerous shrines. The whole process of climbing the mountain is to go through successive steps of self-purification and discipline, culminating, ideally, in reaching the peak before dawn. 'The rising sun at dawn triggers the phenomenon known as "Brocken's spectre", in which the light …, reflected off mists at the mountain's peak, seems to surround an individual figure in a sort of rainbow aura. Pilgrims regard this phenomenon as an encounter with the Buddha, and the epitome of their religious experience.'[49] Ono, Hongo, Yamamoto, and Fuitura directly related industrial activity, such as logging, and environmental degradation on Mount Fuji to a decline in interest in religion, lamenting that a four thousand year history of harmony with nature is in danger of being eroded. The designation of Mount Fuji as a World Heritage site and the recognition of its cultural and spiritual significance is seen as playing a part in reversing this trend by opening a discussion on Japan's environmental and cultural heritage.[50]

The importance of Mount Fuji with its centuries of devotion is recognized in Sandys's mediumistic communications. It is Sandys's diplomat brother, Joe, who has most to say on Mount Fuji, which both confirms and extends the cultural and ethnographic descriptions of the mountain as a sacred site of considerable power. In the first volume of *The Awakening Letters*, Joe told his sister how he was taught by Gandhi to empty his aura and tune into the higher vibrations of white light, being careful to tune out the lower vibrations, and then to carry them back to ashrams and other places where they could be used for healing. Having practised in the Himalaya, Joe went on to see if he could do the same thing on Mount Fuji. He wrote,

> All these mountains have at one time or another, or, as in the case of Fuji, constantly, been looked upon as divine; and they are in almost every case the mouthpiece of divine inspiration. Fuji has the accumulated prayers of many centuries, and you can draw this multi-racial, multi-religion power from her quite easily, especially as you know Fuji.[51]

He described the technique Sandys should use to tap into this source of power, using her imagination, intention, and memory of the mountain to help others, drawing in and redistributing its healing fire. According to Joe, Mount Fuji was too powerful to visit alone in his etheric body: 'I felt the vastness of it and the almost terrifying power. I did not want to go alone again, so with Hugh [their friend Air Chief Marshall Sir Hugh Dowding, 1882–1970], Douglas [his son] and Arthur [Cynthia's husband] we started working upon the Japanese peasants in the surrounding villages.'[52] For Joe the energy of Mount Fuji was quite different to that of the Himalaya. Fuji was seen as having a negative side that had influenced some of the more brutal aspects of the Second World War. Joe's experience of Fuji was 'like a great leviathan of power in a quiescent state. I feared to stir a leaf or stone; the silence was deep and pregnant with subdued wrath.'[53] The group used their technique of harnessing the mountain's white rays to work on the villagers who lived around the mountain, much as they had done in the Himalaya:

> There were those among them who had fought in the last war and had been in contact with the negative ray and used as carriers of that ray of destruction. But there were others who were still impregnated with the inner rays of Fuji, to whom war was a revulsion; and to them we turned in their sleep bodies in order to cure the sickness in those others who were still suffering from the negative ray.[54]

The barrage of white light was apparently too strong for some of the local inhabitants, and they left their homes to find work elsewhere. Families split up and there was a general sense of upheaval, but in the end Joe and his party had enough power to enter the mountain itself. They were helped in this by 'some really great spirits of the angelic nature ... I think they are called the Avatars.'[55] Apparently some of the villagers were also able to see 'these enormously advanced beings of light' and thought 'that the Buddha had returned to lead them into Nirvana … and that the end of the world had come!'[56] As they entered the mountain Joe was aware of the light growing around the villagers as well as around the workers on the etheric plane. 'I had the strong sensation that Fuji was dead, inert and empty. We had the whole strength of the village with us. They were of course in their sleep bodies, but none the less impregnated with the vibrations of the mountain, and they formed the link for the Great Ones, and forced the entry on the material plane.' There ensued a cosmic battle that culminated in great silence 'redolent with majestic power'.[57]

Joe returned later to his work of cleansing on Mount Fuji. He described it not as one great power centre but as 'clusters of large and small whirlpools of energy' that at first seemed almost impossible to disentangle and cleanse.[58] The task was to enter each whirlpool and sense its energy. Where it was under the subservience of a negative earth force, nothing would grow and soil that should have been fertile and productive was barren. They had to persuade reluctant peasants to use their positive energy to give life to the soil. When they succeeded 'almost immediately the germ of life began to take form, and the virginity of the soil gave out at the same time a tiny vibration of psychic energy which flowed into the great spiritual channel which exists in the ether almost everywhere'.[59] These post-mortem descriptions of Mount Fuji affirm the recognition of Mount Fuji as a great power centre. They reinforce Japanese beliefs and practices, from the great cosmic forces that operate at national level, to the individual farmer cooperating with spirits for the fertility of the soil and germination of plants. For many Japanese people the mountain and its forests are seen to hold both negative and positive forces, associated with death as well as with life. This ambiguity is mirrored in *The Awakening Letters*.

Conclusion: Anthropology's 'ontological turn'

For those who consider mountains to be sacred, the notion of invisible powers that can act in and on the world is central. While to some people the scientific possibility of life after death, and concomitantly the possibility of mediumistic communication with those who have died, will seem too obvious to need further proof or explanation, for others it remains so implausible as to be unworthy of further attention. As Sam Parnia observed, interest in the nature and origin of the human psyche or soul and the reality of invisible forces and beings goes back in Western discourses to Aristotle and Plato, and have remained essentially unchanged.[60]

Anthropologists of religion can be found on both sides of the divide. One attempt to bridge the gap is Ingold's notion of world as fluid, temporal, and responsive, rather than something fixed to be acted upon or observed. Making indirect links with Alfred North Whitehead's process theology, Ingold stated, 'Our actions do not transform the world, they are part and parcel of the world's transforming itself.'[61] Ingold has sought to reinstate animism as a legitimate field of study, part of a larger project to see anthropology, and life itself, as a process of opening and indwelling.[62] Throughout his work Ingold emphasizes intentionality in processes of production. We do not just act on a material substrate but grow into the world as the world grows into us. Although he was not referring to sacred or to unseen forces, Ingold's insight that the world and all those within it together constitute a dynamic reality prefigured some of the later discussions within ontological anthropology.

Another useful contribution is Eduardo Viveiros de Castro's perspectivism, which questions Western assumptions that there are different cultural perspectives on the same underlying reality by contrasting this with an Amerindian view, which he refers to as 'multinaturalism'.[63] According to Martin Holbraad and Morten Axel Pederson, this puts questions of ontology at the centre of anthropological debate. Edith Turner's influential article on the reality of spirits challenged anthropologists to take the spirit world seriously as part of the ethnographic landscape.[64] This challenge was taken up by Nils Bubanbdt and Diego Escolar, who incorporated 'tabooed' material into their analysis in the form of interviews with spirits and encounters with a luminous being.[65] Jack Hunter has called this process 'ontological flooding', which he glossed as 'an ethnographic approach that makes use of tools that destabilise ontological certainty, at least in the context of the ethnographic text, but also experientially in the field' that can lead to a 'more honest appreciation of the "non-ordinary"'.[66] My own approach is to treat a wide variety of data 'as if' it could be true in the form of a thought experiment.[67]

From the perspective of an ontological anthropology stories of power, spirits, ancestors, and deities are not inherently impossible or even improbable. This approach enables new questions about the entanglement of thought, body, and place. If intention and world are one and the same thing, or grow into one another, then these forces are not just data about different cultural perspectives but could describe an aspect of reality based on first-hand experience. For those who live in and around power centres such as Mount Everest/Chomolungma or Mount Fuji, learning to live and work with these forces represents particular challenges. Using both conventional ethnographic and historical data alongside mediumistic communications adds a vivid dimension to the narrative, suggesting that the world of spirits, deities, and cosmic forces form part of a universal imaginary, and as such deserve to be part of the 'spiritscape' of anthropology.

Notes

1 Robert Hertz, 'St Besse: A Study of an Alpine Cult', in *Saints and their Cults*, ed. Stephen Wilson (Cambridge: Cambridge University Press, 1995), 55–100.

2 Cynthia Sandys and Rosamond Lehmann, 'Letters from Our Daughters Part 1 Sally & Part 2 Patricia', in *C.P.S. Papers No.1 & 2* (London: Light Publishing, 1971); Cynthia Sandys and Rosamond Lehmann, *The Awakening Letters: Varieties of Spiritual Experience in the Life after Death* (Jersey: Neville Spearman, 1978); Cynthia Sandys, *The Awakening Letters: Volume Two*, selected and edited by Rosamond Lehmann (Saffron Walden: C.W. Daniel, 1986).

3 Tim Ingold, 'The Temporality of the Landscape', *World Archaeology* 25, no. 2 (1993): 152–74, at 153, 157.

4 Gonzalo Oviedo, Sally Jeanrenaud, and Mercedes Otegui, *Protecting Sacred Natural Sites of Indigenous and Traditional Peoples: An IUCN Perspective* (Switzerland, 2005), 2, https://www.iucn.org/sites/dev/files/import/downloads/sp_protecting_sacred_natural_sites_indigenous.pdf (accessed 10 November 2018).

5 Émile Durkheim, *The Elementary Forms of Religious Life*, ed. and trans. Karen E. Fields (New York: Free Press, [1912] 1995), 35.

6 Bas Verschuuren, 'Arguments for Developing Biocultural Conservation Approaches for Sacred Natural Sites', in *Sacred Natural Sites*, ed. Bas Verschuuren, Robert Wild, Jeffrey A. McNeely, and Gonzalo Oviedo (London: Earthscan, 2010), 62–71, at 63.

7 Paola Demattè, 'Itinerant Creeds: The Chinese Northern Frontier', in *Locating the Sacred: Theoretical Approaches to the Emplacement of Religion*, Joukowsky Institute Publication 3, ed. Claudia Moser and Cecelia Feldman (Oxford: Oxbow, 2014), 57–73, at 57.

8 Rudolf Otto, *The Idea of the Holy* (London: Oxford University Press, [1917] 1923), 14–17.

9 Teuvo Laitila, 'A Sympathetic, Yet Critical Reading of Eliade', *Temenos* 43, no. 1 (2007): 99–114.

10 Denis Byrne, 'The Enchanted Earth: Numinous Sacred Sites', in *Sacred Natural Sites*, ed. Bas Verschuuren, Robert Wild, Jeffrey A. McNeely, and Gonzalo Oviedo (London: Earthscan, 2010), 53–61, at 53.

11 Byrne, 'Enchanted Earth', 54.

12   Robert Macfarlane, *The Old Ways* (Harmondsworth: Penguin, 2012), 262.

13   Macfarlane, *Old Ways*, 269.

14   Macfarlane, *Old Ways*, 278–9.

15   Hertz, 'St Besse'. See also Michael Sallnow's depiction of continuity and change in relation to rock cults in the Andes: Michael Sallnow, 'Pilgrimage and Cultural Fracture in the Andes', in *Contesting the Sacred*, ed. John Eade and Michael J. Sallnow (London: Routledge, 1991): 136–53.

16   Jeremy Spoon, 'Tourism Meets the Sacred: Khumbu Sherpa Place-Based Spiritual Values', in *Sacred Natural Sites*, ed. Bas Verschuuren, Robert Wild, Jeffrey A. McNeely, and Gonzalo Oviedo (London: Earthscan, 2010), 87–97, at 91.

17   Spoon, 'Tourism', 91.

18   Spoon, 'Tourism', 92–3.

19   Spoon, 'Tourism', 93.

20   Spoon, 'Tourism', 93.

21   Sherry B. Ortner, 'The Case of the Disappearing Shamans, or No Individualism, No Relationalism'. *Ethnos* 23, no. 3 (1995): 355–90, at 364.

22   Ortner, 'The Case', 363.

23   Ortner, 'The Case', 363.

24   Ortner, 'The Case', 363.

25   Ortner, 'The Case', 365.

26   Ortner, 'The Case', 381.

27   Ortner, 'The Case', 362.

28   Sandys and Lehmann, 'Letters from Our Daughters Part 1', 12.

29   Sandys and Lehmann, 'Letters from Our Daughters Part 2', 14.

30   Sandys and Lehmann, 'Letters Part 2', 15.

31   Sandys and Lehmann, *Awakening Letters*, 148.

32   Sandys and Lehmann, *Awakening Letters*, 156.

33   Sandys and Lehmann, *Awakening Letters*, 156–7.

34   Sandys and Lehmann, *Awakening Letters*, 157.

35   Sandys and Lehmann, *Awakening Letters*, 157.

36   Sandys and Lehmann, *Awakening Letters*, 159–60.

37   Sandys and Lehmann, *Awakening Letters*, 160.

38   Sandys and Lehmann, *Awakening Letters*, 160.

39   Sandys and Lehmann, *Awakening Letters*, 160.

40   Sandys and Lehmann, *Awakening Letters*, 160.

41   'Mount Fuji', Encyclopaedia Britannica, https://www.britannica.com/print/article/221527 (accessed 22 January 2019).

42   Toshihiko Ono, Tetsuro Hongo, Kiyotatsu Yamamoto, and Naoya Furuta, 'Mount Fuji's History as a Spiritual Realm and Means for Its Preservation', in *Asian Sacred*

Natural Sites, Philosophy and Practice in Protected Areas and Conservation, ed. Bas Verschuuren and Naoya Furuta (London: Routledge, 2016), 159–70, at 160.

43 Byron Earhart, *Mount Fuji* (Columbia: University of South Carolina Press, 2015).

44 *Minzokugaku Jiten* (*Dictionary of Ethnology*), ed. K. Yanagida (Tokyo: Tokyo-do, 1952), 646, in Ono et al. 'Mount Fuji's History', 161.

45 Ono et al. 'Mount Fuji's History', 162.

46 Ono et al. 'Mount Fuji's History', 163.

47 Ono et al. 'Mount Fuji's History', 163.

48 Ono et al. 'Mount Fuji's History', 165.

49 Ono et al. 'Mount Fuji's History', 167.

50 Ono et al. 'Mount Fuji's History',167.

51 Sandys and Lehmann, *Awakening Letters*, 159.

52 Sandys and Lehmann, *Awakening Letters*, 161.

53 Sandys and Lehmann, *Awakening Letters*, 161.

54 Sandys and Lehmann, *Awakening Letters*, 161.

55 Sandys and Lehmann, *Awakening Letters*, 161.

56 Sandys and Lehmann, *Awakening Letters*, 162.

57 Sandys and Lehmann, *Awakening Letters*, 162.

58 Sandys and Lehmann, *Awakening Letters*, 165.

59 Sandys and Lehmann, *Awakening Letters*, 166.

60 Sam Parnia with Josh Young, *The Lazarus Effect* (London: Rider, 2014). See in particular chapter 8, 'Brain, Soul, and Consciousness', 177–98.

61 Ingold, 'Temporality of Landscape', 164.

62 Tim Ingold, *Being Alive* (London: Routledge, 2011). The notion of 'indwelling' pervades the book as a whole, as set out in the preface, xii.

63 Eduado Viveiros de Castro, 'Cosmological Deixis and Amerindian Perspectivism', *Journal of the Royal Anthropological Institute* 4, no. 3 (1998): 469–88, at 470–2. See also Viveiros de Castro's chapter 'Perspectivism and Multinaturalism in Indigenous America', in *The Land Within: Indigenous Territory and Perception of the Environment*, ed. Alexandre Surrallés and Pedro García Hierro (Copenhagen: IWGIA, 2005), 36–74, particularly 52–8.

64 Edith Turner, 'The Reality of Spirits: A Tabooed or Permitted Field of Study', *Anthropology of Consciousness* 4, no. 1 (1993): 9–12.

65 N. Bubanbdt, 'Interview with an Ancestor: Spirits as Informants and the Politics of Possession in North Maluku', *Ethnography* 10, no. 3 (2009): 291–316; D. Escolar, 'Boundaries of Anthropology: Empirics and Ontological Relativism in a Field Experience with Anomalous Luminous Entities in Argentina, *Anthropology and Humanism* 37, no. 1 (2012): 27–44.

66 Jack Hunter, ' "Between Realness and Unrealness": Anthropology, Parapsychology and the Ontology of Non-Ordinary Realities', *Diskus* 17, no. 2 (2015): 4–20, at 16.

67   Fiona Bowie, 'Building Bridges, Dissolving Boundaries: Toward a Methodology for the Ethnographic Study of the Afterlife, Mediumship and Spiritual Beings', *Journal of the American Academy of Religion* 81, no. 3 (2013): 698–733.

Bibliography

Bernbaum, Edwin. 'Sacred Mountains and Global Changes'. In *Sacred Natural Sites*, edited by Bas Verschuuren, Robert Wild, Jeffrey A. McNeely, and Gonzalo Oviedo, 33–14. London: Earthscan, 2010.

Bowie, Fiona. 'Building Bridges, Dissolving Boundaries: Toward a Methodology for the Ethnographic Study of the Afterlife, Mediumship and Spiritual Beings'. *Journal of the American Academy of Religion* 81, no. 3 (2013): 698–733.

Bubanbdt, N. 'Interview with an Ancestor: Spirits as Informants and the Politics of Possession in North Maluku'. *Ethnography* 10, no. 3 (2009): 291–316.

Byrne, Denis. 'The Enchanted Earth: Numinous Sacred Sites'. In *Sacred Natural Sites*, edited by Bas Verschuuren, Robert Wild, Jeffrey A. McNeely, and Gonzalo Oviedo, 53–61. London: Earthscan, 2010.

Crombie, Robert Ogilvie. *Encounters with Nature Spirits*, 3rd ed. Rochester, VT: Findhorn Press, 2018.

Demattè, Paola. 'Itinerant Creeds: The Chinese Northern Frontier'. In *Locating the Sacred Theoretical Approaches to the Emplacement of Religion*, Joukowsky Institute Publication 3, edited by Claudia Moser and Cecelia Feldman, 57–73. Oxford: Oxbow, 2014

Durkheim, Émile. *The Elementary Forms of Religious Life*, edited and translated by Karen E. Fields. New York: Free Press, [1912] 1995.

Earhart, Byron. *Mount Fuji*. Columbia: University of South Carolina Press, 2015.

Escolar, D. 'Boundaries of Anthropology: Empirics and Ontological Relativism in a Field Experience with Anomalous Luminous Entities in Argentina. *Anthropology and Humanism* 37, no. 1 (2012): 27–44.

Fenge, Gerry. *The Two Worlds of Wellesley Tudor Pole*. Everett, WA: Starseed, 2010.

Hertz, Robert. 'St Besse: A Study of an Alpine Cult'. In *Saints and Their Cults*, edited by Stephen Wilson, 55–100. Cambridge: Cambridge University Press, 1995.

Holbraad, Martin, and Morten Axel Pedersen. *The Ontological Turn*. Cambridge: Cambridge University Press, 2017.

Hunter, Jack. '"Between Realness and Unrealness": Anthropology, Parapsychology and the Ontology of Non-Ordinary Realities'. *Diskus* 17, no. 2 (2015): 4–20.

Ingold, Tim. 'The Temporality of Landscape'. *World Archaeology* 25, no. 2, Conceptions of Time and Ancient Society (1993): 152–74.

Ingold, Tim. *Being Alive*. London: Routledge, 2011.

Laitila, Teuvo. 'A Sympathetic, Yet Critical Reading of Eliade'. *Temenos* 43, no. 1 (2007): 99–114.

Lehmann, Rosamond. *My Dear Alexias: Letters from Wellesley Tudor Pole to Rosamond Lehmann*, edited by Elizabeth Gaythorpe. Jersey: Neville Spearman, 1979.

Macfarlane, Robert. *The Old Ways*. Harmondsworth: Penguin, 2012.

Minzokugaku Jiten (Dictionary of Ethnology), edited by K. Yanagida. Tokyo: Tokyo-do, 1952.

Ono, Toshihiko Ono, Tetsuro Hongo, Kiyotatsu Yamamoto, and Naoya Furuta. 'Mount Fuji's History as a Spiritual Realm and Means for its Preservation'. In *Asian Sacred Natural Sites, Philosophy and Practice in Protected Areas and Conservation*, edited by Bas Verschuuren and Naoya Furuta, 159–70. London: Routledge, 2016.

Ortner, Sherry B. 'The Case of the Disappearing Shamans, or No Individualism, No Relationalism'. *Ethnos* 23, no. 3 (1995): 355–90.

Otto, Rudolf. *The Idea of the Holy*. London: Oxford University Press, [1917] 1923.

Oviedo, Gonzalo, Sally Jeanrenaud, and Mercedes Otegui. *Protecting Sacred Natural Sites of Indigenous and Traditional Peoples: An IUCN Perspective* Switzerland, 2005, .https://www.iucn.org/sites/dev/files/import/downloads/sp_protecting_sacred_natural_sites_indigenous.pdf (accessed 10 November 2018).

Parnia, Sam, with Josh Young. *The Lazarus Effect*. London: Rider, 2014.

Sallnow, Michael. 'Pilgrimage and Cultural Fracture in the Andes'. In *Contesting the Sacred*, edited by John Eade and Michael J. Sallnow, 136–53. London: Routledge, 1991.

Sandys, Cynthia. *The Awakening Letters: Volume Two*, selected and edited by Rosamond Lehmann. Saffron Walden: C.W. Daniel, 1986.

Sandys, Cynthia, and Rosamond Lehmann. 'Letters from Our Daughters Part 1 Sally & Part 2 Patricia'. In C.P.S. Papers No.1 & 2. London: Light Publishing, 1971.

Sandys, Cynthia, and Rosamond Lehmann. *The Awakening Letters: Varieties of Spiritual Experience in the Life after Death*. Jersey: Neville Spearman, 1978.

Spoon, Jeremy. 'Tourism Meets the Sacred: Khumbu Sherpa Place-Based Spiritual Values'. In *Sacred Natural Sites*, edited by Bas Verschuuren, Robert Wild, Jeffrey A. McNeely, and Gonzalo Oviedo, 87–97. London: Earthscan, 2010.

Spoon, Jeremy. 'Tourism, Persistence, and Change: Sherpa Spirituality and Place in Sagarmatha (Mount Everest) National Park and Buffer Zone, Nepal'. *Journal of Ecological Anthropology* 15, no. 1 (2011): 41–57.

Tucci, G. *The Religions of Tibet*. London: Routledge and Kegan Paul, 1988.

Tudor Pole, Wellesley, and Rosamond Lehmann. *A Man Seen Afar*. Saffron Walden: C.W. Daniel, 1983.

Turner, Edith. 'The Reality of Spirits: A Tabooed or Permitted Field of Study'. *Anthropology of Consciousness* 4, no. 1 (1993): 9–12.

Verschuuren, Bas. 'Arguments for Developing Biocultural Conservation Approaches for Sacred Natural Sites'. In *Sacred Natural Sites*, edited by Bas Verschuuren, Robert Wild, Jeffrey A. McNeely, and Gonzalo Oviedo, 62–71. London: Earthscan, 2010.

Viveiros de Castro, Eduado. 'Cosmological Deixis and Amerindian Perspectivism'. *Journal of the Royal Anthropological Institute* 4, no. 3 (1998): 469–88.

Viveiros de Castro, Eduado. 'Perspectivism and Multinaturalism in Indigenous America'. In *The Land Within: Indigenous Territory and Perception of the Environment*, edited by Alexandre Surrallés and Pedro García Hierro, 36–74. Copenhagen: IWGIA, 2005.

6

Appalachian animism: Religion, the woods, and the material presence of the mountain

Amy R. Whitehead

Introduction

I was born in North-East Tennessee, the uppermost corner in Tennessee where the Blue Ridge Mountains converge with the Smoky Mountains and the Appalachian Mountains. Roan Mountain is one such mountain in this *ménage à trois* of mountain ranges, but is, officially, one of the Appalachians. It is a significant part of my biography and heritage, as well as the biographies and heritages of those who have grown up within the reaches of its shadows. Jared Farmer wrote, 'Holiness has always lived up high.'[1] Farmer was referring to mountains. Yet what happens when 'up high' is not the place where holiness, or the sacred, is found? What is at stake when the sacred is found, indeed encountered, in the dark green folds and ripples that constitute the corporeal form of the mountain, and wildernesses that are teaming with life that it supports? At least this is how it was for me. Like dance partners moving in step with one another, we (mountain inhabitants) were shaped by the material presence of the mountain; and in turn, we gave shape to what Tim Ingold might describe as the 'lines' and cultures that were forged and flowed between the mountain and its inhabitants.

Offering both a personal narrative and a theoretical discussion, this chapter is about that generative relationship. Mutually constitutive sections, 'Animism and Material Religion', 'Mountain Context, Culture, People', 'Material Religion and the Mountain', 'Environmentalism', and 'Animism: Language, Revitalization and Space', are structured to provide an animist relational approach to Roan Mountain and its religions, stories, folkways, and cosmologies. It adds to current academic debates by framing natural landscapes such as mountains in the light of theoretical experimentations that play at the generative and fluid intersections at which landscape studies, animist relational discourses, and studies in material religion meet. It argues that although Roan Mountain appears to be a solid fixture in the vast landscape of East Tennessee, it is not passive to those who live there. Instead it renders itself fluid in terms of the relational and spatial dynamics experienced by those humans and non-humans who are present and participating in the relating.

Animism and material religion

The starting point for any study in the field of material religion is that the 'object' or 'place' (including geographical locations and landscapes) be situated at the foremost centre of investigation. As Brent Plate observed about ideas, beliefs, and doctrines, they emerge from the material world and, in so doing, create material religion which he defined as 'an investigation of the interactions between human bodies and physical objects, both natural and human-made'.[2] Akin to a spider who sits in the centre of her web, all other concerns of the phenomena will radiate outward from this centre where they will then be discussed and explored accordingly. This does not mean that other aspects of phenomena, such as the social, are not significant. Yet what it does mean is that the thing or object of concern is considered first, and is used as anchor from which theory can be grounded and other concerns addressed. This chapter tests this idea. It uses the 'language of animism' to assert that mountains are not only a form of material religion. They are 'kin' to the people who were raised in their folds and the starting place from which investigations into the beliefs, spiritualities, and ideas that inform religious mountain cultures can be rooted and understood.

New animism discourses highlight two things: acknowledging the significance of relationships and a revitalization of language.[3] Animism is a generative concept and practice that acknowledges the fluid assemblages that make up mountain peoples' beliefs and knowledge, and allows for the potential personhood of plants, animals, trees, and other beings that are not so easily explained. It can also include the mountain itself. The idea of 'other-than-human persons' comes from Irving Hallowell's interpretation of the Ojibwe 'world view' that 'persons' are all around us, some are human and others are 'other than human'.[4] This indigenous-based knowledge is unlike Edward Tylor's earlier version of animism that insisted that all religions are based on beliefs in spirits.[5] Animism is useful for this chapter's premise because therein lies the assertion that humans and non-humans carry the possibility, relationally, of bringing each other into co-created forms of personhood. In fact, it is not only 'co-creation' that takes place, but a volatile type of multifactor creation that recognizes place, space, time of day, and even weather conditions (and others) alongside other actors such as humans and non-humans (trees, plants, rocks, insects). The revitalization of the language of animism is a current move in scholarship that encourages a shift away from dualist understandings such as 'sacred and profane', 'mind and matter', 'subject', and 'object'. Brought together with emergent ideas in material religion, it suggests that dualisms be rethought and 'readjusted' to accommodate and engage with a world of potential relations, kin, or persons, many of whom are 'material'.[6] From the perspective of animism, Roan Mountain is better conceived as a potential relational participant in the assemblage of Appalachian culture, religions, and lifeways; and its active personhood can be understood in how it informs, shapes, sustains, and mediates the often conflicting religious beliefs, practices, and folklore.

Mountain context, culture, people

The Blue Ridge Mountains of North-East Tennessee are a segment of the southern Appalachian Highland Mountains that bump into the Smoky Mountains. Roan Mountain is one of the more prominent mountains in the region. Roan Mountain is not, however, what one might consider a classically construed mountain. It does not have a peak that ascends up through the clouds as do some of the Fijian-like volcanic mountains in New Zealand. The Roan consists of five peaks called 'the balds' (due to the fact that there are no trees on them), and they form a five-mile-long ridge top. This ridge is divided into two sections by 'Carver's Gap', and the highest elevation of the peaks is called 'Roan High Top', and it is the seventeenth-highest peak in the United States at 1,916 metres. Wild rivers flow down the mountain, too (Figure 6.1), and the river that I knew best was called the 'Little Doe'. As I grew up, summer for me meant dipping, sometimes more than my feet, often my whole body in this mountain river. These annual immersions renewed my relationship with the mountain continually and with pleasure, even down to the mosquitos that awaited my exit as the sun went down. Now as a scholar I look back and see this as my childhood merging with the mountain.

Yet to contextualize Roan Mountain is not only to put its geographical elements into context, but an account of its people is necessary. The two go hand in hand. Appalachia was first inhabited by the Cherokee and then came to be settled by a diverse range of peoples. In an article, John Redher asked, 'What is Appalachia?' and then answering himself, he wrote,

> The ethnic diversity of the region's original European settlers shaped the traditions today associated with it. Heavy concentrations of Scots-Irish, combined with a fair number of Germans, a sprinkling of French Huguenots, the 'mysterious, almost mythical' Melungeons, Cherokees, and African slaves helped to forge a distinct mountain culture.[7]

Some Cherokee still live in East Tennessee today. In addition to the diverse populous, the distinct mountain culture mentioned by Rehder is forged from how the peoples that settled there combined with the landscape to develop their cultures and ways of being with the land. Landscapes shape, inspire, and form significant aspects of human biographies (indeed, of whole communities). This is the assertion made by Christopher Tilley and Kate Cameron-Daum in relation to a particular heathland landscape in rural South-West England.[8] Among other ideas relating to motility, mediation, place, and agency, they examine 'the biographies of persons and the manner in which the landscape becomes part of whom they are, what they do and how they feel'.[9] Mountains are not, after all, passive, but active in a variety of ways.

Although marginalized by much of the rest of the United States, East Tennesseans have a strong sense of cultural heritage. Much of this is due to our distinct forms of music, food, and oral storytelling traditions. Seasonal festivals are used to highlight local artistry and folkways such as bluegrass music, art, literature, Appalachian traditional (ghost) storytelling, covered bridges, and craftsmanship, as well as local fruits such as apples, blackberries, and plums. All of these events, gatherings, stories, and festivals I now understand as the modes through which we reinforce our belonging to the mountain, to our heritage, and to each other. Growing up, I heard family members construct the identity of the Roan as an entity and a force in its own right. For apart from its naturally treacherous landscape of bears, wild cats, wild rivers, copper heads, and rattle snakes, Roan Mountain is also a source of enchantment. For the people who live with the mountain, it is inhabited by a host of otherworldly beings and the endless accounts of the supernatural. The wind around the Roan is particularly vocal and telling. Some people see and hear different things – the voices of angelic choirs, the sounds of torment and torture accompanied by visions of hell.

Some have scientific reasons – the sound of the wind in the naturally punctured rock faces. Other people choose to ignore the science and relish the supernatural possibility.

As a child, I was both terrified and enthralled by my favourite story about Roan Mountain that told how a female ghost jumped on the bumpers of cars that passed by a cemetery near Dark Hollow Road. Stories about ghosts and voices from beyond the grave ran alongside mountain-related tales of murder and people wandering off beaten paths never to be seen again. Some of my own family members were main characters in these chilling tales. One of my bear-hunting ancestors in particular was celebrated in a song written by Johnny Cash, *Tiger Whitehead*. As the song and his grave stone revealed, in life Tiger Whitehead had killed ninety-nine bears and his ghost still haunts the hills of Eastern Tennessee as he hunts his hundredth bear:

> And when the lightnin' flashes there's the strange thing that the people say they see
> An old grey headed ghost runnin' through the mountains there
> It's Tiger Whitehead after his one hundreth bear.[10]

Areas known as Tiger Creek and Tiger Valley were named after Tiger Whitehead and are the places where my father grew up and went to school as a boy in the early 1940s. Relating to the Roan from afar, as I am doing while writing this chapter, is disconcerting. The sensory disconnect from the landscape is apparent as I look out my office window at Massey University at Auckland over green New Zealand native bush. Yet when I close my eyes, I can easily sense the place and I can see the mountains, the green, and the woods (Figure 6.1).

Figure 6.1 Left: Spring 2012 in the woods in one of Roan Mountain's valleys. Photo: Amy Whitehead. Right: Up Roan Mountain, October 2019. Photo: Rod Whitehead.

Temporally, I can feel the heat and humidity of summer, and I can still smell wet leaves, cool mornings, and thick humid evenings. I can see a particular quality of early evening summer light, just when lightening bugs begin to flicker in the woods surrounding our family home. Shifting into autumn now, I can recall the deep, vivid reds, oranges, and yellows. Then I can hear the sounds of sparrows and crows, and feel the hanging frost and cold starkness of winter. As a child I regularly found 'Indian' arrowheads while digging in the dirt around my home. I also found them on the playground outside my school. I remember how the dirt felt and smelled. I went barefoot, often, too. We were generally described by those who did not know us as 'hillbillies'. I did not care. I spent most of my time growing up outside in the woods where there were worlds to be interacted with and discovered. Reflecting on this, I understand that it was in the woods where I felt most at home. I also understand that this *habitus* would have not only given shape to my scholarship but underpins, informs, and envelops my very being. Landscape, for me, is an interactive presence and source and very powerful.

On Sundays after church services, my father would sometimes drive us up the winding roads that lead to the top of the mountain where we would visit the highest peak and take in the breathtaking views of the Blue Ridge Mountains (Figure 6.2, left). We would notice the weather change, how often it would be cooler, or that the rhododendrons were coming out in bloom. Usually on the way up or down the mountain, we would stop by 'Whitehead Hill' and visit the graves of my ancestors (Figure 6.2, right).

I have distinct memories of 'grave decorations' where every May the wider family would come together to quite informally lay flowers on the graves of our loved ones, talk, and pray. Food played a significant role in these gatherings,

Figure 6.2 Left: Roan Mountain, Tennessee. Right: Whitehead Hill cemetery, grave of my grandparents. Both photos: Rod Whitehead.

and I am told that this tradition is petering out. My grandfather Whitehead, who is now buried on Whitehead Hill, was known to be a 'water witch' and a healer. This means he used a 'water witching stick', a straight stick that forked, to divine the whereabouts of underground water so as to dig a well. I remember a case in particular where he saved a man's infected leg by wrapping it in Elm bark to draw out the infection. My great grandmother, Vienna, painted pictures using paints made from ground berries. She was said to have been an excellent musician, but when she was asked to play piano at local church services, she was told to keep her sleeves down and cuffs buttoned so that her brown skin would be less noticeable to the congregation. The truth is that settler/Indian intermarriages were common, but still, there was a social protocol to uphold.

Colourful language use and humour, hospitality, and kindness occupy some of my more pleasant memories of people growing up in Appalachia. When I visit, I often enjoy hearing the familiar expression 'I appreciate you' instead of 'thank you' in day-to-day interactions and exchanges. I am now both an insider and an outsider to the region. Mountain people are, by nature, mistrustful of outsiders and strangers, and even more suspicious of the government. My own observations and experiences found that mountain people are protective, sometimes poor, guarded, loyal, and clannish, and for the most part, down to earth. These are words I can use confidently in relation to my observation about 'who we are'. 'Rebellious' is another necessary addition. 'Us' (mountain folks) and 'them' (non-mountain folks) is a generative and generational construct that continues to exist in the region today. Mountain pathways and knowledge of 'the hills' were useful cover for when bootleggers had to run from the authorities. They also had no problem making a stand when both necessary and unnecessary. The formidable mountain gave birth to a formidable spirit in its people. Reflecting on the region from here in the antipodes, having put ample distance between us, I see that the Roan, with its shape and the culture it produced, is no ordinary mountain. I can also understand now that 'we' are no ordinary people.

Material religion and the mountain

As suggested in the introduction, one of the purposes of this chapter is to theoretically experiment with the fluid intersections where material religion, animism, and mountain culture meet. Mountains are, after all, material, and are a form of material religion; and as a visual, material presence, Roan Mountain is central to the culture of East Tennessee. Not passive, Roan Mountain and all that it sustains not only inspires but generates forms of religion, spirituality, tradition, and culture. Home to a rich, complex, and often conflicting, patchwork quilt of lived religious traditions, folkways, cultures, customs, heritage, and cosmologies, Catholics, Jews, Buddhists, contemporary Pagans, and environmental activists can all be found residing there today. It also includes Appalachian Granny Magic practitioners, traditional Appalachian people known for their ability to heal with plants, who use divining rods to find water, and who follow the 'old ways'. Yet the predominant umbrella religion of those living in the area is Protestantism under which there are several variations, mainly Evangelical.

Working in the field of material religion, I have learned that it is necessary to ask questions that relate, but are not limited, to what people *do* in relation to objects/spaces (rituals, performances), as well as what these objects and spaces give back. Other questions concern the role of language. What language is used in reference to the thing/place/site, and how does language use motivate or inform how an object or place is housed or treated? Material properties, potential biographies, and other roles are of further concern, as are questions relating to the ways in which things and places/spaces uphold political and social structures and generate a sense of belonging and community. What the before mentioned groups have in common is their relationships to/with the striking material presences of the local mountains and the 'other-than-human persons' who reside there. These 'other-than-human persons' consist of the animals, plants, trees, ghosts, sprites, stories, and more, that emerged with and according to 'place', and play central, significant roles in shaping the cosmologies, epistemologies, and, indeed, the ontologies, that make up the unique, diverse, and sometimes conflicting worlds of East Tennessee religionists. This section will contextualize Roan Mountain by considering how Christianity and the 'alternative' or nature-venerating religions found there have emerged in such a way as to have a vernacular flavour of their own and how it has been co-created and co-inspired in relationship with the material presence of mountains.

For locals of every faith, the Roan inspire awe, creativity, respect, and devotion. However, perspectives on how to conceive and cosmologically frame the mountains often differ. For some Christian groups, the size and grandeur of the mountains represent, or are testimony to, God's glory, creation, mysteriousness, and might, while for others the 'material' mountains and their 'other-than-human' inhabitants are themselves either the focus of veneration or understood as beings with which to peacefully live. Tilley wrote, 'Cosmologies make sense and bring order to the minutiae of similarities and differences observed and encountered through the necessity and practice of dwelling and movement through the medium of landscapes.'[11] Two different narrative perspectives on the origin of the Roan's 'Balds' exemplify this, as relayed by Jennifer Bauer Laughlin, the first being Cherokee, the second being that of early European Christian settlers. First,

> They say that there was once a giant yellow jacket known as Ulagu that terrorized a particular Cherokee village by swooping down, carrying off young children, and flying away faster than the village's warriors could follow. After much anguish, the Indians hit upon the idea of posting sentinels along the tops of mountains as a means of tracking Ulagu's flight to its home. That accomplished, the Cherokees prayed to the Great Spirit for aid, and the Great Spirit obliged by sending a bolt of lightening to split open the mountain where Ulagu lived. The warriors then proceeded to hunt down the beast and kill it. So pleased was the Great Spirit by the Cherokees' resourcefulness, by their piety in beseeching him for help, and by their bravery in finally killing Ulagu that he rewarded them by keeping the tops of the mountains bare of trees, so they could serve as sentry posts should the need ever arise again.

And then,

> It was said that the balds came about whenever the devil went walking in the mountains, with each of his footsteps causing the growth to be permanently stunted.[12]

The first story tells of a giant yellow jacket and how 'a type of spirit being' helps the Cherokee by altering the landscape, while the devil is the main character of the second. Within the framework of East Tennessee's predominantly Christian cosmology, the notion of 'otherworld beings' should spark fears of devilry. Yet having been raised a Protestant in the mountains, I have observed on countless occasions that vernacular Appalachian Christians either typically believe in, or have experienced, some type of supernatural encounter that cannot be explained either through use of logic or the Bible. Discussions about vernacular religion point toward the fact that no 'pure' form of a religion exists, and that all religions take root and grow in relation to their place where they take on distinct place-oriented characteristics, such as the influence of the balds of Roan Mountain.

Further, inspired by European Christian expansion and early attempts to suppress if not obliterate pagan practices, Christianity officially dissuades the notion that particular mountains, groves, and rivers can be anything special, for in their eyes all of God's creation is special, and particular places are to be absorbed into one large feeling of awe that transcends specific locales. Yet local

Christians, in their hollows and settlements, live alongside and are intimately entangled with the mountain and its rather active folklore. Breathing mountain air means being with and part of the mountain. The Roan is also ever present. Depending on where one is, it either sits as a solid looming backdrop to daily life or it envelops and enfolds daily activities. Humans are not separate from their place, and the particular environment of the Roan lends itself to housing tales of strange beasts such as the story of the black, red-eyed beast the size of a wolf who is often glimpsed at forest edges, woodland sprites, plant lore, tales of mountain witchery, Evangelicals, and Jesus.

Apart from the latter two, while these stories do not typically sit comfortably within Christianity, they will often run parallel to traditional or more doctrinally informed beliefs. To Appalachian Christians, nature and all that comes with it has inherent value. Joseph D. Witt accurately referred to this as 'Appalachian vernacular nature religion'.[13] Such an expression serves as an umbrella term and describes why so many people in different parts of Appalachia have struck out so strongly against and resisted mountaintop removal for the sake of coal mining.

In terms of their religious material cultures, Roan Mountain forms the backdrop to mountain religious life of many descriptions, and their material cultures and practices reflect this. Plate observed that people 'need their objects that bring a sense of value, meaning, and order into their lives ... The objects may be natural, such as a mountain in view or a stone in the hand, a river to bathe in or water in a font'.[14] The roles that objects, spaces, and places play in the ontological perspectives of humans, while often muted in terms of cultural discourse, are silently potent and powerful. Landscapes such as mountains are no different. In Appalachian Christianities, baptismal services are sometimes held at local rivers. I have observed how revivals are often held outside in church grounds and in marquee tents. I know that Snake-handling congregations handling poisonous mountain snakes such as copperheads to test their own faith, and bibliomancy, is a regular practice. In contrast, Appalachian Pagans and Granny Magic practitioners have knowledge about and utilize healing herbs, particular forms of bark, and other nature-found remedies. It is common knowledge that magic, forms of spell and witchcraft, as well as divination are practiced, often through the mediums of tea leaves, scrying with a bowl of water, and watching for signs in the clouds. As a scholar of material religion and alternative religions, I have noted that these practices appear to be syncretic; they are fusions constructed between traditional knowledges from 'the old worlds' of Scotland, England, Wales, and Ireland, and the Appalachian mountains themselves. From my observation, they also appear to differ from Wicca and other, more globalized forms of Paganism, with the emphasis being placed on the local cultures of 'Appalachia'. Currently, my experience dictates that there is a revival of these magical and nature-venerating cultures taking place in the mountains of East Tennessee.

What I would define as the mountain nature religions of East Tennessee are not necessarily organized but quite readily fall into the category of alternative religions, contemporary Paganism or Animism specifically. They can even include forms of Appalachian Christianity. Further, Pagan and earth-based traditions exemplify what can be considered quintessential forms of material religion because, like studies in material religion, they take nature (matter, *mater*, mother) as the central starting point from which to understand and know the rest of life and its goings-on. Animists, along with others who practice a variety of 'earth traditions', acknowledge and celebrate nature, its cycles and bounty rather than something that will eventually be transcended (unlike the monotheistic faiths), and they venerate it accordingly.

Environmentalism

As has so far been discussed, a variety of nature-venerating religious traditions and folkways exist in the mountains, many of whom have responded to growing environmental awareness and concerns in Appalachia. Furthermore, many have found that their beliefs and their connections to the mountains have been passionately reinforced through their activism. In addition to Christians, contemporary Pagan groups, Buddhists, and others are coming together to stop activities such as mountaintop removal in West Virginia. Witt's research in Appalachia outlined the often conflicting religious perspectives of those who were campaigning for or against the process that continues to this day.[15] Witt's work is significant to this chapter because he offers accounts from interviewees that clearly outline the 'nature-venerating spiritualities' and activist practices found in Appalachia, the notion of stewardship among Christian groups, and the language that these groups use in reference to the mountains.

Witt revealed an account given to him by his research interviewee, Martin. Martin was an activist and campaigner against mountaintop removals. He described his connection to the woods as such:

When I'm out in the woods, I get a similar feeling, that endorphin rush. It just
feels so good. It takes that sigh out of your chest, and when we just saw [on the
Hobet mine] puts the sigh in there, just cramps up your insides … I've been in
places in the mountains, in the woods, that feel like cathedrals. They just have a
holy feel about them. And if there is a God he sure as hell isn't going to be found
over that strip mine; more likely to be found in these woods. I love'em, I love'em,
I love the trees! I'm a tree hugger! And I love the bullfrogs. But I don't love that
shit over there [at the Hobet mine]; that's ugly, that takes all the love out of this
land.[16]

It was Martin's spiritual connection to the land that he was defending, and he
felt physical pain in his body when he saw the damage done by the coal mining
companies. Witt wrote, 'For Martin, the forests and mountains of Appalachia
themselves were worthy of reverence and care without an appeal to transcendent
powers or divine laws. The ecosystem had an inherent, spiritual value.'[17]

Thus, language used to express understandings of the wilderness around the
Roan Mountain region ranged from 'divine' and 'holy' to 'awe' and 'sacred', even
by those who did not self-identify as Christian. In support of Witt's account
of Martin, I remember a family member once referring the tree canopy in the
woods as her temple. Many others I knew growing up there would echo this
sentiment as we searched for alternatives to the Protestant norm. For many
people in Appalachia, including me, the woods are the place to go when thinking
is needed, and when one needs to get back to nature. And I, too, remember
having a sense of awe in the wild, and I still do when I visit the woods on my
annual visits home.

Witt observed that, as he continued his research, he 'noticed more examples
of local activists making similar statements about their affective, spiritual
connections to the specific landscape of Appalachia' and how they used
similar language to Martin.[18] Witt further observed how many of these people
rejected mainstream religious affiliations and practices, choosing agnosticism
instead, or affiliations to other non-Christian religious traditions such as
'Buddhist philosophy, mystical traditions, American Indian stories, or simply
used language of the sacred to describe the complex ecosystems of Appalachia
(like Martin)'. They shared 'a deep sense of belonging to and connectedness in
nature, while perceiving the earth and its living systems to be sacred'. They were
all exemplars of 'nature-venerating spiritualities', including what Bron Taylor
termed 'dark green religion'.

As a term, 'dark green religion' is a theory that emerged from Taylor's research
among environmental activists, surfers, New Agers, and contemporary Pagans

(among others) – people who claim no religious affiliations to any organized religion, but who hold (and relate to) nature as sacred and act accordingly.[19] Taylor's 'dark green religion' is significant to these discussions because it addresses and accounts for a newly recognized form of religiosity and its relationship to contemporary Pagan understandings of nature as living. Dark green religion also has a relationship to the term 'animism' as more recently conceived by Nurit Bird-David, Graham Harvey, and many others (including myself) who are currently involved in resurrecting the term in a more useful way than what Edward Tylor had offered nearly 150 years ago in his prolific work, *Primitive Culture* ([1871] 1913).[20] This paper is not, however, about activism per se. What is significant here is that Taylor's description of 'dark green religion' and Joseph Witt's descriptive accounts of the beliefs and practices of mountaintop removal activists both outlined a certain flavour, or understanding of the kind of 'nature connectedness' that I experience in Appalachia, as well as that of many of my relatives, and a few friends. Pagan groups, Buddhists, and Granny Magic practitioners in the region report similar understandings, and while some Christians may also have connections or relationships with nature, or with the mountains, their relationships could easily suffer theological and cognitively dissonant restraint.

Reflecting again on mountaintop removal activists, Witt observed that many of those who participated in his study understood the natural world as 'kin'. This is marked by a general 'feeling of the inherent worth of nature, and a longing to bring about a future society marked by increased cooperation and equality among beings and decreased exploitation of nature'.[21] This last reflects the aims and objectives of many of those involved in 'dark green' religious movements more broadly, and particularly 'animism', which conceives of a world that is full of potential persons, some of whom are relations. It also reflects my own animist understanding of Roan Mountain as kin to me.

Demonstrating the deep connection that I personally feel with the Roan requires one last account. It was the beginning of summer. I was 24 years old. I had already moved to the UK, but had gone home to spend some time with family. My sister and I stopped at our favourite local deli and picked up a sandwich before heading up to Whitehead Hill. Once there, we planted ourselves on the side of the hill to have lunch with the graves of our ancestors and the wildflowers, buttercups. As we settled and started looking properly, we saw that several of tall, old trees in the field in front had been felled, and were lying on the ground, undignified and disregarded. The same feeling came over us at the same time. Instead of seeing 'just trees', we saw 'tree corpses', beings who were once noble and tall and who had fallen, and we were simultaneously saddened. It was, as Martin said, 'ugly'. We used the words 'horrible' and 'unnecessary'. Any number of reasons can be given as to why the trees had been felled. For example, they could have been sick, but it did not seem that way. A deeper look revealed that the felled trees were lying among the unkempt, overgrown, forgotten, and now uneven graves perhaps of past relations due to the place of their burial, who had fought in the Confederate Army. For those forgotten soldiers, just as the felled trees lying across their graves, we used the words 'horrible' and 'unnecessary': trees and soldiers together. Surrounded and inspired by the woods, rivers, birds, bears, and natural springs, as well as by Appalachian folk tales, fairy tales, and the tales of ghosts and witchery, it is no wonder that I was later to be led to animism as an area of research and personal interest.

Animism – language, revitalization, and space

Religious sites, objects, places, clothing, statues, and architecture sit at the heart of religious communities around the world, and while being material themselves, they are frequently tasked with either mediating relationships between 'here' and 'there' or sitting on the borders of what are often perceived as 'the sacred' (beyond) and 'the profane' (worldly). This highlights one of the appeals of structuring mountains as sites of sacred significance. With their majestic height, they appear to border the beyond. To elaborate, Protestantism and its emphasis on Christianity being a religion of hearing instead of seeing fosters a view and thus a language of metaphor and representation in most things apart from food. In addition to this, however, most Protestants view all of God's creation (including mountains) as representing God's might, glory, and artistry. As mentioned before, mountains demonstrate God's ability where the more dramatic aspects of the earth and thus creation can be witnessed and observed. As I found in my previous research into religious artefacts and fetishism, Christianity generally emphasizes mind or spirit over matter, or the earth, or suggests that that which is intangible or transcendent is superior to that which we can touch, see, feel, and know with our whole bodies and senses.[22] In many ways they have co-structured and co-produced many of the norms, values, and constructs that are responsible for the distance that has come between humans and their landscape, mountains, and, indeed, their nature. This distance is reflected in the before-mentioned language use of sacred, or the divine because they imply, by default, that there is an opposite (the profane). The question that can be raised is whether this applies to non-Christians who use the language of the sacred. The category of the sacred, is, however, viable if rendered fluid and relational according to who or what is doing the relating. This can include Appalachian activists, East Tennessee religionists, or modernist observers alike.

Encounter, perception, and 'place-making' are fluid, generative, and relational. Applied to Roan Mountain, not all mountain community dwellers will see or understand the mountain as sacred, or feel a cognitive connection to it, although they may connect with the mountain's presence in the landscape to the point where familiarity becomes entangled with being in the world. My own perspective growing up lent itself to an awareness of the mountains and their grandeur. Growing up, God, as I knew him/it, was tangible as well as intangible, and the earth was alive. I understand now that my animist perspective, then, originates from my being born into the Roan Mountain region, and my mountain heritage is responsible for my perspective as a researcher today. Living now in Aotearoa New Zealand where Maori and non-Maori alike will often self-identify in relation to 'place' (often down to the nearest river, tree, or mountain), never have I been more called upon to be aware that *my mountain* is the Roan, *my river* is the Little Doe, and that my ancestors are from different lines that criss-cross in North America and go back to Northern Europe. This change of language, where I refer to my mountain and my river, takes me home in myself and firmly plants me back on the mountainside of the Roan. Language is, after all, a powerful and emotive tool.

The complexity of these relationships is often conceptually unaccounted for as a result of limited, dualistic, and categorical language use, such as 'nature and culture', 'subject and object', 'transcendent and imminent', and the forever popular 'sacred and profane'. Therefore arguably, the way that these language tools are employed gives shape to how locals perceive, understand, and relate to the mountain, which oftentimes relay a sense of distance or disconnect. Harvey observed that 'language is as central to people's construction and experience of the world as it is the relationships in which they communicate about ways of being in the world'.[23] Utilizing Harvey's useful suggestion that we adjust our styles of communication, as indicated earlier on, this chapter is proposing that the language of animism, personhood in particular, is a good way to both understand and express the complex relationships that people living in Appalachia/East Tennessee have with their mountain.[24]

Building on this, and in terms of 'space' (different from 'place') Thomas Tweed wrote that space itself is relational. It is not a static thing, or 'a pre-existing static container isolated from other spaces. Space is not an absence waiting for a presence.[25] It is also not metaphorical. Mountains, like religious and other objects, exist on a fluid continuum of relational possibilities, all of which are dependent upon the nature and culture of encounters. They can even be sacred. In support of this, Tweed observed, 'Never inert pre-existing containers, devotional spaces are both generated and generative. They make and are made.'[26] As suggested by my relative, the canopy of the trees in the mountain woods is her temple. She finds the divine there. That devotion in that space, therefore, provides a generative zone that is full of a host of creative, unique ontological possibilities. Tweed further observed how 'Spaces do things. We might say playfully: spaces are people, too.' Space forms around that which moves through it or resides within. Here, human and other-than-human persons can emerge in relation to space, time, landscape, material, and encounter, all of which can be understood as sacred or divine. Further still, Tweed proposed, 'Some scholars have suggested that images perform actions – weep, cajole, and comfort – and, in a similar way, spaces are structures that exert agency. We might re-imagine them as characters – not just settings – in our scholarly narratives.'[27] Building on this perspective, as both places and spaces with their own biographies and forms of life, mountains are more than characters. They are also more than sacred. With their material presence they are not only relational participants in devotion, they are life-sustaining actors in their own cosmologies. This understanding of Roan Mountain as a person sidesteps modern, anthropocentric understandings of mountains as things, and firmly confers their membership in the 'larger than human world' category. Harvey observed that dialogue can be had between all manner of species in the world and that 'communication *about* that world is also generative of rituals and discursive practices, including initiations and story-telling. Those of us who seek better ways of communicating about animism and materiality can be inspired by and within these dialogical relations.'[28]

Adding visually prominent features of the environment such as mountains that include stories and rituals in addition to all manner of species provides another space from which to deconstruct anthropocentric notions and to begin rethinking our position in the world in relation to its totality. Rethinking animism offers a tool of expansion. Further including debates in the growing field of material religion forms yet another step in facilitating a 'more than' approach to understanding the world in which we inhabit, for example, material objects are 'more than' material. They can be active participants in encounters. Mountains are also 'more than' material, dirt, soil, plants, and geological strata. Once we begin to see/understand that the world is full of a variety of inhabitants, otherworlds begin to emerge. Ingold noted that the environment might be better envisaged as a domain of entanglement. It is within such a tangle of interlaced trails, continually ravelling here and unravelling there, that beings grow or 'issue forth' along the lines of their relationships (Ingold 2003: 305–6) [*sic*]. This tangle is the texture of the world. In the animic ontology, beings do not simply occupy the world, they *inhabit* it, and in so doing – in threading their own paths through the meshwork – they contribute to its ever-evolving weave.[29]

The 'meshwork' can be applied to the assemblages that make up the constituent parts of Roan Mountain. Putting the relational discourses of animism and personhood to proactive use indicates how human beings might better placed to actively acknowledge these engaged relationships in modern contexts. As Ingold noted, 'Knowing must be reconnected with being, epistemology with ontology, thought with life. Thus has our rethinking of indigenous animism led us to propose the re-animation of our own, so-called "western" tradition of thought.'[30]

Revitalizing the language of animism in relation to mountains, materiality, and religion in contemporary Appalachia is one such attempt at reconnecting knowing with being, or thought with life. Developing Western models for such engagements is paramount to not only having a better understanding of our world and its many 'entanglements' but also in forging paths towards more active and respectful relationships.

Personhood, legal and otherwise

The final subsection of this chapter explores the ways in which a mountain such as the Roan can be considered using the language of animism. For example, can the Roan be considered a person? Such a term does not equate mountains with humanity, but rather the combination of material properties and natural inhabitants, including humans, generates the mountain's personhood (soil, minerals, grass, shrubs, trees, rocks, animals, rivers, fish, and a host of other beings). The personhood of the Roan is also generated by the tales, stories, isolation, legends, and other intangible forms of heritage. It is intersubjective, generated and generational, co-inspired and co-created, not only between human persons and the mountains but also within the complex interfaces that comprise networks and meshworks of the mountain's vast relations. Thus, I am suggesting that mountains are not living persons in the biological sense, but living, life-sustaining beings, who play prominent and significant roles in the lives of local peoples and their cultures. The personhood of the Roan can therefore be considered in three different ways: first, through the way that it is related to and regarded by many locals; second, because it actively sustains life and generates feelings of awe and connection; and third, because it is protected and conserved.

In Aotearoa New Zealand, Mt Taranaki has been granted the status of 'legal person'. Legal personhood is a status which means that the mountain is both recognized and protected environmentally and, significantly, that it honours the ontologies of the eight local *iwi* (tribes, or groups) that know Mt Taranaki as an ancestor. Using the words 'legal personhood' is a clear environmental strategy. This strategy speaks to modernist observers and lawmakers in a way that denotes value. Persons are (usually) valuable, so acknowledging the personhood of the mountain means that a change in value has taken place whereby the mountain is no longer an object or a thing that can be violated, littered, or used for industrial and other resources. This move followed the granting of legal personhood to the Whanganui River (close to Taranaki) four years previously. New Zealand's government has been informed by consultations with, and listening to, the voices of Maori peoples. However, according to Harvey, the nature of personhood is debated by both Maori and non-Maori alike. For multinational corporations, the granting of the status of personhood is concerned with rights and protections. Yet in thinking about rivers in terms of animist relationality, it can be argued that the river acts 'relationally with others who live with and within them'.[31] Harvey wrote, 'Rivers, like humans, have multiple relationships, for example, with fish, plants, local humans, tourists, engineers, soils, and so on.'[32] This is similar to how Roan Mountain is the sum of all of those beings, stories, rituals, and traditions. Harvey observed, 'Indeed, rivers are the sum of all those who compose them: water, fish, plants, fishers, bacteria, banks, and all. These relationships and constitutions also help us see human personhood more clearly. Like rivers, we are multiple beings both in the sense that "our" bodies work with others (particularly hosts of necessary bacteria in our guts) to share nutrition.'[33] Yet, according to Harvey, it is not enough to acknowledge the multispecies persons who inhabit rivers. More than this is needed to understand the nuances found in animist ontologies.[34]

Although in the past the Cherokee inhabited part of Roan Mountain, the personhood of Roan Mountain is not ontologically or legally supported in the same way as both Mt Taranaki and the Whanganui River. It is, however, protected by local and state governments, and is conserved in the form of an enormous state park known as Roan Mountain State Park. In terms of personhood, I have argued elsewhere that humans and other-than-human religious statues (statue-persons) are capable of bringing each other into co-relational, co-inspired, forms of ontological being. This used the concept of relationality as radically applied to religious statues, and offered a way in which to reimagine and re-conceptualize human and other-than-human relationships.[35] I later discovered through a colleague that the arguments made for the legal personhood of the River Ganges was made using the example of the legal personhood granted to Hindu statues in India, whereby Hindu statues can own land. This was, however, later overturned. Through my research in Andalusia, Spain, I found that a statue of the Virgin Mary, the Virgin of Alcala de los Gazules, is not only the legal owner of the land on which her shrine sits, but that she also owns her shrine building. Applying this argument to mountains, if personhood can be granted to religious statues who play central roles in the lives of their devotees, then it can be granted to mountains who sustain billions of life forms and are a 'thing' or 'person' in and of themselves. Here again, if permitted, the language of personhood can assist in pushing the boundaries of what can be considered a 'thing', and it is possible to begin to see the thing as a living thing with agency.

A further site that illustrates how the notion of personhood is being utilized in fights for the rights of nature/the environment can be found currently in the case of Pachamama in Ecuador. In the case of the legal personhood of Pachamama, Rafi Youatt asserted that the language found in Article 71 of the legalization document is 'remarkable'. It reads,

> Nature, or Pacha Mama [*sic*], where life is reproduced and occurs, has the right to integral respect for its existence and for the maintenance and regeneration of its life cycles, structure, functions and evolutionary processes. All persons, communities, peoples and nations can call upon public authorities to enforce the rights of nature. To enforce and interpret these rights, the principles set forth in the Constitution shall be observed, as appropriate. The State shall give incentives to natural persons and legal entities and to communities to protect nature and to promote respect for all the elements comprising an ecosystem.[36]

Although appropriate political history is needed to understand the position from whence this came, damages done by oil companies, issues with indigenous rights, and so on, it raises a significant point about how changes are being made in different parts of the world that value both 'rights' and 'nature' in the same space. The mountains whose tops have been destroyed by coal mining companies in West Virginia, Virginia, Kentucky, and Tennessee would benefit greatly from being granted the status and protection of legal personhood. In fact, at present, although there are several 'sacred' mountains and sites in the United States that could be considered persons to Native American tribal peoples, none of them have been granted legal personhood. Neither the voices of indigenous groups, nor the vernacular religions, nature religions, nor material religions of Appalachia are powerful enough to stop such atrocities. However, a signal for change has been sent out as efforts are made to adjust styles of communication through the revitalization of the language of animism as well as other efforts that seek to cultivate respectful and non-anthropocentric relationships with the other-than-human world.

Conclusion

This chapter has had two main objectives. Providing both an insider's account of having been born and raised in the mountains of East Tennessee, and an animist scholarly perspective, it has explored the intersections at which stories, traditions, heritage, practices, and spiritualities assemble through the medium, indeed the presence, of Roan Mountain, to form Appalachian-specific nature religions. Enhancing debates in the emerging field of material religion, this chapter has framed East Tennessee's Roan Mountain as not only a backdrop but also part and parcel to all of the species that make up the totality of mountain life, culture, and religion. Animist discourses have been presented as a framework through which to re-conceptualize relationships with the mountain that go beyond notions of the symbolic and the sacred. In addition to the sacred and the symbolic, animist discourses both highlight and account for the multifaceted, relational webs of entanglement that continually emerge through encounters. Central to the chapter is the assertion that the language of animism is the appropriate tool with which to consider the mountain as a central form of religious materiality, albeit one that is teaming with intensity and life, and includes the earth and landscape categorically in that which can be considered both 'material' and 'religious'. After all, the presence of the mountains, along with the 'other-than-human persons' who reside there, plays central, significant roles in shaping the cosmologies that make up the unique and diverse worlds of East Tennessee religionists. They are the motivating factors that inspire locals into either/both environmental action or spiritual/religious practice, and their effect is powerful for both Christians and Pagans alike. As my own narrative perspective has suggested, Roan Mountain, the woods, and the life it sustains are 'kin' to me. The mountain gave birth to me and my relations, as well as my own unique form of Appalachian animism.

Notes

1 Jared Farmer, *On Zion's Mount: Mormons, Indians, and the American Landscape* (Cambridge, MA: Harvard University Press, 2008), 142–3.

2 Brent Plate, *Key Terms in Material Religion* (London: Bloomsbury, 2015), 4.

3 Miguel Astor-Aguilera and Graham Harvey, *Rethinking Relations and Animism: Personhood and Materiality* (London: Routledge, 2018), 2–3.

4 Irvin Hallowell, 'Ojibwa Ontology, Behavior, and World View,' in *Culture in History: Essay in Honor of Paul Radin*, ed. S. Diamond (New York: Columbia University Press, 1960), 19–52. Reprinted in *Readings in Indigenous Religions*, ed. G. Harvey (London: Continuum, 2002), 18–49.

5 Edward Tylor, *Primitive Culture*, 2 vols. Reprint (London: John Murray, [1871] 1913).

6 Graham Harvey, 'Adjusted Styles of Communication (ASCs) in the Post-Cartesian World,' in *Rethinking Relations and Animism: Personhood and Materiality*, ed. Miguel Astor-Aguilera and Graham Harvey (London: Routledge, 2018), 35–52, at 35.

7 John Rehder, *Appalachian Folkways* (Baltimore, MD: Johns Hopkins University Press, 2004), 59.

8 Christopher Tilley and Kate Cameron-Daum, *Anthropology of Landscape: The Extraordinary in the Ordinary* (London: UCL Press, 2017), 2.

9 Tilley and Cameron-Daum, *Anthropology of Landscape*, 2.

10 *Tiger Whitehead*, songwriters John Cash and Nat Winston. Lyrics © BMG Rights Management.

11 Christopher Tilley, *Interpreting Landscapes: Geologies, Topographies, Identities; Explorations in Landscape Phenomenology 3* (New York: Routledge, 2010), 35–6.

12 Jennifer Bauer Laughlin, *Roan Mountain: A Passage of Time* (Johnson City, TN: Overmountain Press, 1999), 31.

13 Joseph D. Witt, *Religion and Resistance in Appalachia: Faith and the Fight against Mountaintop Removal Coalmining* (Lexington: University Press of Kentucky, 2016), 150.

14 Plate, *Key Terms in Material Religion*, 4–5.

15 Witt, *Religion and Resistance in Appalachia*.

16 Witt, *Religion and Resistance in Appalachia*, 146.

17 Witt, *Religion and Resistance in Appalachia*, 147.

18 Witt, *Religion and Resistance in Appalachia*, 147.

19 Bron Taylor, *Dark Green Religion: Nature Spirituality and the Planetary Future* (Berkley: University of California Press, 2010).

20 Nurit Bird-David, 'Animism Revisited: Personhood, Environment, and Relational Epistemology', *Current Anthropology* 40, no. S1, Special Issue *Culture – A Second Chance?* (February 1999); Graham Harvey, *Animism: Respecting the Living World* (London: Hurst); Tylor, *Primitive Culture*.

21 Witt, *Religion and Resistance in Appalachia*, 160–1.

22 Amy Whitehead, 'Touching, Crafting and Knowing: Religious Artefacts and the New Fetishism,' in *Sensual Religion: Religion and the Five Senses*, ed. Graham Harvey and Jessica Hughes (London: Equinox, 2018), 219–20.

23 Harvey, *Animism*, 33.

24 Harvey, 'Adjusted Styles of Communication', 47.

25 Thomas Tweed, 'Space', in *Key Terms in Material Religion*, ed. S. Brent Plate (London: Bloomsbury, 2015), 224.

26 Tweed, 'Space', 227.

27 Tweed, 'Space', 228.

28 Harvey, 'Adjusted Styles of Communication', 49.

29 Tim Ingold, 'Re-Thinking the Animate, Re-Animating Thought', *Ethnos* 71, no. 1 (2006): 14.

30 Ingold, 'Re-Thinking the Animate', 7.

31 Harvey, 'Adjusted Styles of Communication', 47.

32 Harvey, 'Adjusted Styles of Communication', 47.

33 Harvey, 'Adjusted Styles of Communication', 47.

34 Harvey, 'Adjusted Styles of Communication', 47.

35 Amy Whitehead, *Religious Statues and Personhood: Testing the Role of Materiality* (London: Bloomsbury, 2013).

36 Rafi Youatt, 'Personhood and the Rights of Nature: The New Subjects of Contemporary Earth Politics', *International Political Sociology* 0 (2017): 9.

Bibliography

Astor-Aguilera, Miguel, and Graham Harvey, eds. *Rethinking Relations and Animism: Personhood and Materiality*. London: Routledge, 2018.

Bird-David, Nurit. 'Animism Revisited: Personhood, Environment, and Relational Epistemology'. *Current Anthropology* 40, no. S1, Special Issue *Culture – A Second Chance?* (February 1999): S67–S91.

Farmer, Jared. *On Zion's Mount: Mormons, Indians, and the American landscape*. Cambridge, MA: Harvard University Press, 2008.

Hallowell, Alfred Irving. 'Ojibwa Ontology, Behavior, and World View'. In *Culture in History: Essay in Honor of Paul Radin*, edited by S. Diamond, 19–52.

New York: Columbia University Press, 1960. Reprinted in *Reading in Indigenous Religions*, edited by Graham Harvey, 18–49. London: Continuum, 2002.

Harvey, Graham. *Animism: Respecting the Living World*. London: Hurst, 2005.

Harvey, Graham. 'Adjusted Styles of Communication (ASCs) in the Post-Cartesian World'. In *Rethinking Relations and Animism: Personhood and Materiality*, edited by Miguel Astor-Aguilera and Graham Harvey, 35–52. London: Routledge, 2018.

Ingold, Tim. 'Rethinking the Animate, Re-Animating Thought'. *Ethnos* 71, no. 1 (2006): 9–20.

Laughlin, Jennifer Bauer. *Roan Mountain: A Passage of Time*. Johnson City, TN: Overmountain Press, 1999.

Plate, Brent, ed. *Key Terms in Material Religion*. London: Bloomsbury, 2015.

Rehder, John B. *Appalachian Folkways*. Baltimore, MD: Johns Hopkins University Press, 2004.

Tilley, Christopher. *Interpreting Landscapes: Geologies, Topographies, Identities; Explorations in Landscape Phenomenology 3*. New York: Routledge, 2010.

Tilley, Christopher, and Kate Cameron-Daum, *Anthropology of Landscape: The Extraordinary in the Ordinary*. London: UCL Press, 2017.

Tweed, Thomas. 'Space'. In *Key Terms in Material Religion*, edited by S. Brent Plate, 223–30. London: Bloomsbury, 2015.

Tylor, Edward. *Primitive Culture*, 2 vols. Reprint. London: John Murray, [1871] 1913.

Whitehead, Amy. 'Touching, Crafting and Knowing: Religious Artefacts and the New Fetishism'. In *Sensual Religion: Religion and the Five Senses*, edited by Graham Harvey and Jessica Hughes, 260–70. London: Equinox, 2018.

Witt, Joseph D. *Religion and Resistance in Appalachia: Faith and the Fight against Mountaintop Removal Coalmining*. Lexington: University Press of Kentucky, 2016.

Youatt, Rafi. 'Personhood and the Rights of Nature: The New Subjects of Contemporary Earth Politics'. *International Political Sociology* 0 (2017): 1–16.

Part Four

Storied conversations

7

Mountains talk of kings and dragons, the Brecon Beacons

Bernadette Brady

This chapter turns to the Brecon Beacons in Wales and approaches the nature of a 'place' as it draws together the diverse threads of local folklore, sky and star movements, the contemporary use of the place of the Brecon Beacons, and the location's larger cultural themes of the dragon of Wales and its links to kingship. With so many diverse layers of mythology and topography, these two twin peaks present what Belden Lane defined as a place that 'talks back', a place that participates with humanity in its expression.[1] The case study slowly reveals that the roof of the Brecon Beacons, rich in its cultural roots, is a place 'singing to itself' and as such draws sacredness or meaning towards itself independent of human conscious actions.

The Brecon Beacons is a mountain range comprised of six main peaks shaped into a long winding ridge which geographically defines the border between south and mid Wales. At either end of the ridge are mountain ranges: to the west, Black Mountain; and to the east the similarly named, Black Mountains. The actual name of the Brecon Beacons is thought to relate to their use of beacon lighting to warn of attacks. The beacons were also lit to celebrate the millennium. One of these six peaks is the highest in southern Britain. Named Pen y Fan and standing at 886 metres, it is connected by a ridge to the west to the second highest peak, Corn Du, with a height of 873 metres. The two peaks and their joining ridge thus combine to form a 'beam' in the roof of the Brecon Beacons. From this high ridge two U-shaped glacial valleys flow, one running down to the south, called the Tâf Fechan Valley, and the other to the north, containing a glacial lake, Llyn cwm Llwc (Figure 7.1, top).

From 1896 to 1902 a section of the Tâf Fechan Valley was flooded to form the Upper Neuadd Reservoir. The reservoir was built in a rectangular shape with a

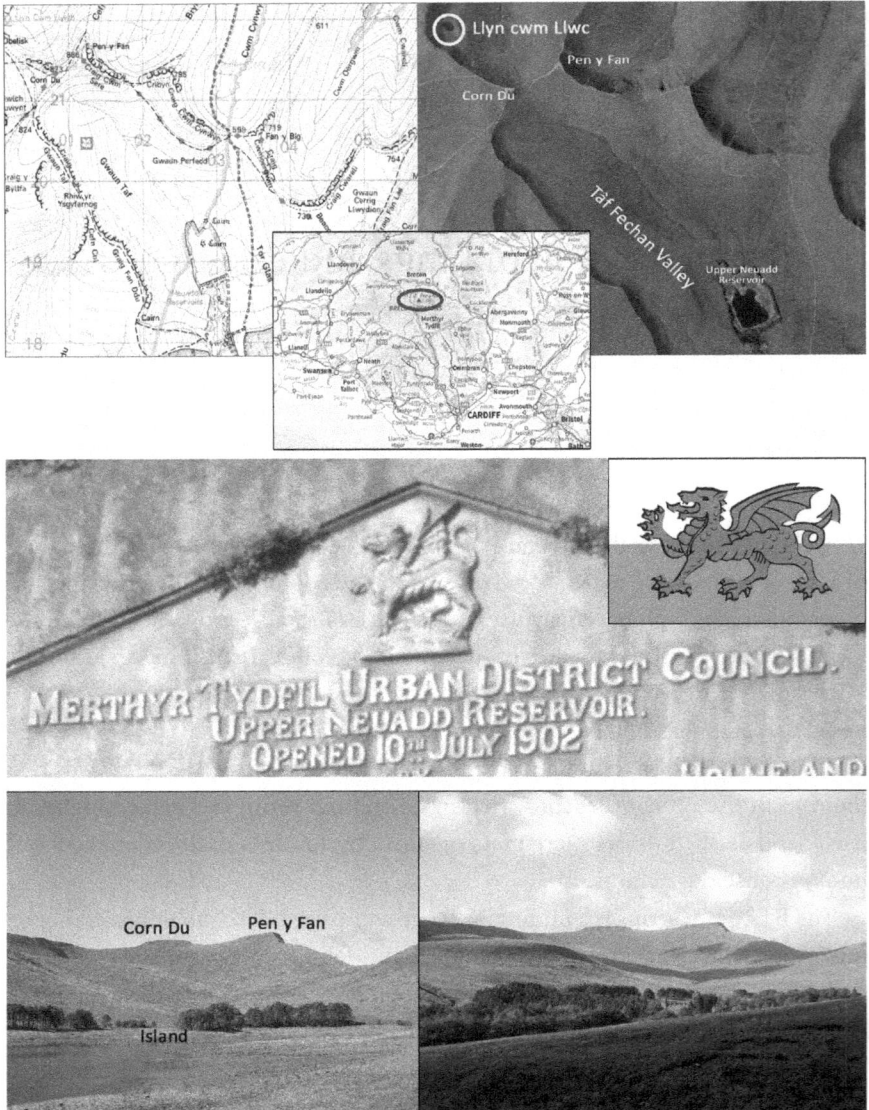

Figure 7.1 Top: Ordinance Survey map of the two valleys that flow northerly and southerly from the twin peaks of Pen y Fan and Corn Du in the Brecon Beacons, South Wales, plus the image of the same area from Google Earth showing the Upper Neuadd Reservoir, the contours of the ridge, and the small glacial lake of Llyn cwm Llwch in the top left edge of the map. Middle: The plaque on the outflow of the Upper Neuadd Reservoir, showing a Welsh Dragon image before the emblem was standardized into its national icon in 1959. Photo: B. Brady. Insert: The style of the nationalized Welsh dragon. Bottom left: The view of Cadair Arthur, looking north from the side of the Upper Neuadd Reservoir showing the island on which there is a round barrow cemetery. Bottom right: The view of Cadair Arthur from outside the valley looking north. The wall of the outflow to the Upper Neuadd Reservoir can be seen as the small structure in the middle of the image. Photos: B. Brady.

massive outflow wall across a natural narrowing in the valley. Upon this outflow wall there is a plaque proclaiming the date of opening, 10 July 1902, and topped by a 1902 version of a Welsh dragon (Figure 7.1, middle). This is not the dragon one normally associates with Wales, for it was only in 1959 that the dragon's image took on its official Welsh form that we know today (Figure 7.1, middle insert).[2]

Additionally, in more recent times, the Merthyr Tydifil Angling Association has been given permission to stock the upper reservoir with wild brown trout. This area is now considered to be a premier fly-fishing area, although warnings are given that the trout are rare and extremely hard to catch, with a bag limit of only two per day. According to a fly-fishing website for the area,

> Fly fishing is the only permitted method and small imitative patterns are recommended. The trout will not be large and they will not be easy to catch, but it is hard to imagine a more beautiful or more isolated place in which to fish this side of the Scottish border.[3]

Although the valleys are now mainly home to day trekkers and fly-fishers, these two valleys have, in the past, seen much human activity. Apocryphal stories tell of a Roman road or trail that runs through Tâf Fechan Valley over the escarpment and through to the northern side of the Beacons. Jenny Hall and Paul Sambrook Trysor pointed out, however, that there was no archaeological evidence of such a road, although they noted that there was an old trackway which crossed to one side of the Tâf Fechan Valley and this followed a stream called Nant yr Hen Heol (the Stream of the Old Road).[4] Notwithstanding this lack of Roman stonework, the Tâf Fechan Valley and the high ridge between Pen y Fan and Corn Du hold substantial evidence of Neolithic and Bronze Age activity. Under or near the water of the Upper Neuadd Reservoir there are at least six cairns or round hut foundations, with some located on a natural island in the reservoir. Those on the island, according to the RCAHM in 1997, have the appearance of sepulchral cairns.[5] In 2006 this entire grouping of the submerged cairns and those on the island were defined by the Clwyd-Powys Archaeological Trust as a round barrow cemetery.[6] In addition to these structures, both Pen y Fan and Corn Du have round barrows on their summits, with the barrow on Pen y Fan containing a bronze horde.[7] Thus the Tâf Fechan Valley with its high location and its naturally raised area of ground — the island in the reservoir — was considered important and probably even sacred by Neolithic and/or Bronze Age people, a place of burial with the peak of Pen y Fan deemed worthy of the gift of a precious horde of metal.

The story of these valleys does not end there, however. At this juncture one could, using the evidence of the ancient metal horde and the Neolithic or Bronze Age cemetery, speculate about the human-bestowed sacredness of the place. Such an argument would, of course, be complemented by the natural liminal nature of mountains for, as Christopher Tilley wrote, mountains are 'considered to be the dwelling-places of spirits and places where shamans go to practise magic'.[8] Yet there are other features in this high ancient burial ground. The ridge between Corn Du and Pen y Fan is orientated at a true azimuth of around 70°, azimuth being the compass bearing measured from due north at 0°. Hence the ridge creates a high horizon which runs roughly east-west. If a person stands on the raised land, which is now the island in the reservoir, and looks north to the ridge they would see a raised, clear, and well-defined level horizon line at an altitude of around 10°.[9] As a result, the view of the stars touching the ridge is free from horizon haze, thus the circumpolar stars, the never-setting northern stars, are clear and sharp as they skim along the top of the ridge. In this way the natural liminal place of the burial ground and high mountains gains an additional feature of being a place where special stars, non-setting stars, commune with the earth. Adding to this feature is the fact that all northern hemisphere stars reach their lowest point in the sky when they are at a bearing of due north. Hence a star seen to just skim the ridge would act as a marker of the direction of due north. This feature is one of the threads of meaning in the valley, for north is linked to the mythical king of the Britons, Arthur, and indeed by coincidence the ridge and twin peaks are known as Arthur's Chair.

In 1188 Gerald of Wales, in his work *Journey around Wales*, focused his attention on the glacial lake in the northern valley named Llyn cwm Llwc. He defined the lake as 'miraculous' and gave its location as lying 'to the south by a range of hills the chief of which is Cadair Arthur, or Arthur's Chair, so called from two peaks which rise up in the form of a throne'.[10] This visual phenomenon of a chair is formed by the ridge between the peaks dipping a little below the level of the two peaks, with the peaks forming the arms of a chair (Figure 7.1, bottom). Gerald explained the link to Arthur and the throne as, 'This summit is a very lofty spot and most difficult of access, so that in the minds of simple folk it is thought to have belonged to Arthur, the greatest and most distinguished King of the Britons.'[11] The name of Cadair Arthur or Arthur's Chair persisted on maps until the early twentieth century and is still so named by websites which discuss hiking in the area. This name, however, is by no means unique to these twin peaks. Thomas Green listed at least nine other places, ranging in locations from Edinburgh to Tintagel in Cornwall. Although one can make no claim as to which of these 'chairs' was the earliest, many of them appear to be named at dates later than the observations made by Gerald of Wales of Pen y Fan and Corn Du.[12] Nevertheless, while all have similar topography of a high ridge with raised sides, they do not necessarily have an east-west orientation and thus one cannot observe the northern sky behind the chair.

Having dismissed the folk stories of Cadair Arthur, Gerald detailed the magical qualities of the peaks. He described the peak of Pen y Fan where,

> On the topmost point of this mountain a spring of water bubbles forth. Its deep basin is square in shape and like a well, but no stream ever runs from it. Trout are said to be found there from time to time.[13]

Gerald considered the mountain a place of magic, a notion supporting Tilley's link between high places and magic cited earlier. For Gerald, this magic was twofold, embracing the deep spring which was like a well and held water that never flowed as a stream and the periodical presence of trout in this well. Gerald then wrote of the small lake in the northern valley, Llyn cwm Llwc, to which he attributed even greater magical powers. According to Gerald, this lake could at different times turn into rich pasturelands or become adorned with gardens and an orchard, while at other times it could be covered with buildings or groan horribly when iced over. Yet its central miraculous property lay not in its shape-changing. In the time of 'the cold winter season' when waterfowl were on its surface, it had the power to recognize the true heir to the kingship of Wales.[14]

Gerald explained this myth through an anecdote. He recounted an earlier story of three men – Milo, Earl of Hereford (f. 1139); Gruffydd, son of Rhys ap Tewdwr (d. 1137); and Payn FitzJohn (d. 1137) – who rode by the lake when it was occupied by waterfowl. Milo challenged Gruffydd to let the birds test his claim that the blood of Welsh princes ran in his veins. Gruffydd replied that, since Milo had great power in the country, he should speak to the birds first. Yet neither Milo nor Payn could make the birds sing. When Gruffydd, however, claimed loudly that he was the true heir of the ancient Welsh throne, 'all the birds, each according to his kind, beat the water with their wings and began to sing with one accord and to proclaim him master'.[15] Gerald's claim was that the lake could recognize and announce the true king of Wales and the timing of such announcements was winter, when the waterfowl gathered there. This story of Welsh kingship fits seamlessly into the local name of the ridge and peaks, that of Cadair Arthur, with Arthur being, as Gerald claimed, 'the greatest and most distinguished King of the Britons'.

Thus stories, folklore, history, and legends have gathered around these two mountains, making them a 'thick' place, one rich with meaning. Tim Ingold has argued that the construction of 'place' is where different threads meet and overlap, 'in which every linear segment serves as a joint, welding together the elements of the pattern into a totality of a higher order'.[16] In the case of these two mountains, the components that imply Ingold's 'totality of a higher order' are the 'welding together' of the material evidence of sacredness of burials and bronze hordes from the time of pre-history, the topographical features of liminality of the highest mountains in southern Britain, and the evidence in the literature of stories of magic, wonder, or 'otherworldliness' which are linked to the theme of Welsh kingship. These components are sufficient to produce the thick description of this location, yet to this potent place, with its emphases on winter, a starry dragon joins the blend.

The Roman sky

Celestial cartography, and thus the images within the starry sky, has been consistent in Western culture since the Greeks. The constellations of modern Western celestial cartography were enshrined in poetry by Aratus in the third century BCE:

> Through the two Bears the breathtaking
> *Dragon* meanders like a river, snaking
> At great length far and wide, On either side
> Of his extent, the Bears wheel with the tide
> Beneath them.[17]

These poetic images were then immortalised in the first century CE by Claudius Ptolemy in his work, the *Almagest*, where, for example, he located the constellation of Draco, the Dragon, star by star in the sky, defining the position of 'the star on the tongue, the star in the mouth, the star above the eye, the star on the jaw, the star above the head', and so on, listing not only the thirty-one stars for the constellation of Draco but also their location in the constellation image and their magnitude.[18] The Romans inherited these sky images from the Greeks and, as they were a useful for navigation and calendar matters, they became culturally robust.[19] Indeed so culturally robust were these Greco-Roman sky images that when they encountered the well-established sky cartography of the Egyptians, the Egyptian cartography was slowly lost.[20] Hence when the Romans marched into Wales in 77 CE, so too did their sky.[21] Their sky is our sky, one where the area around the north celestial pole is encircled by the two bears, Ursa Major and Ursa Minor, with the dragon, Draco, curled between them.

Evidence that Greco-Roman cartography had been injected into the Welsh culture can be seen in the work of Geoffrey of Monmouth (*c.*1100–55). In his *Prophecies of Merlin*, he wrote of the world in chaos which he defined by zodiac constellations in disarray:

> The twins shall surcease from their wonted embrace, and shall call the Urn unto the fountains. The Scales of the Balance shall hang awry until the Ram shall set his crooked horns beneath them.[22]

Granted, as Mark Williams pointed out, there is little to no evidence before the time of Geoffrey's work of the zodiac (and thus Greco-Roman celestial cartography) in Welsh early medieval literature.[23] Nevertheless, an absence of evidence is not evidence of absence. Wales, particularly south Wales, was dominated in the first century CE by Roman culture; thus around the sixth century, at the time of the legendary kingship of Arthur, the Greco-Roman celestial cartography with its northern bears and dragon would have populated the heavens over southern Wales.

Of all the circumpolar constellations Draco traces the longest line through the sky, winding upwards and around the bears. Additionally, a feature of Draco is that at its lowest culmination, the dragon's head points directly downwards and thus its head on, or near, the ground indicates due north. At the latitude of the valley (51°N 53' 1.8"), if one stands in the mouth of the valley, or even further away, and looks towards Cadair Arthur, the sky dragon will appear to butt its head on or just above the horizon of the ridge, near the peak of Pen y Fan (Figure 7.2, left). The constellation Draco has maintained this visual orientation despite the effects of precession, the slow shift of the stars against the seasons, over the last few thousand years. Precession is slowly lowering the dragon's head onto the ridge; however, in the course of the last 3,500 years, the head of Draco has only lowered by 4°, with little change to the actual time of the year when this is seen.

The actual nights when Draco will be seen at its lowest culmination and engaging with Arthur's Chair will depend on the time of the year. Gerald commented that the waterfowl that could proclaim the king gathered on this high-altitude lake in 'the cold winter season'. For the Bronze Age, and in Gerald's time, and for today, Draco will only be seen with its head on the ridge during the nights of the winter months (Figure 7.2). This annual rhythm forms a

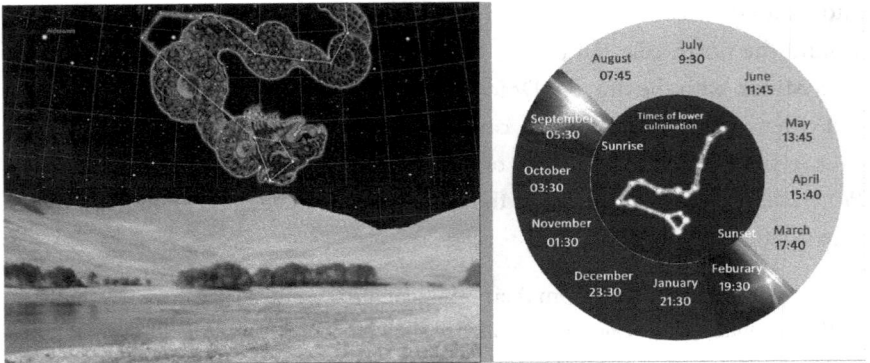

Figure 7.2 Left: An artistic rendition of Draco at its lower culmination for 1000 CE (indicating due north) over Cadair Arthur from a location adjacent to the reservoir. Image: B. Brady. Right: The local mean times to the nearest five minutes of the lower culmination of Draco for the year 1000 CE for the fifteenth day of each month (Gregorian calendar). The night hours are dark, while the daylight hours are light. Draco's lower culmination is only visible in the nights of the winter months. This pattern is still applicable today. Image: B. Brady.

correlation with Gerald's discussion of the magical Llyn cwm Llwc which could only proclaim a Welsh king in the winter months. Draco can only be seen to 'sit' in Arthur's Chair in nights of the winter months.

The dragon in Wales

As the Romans colonized Britain, and later Wales, they brought with them the image of the dragon as an icon of military might. As noted by Pat Southern and Karen R. Dixon, it was in the second century CE that Roman cavalry adopted the *draco* standard. This standard was a dragon represented as a flag-like banner that flowed from the top of a pole but in the shape of a windsock so it could capture the air and, at times, even makes sounds.[24] John Tatlock commented that the dragons of these Roman forces were either coloured red or purple and were used not only in warfare but also in ceremonial ways.[25] As the Roman legions and cavalry moved across Britain, they introduced the notion of the dragon as a creature of the air and of military might which should be feared.

Evidence for the Welsh adoption of the dragon stands, according to Tatlock, on uncertain ground.[26] Nevertheless, the dragon within Welsh or early British culture was viewed in a positive manner and linked to kingship and military might. In the sixth century the monk, Gildas (*c.*500–70) wrote a work named *De Excidioi Britanniae* (*Ruin of Britain*). This work Ronald Hutton considered to be 'the nearest thing that we possess to an account of the sub-Roman period in Britain written by somebody who was part of it'.[27] In this work Gildas gave his opinion of a welsh king, Maglocune, who is believed to be Maelgwn Gwynedd, king of north Wales, and Gildas spoke of him as 'O thou dragon of the island' and then referred to him as 'exceeding many in power' in his role of kingship.[28] Furthermore, the *Historia Brittonum*, a work of around 800 CE considered to be authored by the Welsh monk, Nennius, described a Red Dragon as the symbol of the British people in their wars against the White Dragon of the Saxons. He wrote of a dream or vision of the two dragons fighting within a pool,

> The pool is the emblem of this world, and the tent that of your kingdom: the two serpents are two dragons; the red serpent is your dragon, but the white serpent is the dragon of the people who occupy several provinces and districts of Britain.[29]

Such accounts reinforce the view that the Welsh linked the dragon to their own fighting identity against the invading Saxons.

This Welsh association with the dragon and its link to a warrior king offers an insight into why the Welsh alone in all of Europe maintained a positive view of the dragon. In other parts of Europe the dragon fell victim to the Christian Book of Revelation and became an evil creature associated with Satan.[30] Hutton argued that in the Early Middle Ages the dragon throughout most of Europe was considered a 'fire-breathing, flying reptilian monster' which carried off livestock; yet, Hutton continued, such an evil creature, in this difficult guise, did not exist in Celtic Britain.[31] The dragon as warrior king was instilled in British/Welsh culture quite early and may have been adopted or copied from the Romans. It would have then been reinforced in the Welsh culture as they fought against other invading tribes and thus well-established before the arrival of Christianity with its Book of Revelation in the sixth century.

For Celtic Britain, the dragon's kingly association is with Arthur and his father. In the poetic history of Geoffrey of Monmouth, the source of most of the Arthurian legendary material, it is not surprising that Geoffrey named Arthur's father as Uther Pendragon, where 'pendragon' means head dragon.[32] Arthur's birth was also, according to Geoffrey, foretold by the appearance of the Dragon Star, a type of Celtic star of Bethlehem, which appeared in the sky in the shape of two dragons. Additionally, in the medieval Welsh manuscript the *Mabinogi*, the *Dream of Rhonabwy*, Arthur's sword is described as two fire-breathing serpents that, when unsheathed, produced 'two flames of fire, so dreadful that it was not easy for anyone to look'. He, Arthur, also sat upon 'a chair so large that three armed warriors could sit in it' while he was wrapped in a mantle that bestowed on its wearer the ability to see everyone while being unseen by all.[33] Tatlock also pointed out that Arthur wore a golden helmet sculptured as *simulacro draconis*.[34] All of these attributes have strong sky components: the Dragon Star, huge high seats where all can be seen, and a golden helmet which could be a reference to the sun. Hutton suggested that it is entirely possible that the notion of Arthur was a humanization of a 'pagan god, probably of the sun, who was turned into a human hero after the coming of Christianity'.[35] He added the caveat, however, that nineteenth-century authors had the tendency to link mythic heroes to forces of nature. Nevertheless, Green made the case that the name Arthur had its origins in the Gallo-Brittonic *arto-* 'bear, warrior and hero' and he defined Arthur as

> a story-cycle focused on a folkloric Protector of Britain and a peerless warrior, a character of local wonder-tales and the wild parts of the landscape who is intimately connected with the Otherworld.[36]

Green noted that the bright star in the northern hemisphere, Arcturus, carries the proper name made of the Greek *arktos*, 'bear' + *ouros*, 'guardian, keeper' meaning guardian of the bear, or guardian of the north, thus adding to the star or sky theme of Arthur and the dragon.[37] Further links between Arthur and the north are seen in an alternative name for Ursa Major as being Arthur's Wain.[38] Finally there is the fact that the word 'bear' was also used in the Greek to indicate the north.[39] Whether Arthur was a real figure or a sky phenomenon or a combination of both, it is generally accepted that among his attributes are the dragon, links to the north, and a tendency to dwell in high places, or liminal areas, thereby maintaining his otherworldliness.

These links of the north, Welsh kingship, and dragons all reside in the twin summits of the Brecon Beacons. At a local level the area's folklore of kingship is in rapport or enhanced by the sky's movement against the local landscape, as it places the constellation of Draco on the ridge only in the winter months. These local stories are, however, moved into a national sphere through the ethno-topography of the ridge being acknowledged as Cadair Arthur, the lost king of the Welsh. Arthur's attributes, whether consciously understood or not, are also supplied by the northern view provided by the high ridge and the Welsh symbol of the dragon visible sitting on the great king's throne, Arthur's Chair.

The power of place

In contemporary thought landscapes tends to be viewed as inert in that it is a place upon which humanity acts. Tilley, however, suggested that such storied landscapes become humanized and encultured as they become saturated with place names which are intertwined with topography and human intentionality and even mythological characters.[40] To this idea of intertwined intentions and landscape the classical notion of place as presented by Aristotle (384 BCE–322 BCE) gains relevance. Aristotle defined place as coextensive with its occupying body, like a vessel that gives shape to water but is independent of that water.[41] Edward Casey argued that this Aristotelian approach viewed place as holding its own quality independent of its contents.[42] He expanded his comments on Aristotle's view of place by stating,

> This is the acknowledgment of place as a unique and nonreducible feature of the physical world, something with its own inherent powers, a pre-metric phenomenon (thus both historically and conceptually pre-Euclidean in its specification). And above all something that reflects the situation of being in, and moving between, places.[43]

It is this very notion of motion, moving between places, that Aristotle ascribed to the power of place. He argued that the motion of any body, which was composed of the natural elements of fire, earth, air, and water, 'show not only that place is something, but also that it exerts a certain influence'.[44] He saw this influence of place as a form of gravity that drew bodies towards certain places, places which somehow reflected that body. When a body found itself in such a place Aristotle considered that it was in its 'proper place' for 'the movement of each body to its own place is motion towards its own form'.[45] This location of a body in its proper place was recognized by Aristotle as a state where the body experiences a sense of wholeness and a form of stillness.[46]

This Aristotelian notion of place could be dismissed as the outdated views of classical physics. Aristotle's views, however, were informed not by experimentation but by his powers of observation. Today, therefore, his views on the power of place speak of the human experience of place. His thinking on how a body is drawn to its proper place, a place where it finds a sense of wholeness, completeness, and stillness, is a form of phenomenological gravity, the force that draws an individual or indeed any form of life to where they feel whole, complete, and thus find stillness. Examples of this notion of an individual in their proper place are evident in the art of portraiture where the artist seeks to place the individual in the setting and clothing that makes them complete and whole so that their true character is expressed. But it also extends to all levels of life, whether it is a tidy room with all things in their proper place or the chosen lifestyle of an individual which nurtures that individual with feelings of completeness and wholeness.

As an area becomes rich with cultural layers, then according to Aristotelian thinking, it will grow in its potential to influence human activity, such activity as wanting to maintain place names and taking measures to protect a storied location. Society will generally seek to maintain a tradition or protect the history of its areas, whether this is a town street, a sports stadium, or a national park. This is achieved by resisting change to that area and bringing into the area events and things which are deemed to be traditionally correct for that place. This in turn promotes stillness, stillness in the sense of a resistance to change, a level of consistency. Thus, according to Aristotle's views, a landscape can gain agency by the power of place.

The song of the Beacons

In returning to the twin summits of the Brecon Beacons, recently the area has been made into the Brecon Beacon's National Park in order to maintain its wilderness. Additionally, the whole of the Brecon Beacons has been declared a Dark Sky Area so that the brilliance of the starry sky can be returned to the region, which by default ensures that the starry dragon will not be lost to light pollution. Furthermore, some eight hundred years after Gerald wrote his story of well and fish, this, too, is being reproduced by human activity. The construction of the rectangular Upper Neuadd Reservoir reflects Gerald's magical deep square well. Gerald's claim that no spring flowed from this well is also maintained, for the reservoir is a holder of water from which no streams flow. Only pipelines and the occasional drainage are its outlet. Continuing the parallels between Gerald's well and the reservoir is the issue of the trout. Gerald claimed that in the well 'trout are said to be found there from time to time'.[47] The reservoir has been stocked by the Merthyr Tydifil Angling Association with brown trout, a fish considered elusive as it rarely rises to a fly so that they give the impression of 'disappearing' in the reservoir. It is almost as if the Merthyr Tydifil Anglers had intentionally followed Gerald's description of the well. There may also be good reason for the 1902 image of the proud dragon standing at the top of the plaque on the outflow of the reservoir (Figure 7.1, middle). Although placed there with Welsh pride by the reservoir builders, this too could be part of the place's voice. For the dragon traditionally lives in lonely and desolate spots remote from humankind, lofty with big airy skies, and often near water.[48] The dragon has also crept into the promotional material of Brecon Beacon's National Park which uses a photo of two people looking at a starry sky. In the background, understandably, is Arthur's Chair, the twin peaks, but if one looks closely at the peaks, the photo just happens to have captured the dragon sitting on the ridge.[49] These may be a string of coincidences, a fluke of human activity which just happens to be fulfilling the local legends around the peaks and its valleys. But if mountains have agency, then here is evidence of these mountains slowly restoring the magical habitat of the native Welsh dragon, a creature that can be viewed sitting on Arthur's Chair on dark winter nights, even in the mountain's promotional material.

There is sacredness here as well, the sacredness which comes from the power of a place to maintain itself. Its most obvious level is the natural sacredness of a high place and the quiet sacredness of a burial ground. This is sacredness which emerges from stillness as a timelessness sits upon it. Being largely deserted, it has a sense of being left alone to its own thoughts. Yi-Fu Tuan claimed that 'if we think of space as that which allows movement, then place is pause'.[50] This place requires pause. The fly-fishers have to wait for hours in the stillness as they hunt the elusive fish, hikers pause on the peak of Pen-y-Fan to savour the view and the moment, and even the water is 'paused', held back from its normal eagerness to run down the valley by the reservoir. This is a place still and wild, paused yet alive. It holds many layers of local and national stories and through the helpful hands of eager humans, it is expressing the material features of its own story. This place, to use Beldon Lane's words, 'demands its own integrity, its own participation in what it "becomes," its own voice'.[51]

This notion of the 'voice' of a place is described by Sean Kane as 'the song of the place to itself'. Kane considers that this song is created when folklore and nature combine in an annual rhythm which 'preserves a place whole and sacred, safe from human meddling'.[52] In Kane's example, the annual rhythm is that of a salmon run up a river which becomes sanctified with local mythology and where salmon, myth, and forest combined as the river's song, sung not for human ears, but for the simply joy of its singing. In the case of the roof of the Brecon Beacons, the natural rhythm that produces the song is the annual winter appearance of the dragon in Arthur's Chair. Importantly, this is independent of whether this is noticed or understood or even 'heard' by humans. The song that the two mountains and the valley 'sings to itself' is a song of dragons, kings and thrones, trout, and deep wells.

It is only our ontologies that cast landscape as an inactive canvas. Lane argued that scholarly discourse about sacred place often lacks any basis for appreciating the native traditions that nature 'talks back', that it participates in the experiences humans have of it.[53] With Lane's arguments in mind, the mountains and the ridge of Arthur's Chair can be considered as 'talking back', and the evidence of this conversation with humanity is suggested in the materialization of the components of its song, the dragon's habitat being protected by the human-maintained wildness and the human-maintained dark skies, the magical stories expressed by the human-built deep well, the human stocking of the water with elusive trout, all of which sit in a stillness which is maintained quite instinctually by the human visitors. Humanity is in conversation with these mountains.

Notes

1   Belden C. Lane, *Landscapes of the Sacred: Geography and Narrative in American Spirituality*, expanded ed. (Baltimore, MD: Johns Hopkins University Press, 2001), 42.

2   Carl Lofmark and G. A. Wells, *A History of the Red Dragon* (Llanrwst: Gwasg Carreg Gwalch, 1995), 74.

3   'Fishing in Kite Country', http://www.fishing-in-kite-country.co.uk/fishing/neuares. html (accessed 1 November 2013).

4   Jenny Hall and Paul Sambrook Trysor, 'Uplands Initiative Brecon Beacons (East) Archaeological Survey (Part One)' (The Royal Commission on the Ancient and Historical Monuments of Wales, 2009), 30.

5   *An Inventory of the Ancient Monuments in Brecknock (Brycheiniog). The Prehistoric and Roman Monuments. Part 1: Later Prehistoric Monuments and Unenclosed Settlements to 1000 A.D.* (London: Royal Commission on the Ancient Historical Monuments of Wales, 1997), 110–11.

6   N. W. Jones and W. J. Owen, *Prehistoric Funerary & Ritual Sites: Eastern Brecon Beacons* (Cadw Welsh Historic Monuments, 2006), 26.

7   *An Inventory of the Ancient Monuments in Brecknock*, 117; Alex Gibson, *Survey on Pen-y-Fan and Corn Du, Brecon Beacons, Powys, April–May 1990* (National Trust, 1990), 6.

8   Christopher Tilley, *A Phenomenology of Landscape* (Oxford: Berg, 1994), 56.

9   All field measurements were taken with a Suunto compass and clinometer by the author in October 2013 on the easterly side of the lake. This altitude measurement is approximated, as one cannot now stand on the island.

10 Cambrensis Giraldus, *The Journey through Wales/the Description of Wales*, trans. Lewis Thorpe (Harmondsworth: Penguin, 1978), 95.

11 Giraldus, *Journey through Wales*, 96.

12 Thomas Green, *Arthuriana: Early Arthurian Tradition and the Origins of the Legend* (Lincolnshire: Lindes Press, 2009), 108–9.

13 Giraldus, *Journey through Wales*, 96.

14 Giraldus, *Journey through Wales*, 94.

15 Giraldus, *Journey through Wales*, 95.

16 Tim Ingold, *Lines: A Brief History* (London: Routledge, 2007), 74.

17 Aratus, *Phaenomena*, trans. Aaron Poochigian (Baltimore, MD: John Hopkins University Press, 2010), L.45–9.

18 Claudius Ptolemy, *Ptolemy's Almagest*, trans. G. J. Toomer (New Jersey: Princeton University Press, 1998), VII 5, III. H44.

19 Bernadette Brady, 'Images in the Heavens: A Cultural Landscape', in *The Imagined Sky*, ed. Darrelyn Gunzburg (Sheffield: Equinox, 2016), 234–58.

20 Bernadette Brady, 'Images in the Heavens: A Cultural Landscape', *Journal for the Study of Religion, Nature and Culture* 7 (2013): 461–84.

21 Peter Guest, 'The Early Monetary History of Roman Wales: Identity, Conquest and Acculturation on the Imperial Fringe', *Britannia* 39 (2008): 33–58, at 33.

22 Geoffrey of Monmouth, *History of the Kings of Britain*, trans. Sebastian Evans (London: J. M. Dent, 1904), 188.

23 Mark Williams, *Fiery Shapes, Celestial Portents and Astrology in Ireland and Wales 700–1700* (Oxford: Oxford University Press, 2010), 108.

24 Pat Southern and Karen R. Dixon, *The Late Roman Army* (London: Yale University Press, 1996), 126.

25 J. S. P. Tatlock, 'The Dragons of Wessex and Wales', *Speculum* 8 (1933): 223–35, at 223.

26 Tatlock, 'Dragons of Wessex and Wales', 228.

27 Ronald Hutton, 'The Early Arthur', in *The Cambridge Companion to the Arthurian Legend*, ed. Elizabeth Archibald and Ad Putter (Cambridge: Cambridge University Press, 2009), 21–35, at 24.

28 Gildas, 'On the Ruin of Britain', trans. J. A. Giles and T. Habington (1842), 23–4, http://www.heroofcamelot.com/historic-documents/on-the-ruin-of-britain (accessed 1 October 2013).

29 Nennius, 'Historia Brittonum', in *Six Old English Chronicles*, trans. J. A. Giles (London: Henry G. Bohn, 1848), Section 42, http://www.bsswebsite.me.uk/History/Nennius/NenniusHistory2.html – (accessed 12 October 2013).

30 *Revelation* 12:3, 12:9.

31 Ronald Hutton, *The Pagan Religions of the Ancient British Isles: Their Nature and Legacy* (Oxford: Blackwell, 1991), 125–6.

32 Monmouth, *History of the Kings of Britain*, 292; Marged Haycock, *Legendary Poems from the Book of Taliesin* (Aberystwyth: CMCS, 2007), 503.

33 Jeffrey Gantz, *The Mabinogion*, trans. Jeffrey Gantz (Harmondsworth: Penguin, 1976), 184–5.

34 Tatlock, 'Dragons of Wessex and Wales', 229.

35 Hutton, 'Early Arthur', 28.

36 Thomas Green, *Concepts of Arthur* (Stroud: Tempus, 2007), 188.

37 Green, *Concepts of Arthur*, 188.

38 Gertude Jobes and James Jobes, *Outer Space: Myths, Name Meanings, Calendars* (New York: Scarecrow, 1964), 260.

39 Paul Kunitzsch and Tim Smart, *A Dictionary of Modern Star Names* (Cambridge: Sky, 2006), 19.

40 Tilley, *Phenomenology of Landscape*, 24.

41 Aristotle, 'Physics', in *The Complete Works of Aristotle*, Volume 1, ed. Jonathan Barnes, trans. R. P. Hardie and R. K. Gaye (Princeton, NJ: Princeton University Press, 1984), 315–446: 4.2, 209a 8–9, at 32–3.

42 Edward S. Casey, *The Fate of Place: A Philosophical History* (Berkeley: University of California Press, 1998), xii, 51–3.

43 Casey, *Fate of Place*, 70.

44 Aristotle, 'Physics', 208b11.

45 Aristotle, 'On the Heavens', in *The Complete Works of Aristotle*, Volume 1, ed. Jonathan Barnes, trans. J. L. Stocks (Princeton, NJ: Princeton University Press, 1984), 447–511: IV 3, 310a, at 35.

46 Aristotle, 'Metaphysics', in *The Complete Works of Aristotle*, Volume 2, ed. Jonathan Barnes, trans. R. P. Hardie and R. K. Gaye (Princeton, NJ: Princeton University Press, 1984), 1552–728: IV, 1014b, at 16–26.

47 Giraldus, *Journey through Wales*, 96.

48 Lofmark and Wells, *History of the Red Dragon*, 24–5.

49 Brecon Beacons, Our National Park, *Ten Places to Go Stargazing*, http://www. breconbeacons.org/stargazing-ten-places (accessed 12 August 2017).

50 Yi-Fu Tuan, *Space and Place: The Perspective of Experience* (London: Arnold, 1977), 6.

51 Belden C. Lane, *Landscapes of the Sacred: Geography and Narrative in American Spirituality*, expanded ed. (Baltimore, MD: Johns Hopkins University Press, 2001), 4.

52 Sean A. Kane, *Wisdom of the Mythtellers* (Ontario: Broadview Press 1998), 46, 50.

53 Lane, *Landscapes of the Sacred*, 41.

Bibliography

An Inventory of the Ancient Monuments in Brecknock (Brycheiniog). The Prehistoric and Roman Monuments. Part 1: Later Prehistoric Monuments and Unenclosed Settlements to 1000 A.D. London: Royal Commission on the Ancient Historical Monuments of Wales, 1997.

Aratus, *Phaenomena*, translated by Aaron Poochigian. Baltimore, MD: John Hopkins University Press, 2010.

Aristotle. *Metaphysics*. In *The Complete Works of Aristotle*, volume 2, edited by Jonathan Barnes, translated by R. P. Hardie and R. K. Gaye, 1552–728. Princeton, NJ: Princeton University Press, 1984.

Aristotle. *On the Heavens*. In *The Complete Works of Aristotle*, Volume 1, edited by Jonathan Barnes, translated by J. L. Stocks, 447–511. Princeton, NJ: Princeton University Press, 1984.

Aristotle. *Physics*. In *The Complete Works of Aristotle*, volume 1, edited by Jonathan Barnes, translated by R. P. Hardie and R. K. Gaye, 315–446. Princeton, NJ: Princeton University Press, 1984.

Brady, Bernadette, 'Images in the Heavens: A Cultural Landscape'. *Journal for the Study of Religion, Nature and Culture* 7 (2013): 461–84.

Brady, Bernadette. 'Images in the Heavens: A Cultural Landscape. In *The Imagined Sky*, edited by Darrelyn Gunzburg, 234–58. Sheffield: Equinox, 2016.

Brecon Beacons, Our National Park, *Ten Places to Go Stargazing*, http://www.breconbeacons.org/stargazing-ten-places (accessed 12 August 2017).

Casey, Edward S. *The Fate of Place: A Philosophical History*. Berkeley: University of California Press, 1998.

'Fishing in Kite Country', http://www.fishing-in-kite-country.co.uk/fishing/neuares.html> (accessed 1 November 2013).

Gantz, Jeffrey. *The Mabinogion*, translated by Jeffrey Gantz. Harmondsworth: Penguin, 1976.

Gibson, Alex. 'Survey on Pen-Y-Fan and Corn Du, Brecon Beacons, Powys, April–May 1990'. National Trust, 1990.

Gildas, 'On the Ruin of Britain', translated by J. A. Giles and T. Habington, 1842, http://www.heroofcamelot.com/historic-documents/on-the-ruin-of-britain (accessed 1 October 2013).

Giraldus, Cambrensis. *The Journey through Wales/the Description of Wales*, translated by Lewis Thorpe. Harmondsworth: Penguin, 1978.

Green, Thomas, *Concepts of Arthur*. Stroud: Tempus, 2007.

Green, Thomas. *Arthuriana: Early Arthurian Tradition and the Origins of the Legend*. Lincolnshire: Lindes Press, 2009.

Guest, Peter. 'The Early Monetary History of Roman Wales: Identity, Conquest and Acculturation on the Imperial Fringe'. *Britannia* 39 (2008): 33–58.

Hall, Jenny, and Paul Sambrook Trysor. 'Uplands Initiative Brecon Beacons (East) Archaeological Survey (Part One)'. The Royal Commission on the Ancient and Historical Monuments of Wales, 2009.

Haycock, Marged. *Legendary Poems from the Book of Taliesin* Aberystwyth: CMCS, 2007.

Hutton, Ronald. *The Pagan Religions of the Ancient British Isles: Their Nature and Legacy*. Oxford: Blackwell, 1991.

Hutton, Ronald. 'The Early Arthur'. In *The Cambridge Companion to the Arthurian Legend*, edited by Elizabeth Archibald and Ad Putter, 21–35. Cambridge: Cambridge University Press, 2009.

Ingold, Tim. *Lines: A Brief History*. London: Routledge, 2007.

Jobes, Gertude, and James Jobes. *Outer Space: Myths, Name Meanings, Calendars*. New York: Scarecrow, 1964.

Jones, N. W., and W. J. Owen. 'Prehistoric Funerary & Ritual Sites: Eastern Brecon Beacons'. Cadw Welsh Historic Monuments, 2006.

Kane, Sean A. *Wisdom of the Mythtellers*. Ontario: Broadview Press, 1998.

Kunitzsch, Paul, and Tim Smart. *A Dictionary of Modern Star Names*. Cambridge: Sky, 2006.

Lane, Belden C., *Landscapes of the Sacred: Geography and Narrative in American Spirituality*, expanded ed. Baltimore, MD: Johns Hopkins University Press, 2001.

Lofmark, Carl, and G. A. Wells. *A History of the Red Dragon*. Llanrwst: Gwasg Carreg Gwalch, 1995.

Geoffrey of Monmouth. *History of the Kings of Britain*, translated by Sebastian Evans. London: J. M. Dent, 1904.

Nennius. 'Historia Brittonum'. In *Six Old English Chronicles*, translated by J. A. Giles. London: Henry G. Bohn, 1848, http://www.bsswebsite.me.uk/History/Nennius/NenniusHistory2.html (accessed 12 October 2013).

Ptolemy, Claudius. *Ptolemy's Almagest*, translated G. J. Toomer. New Jersey: Princeton University Press, 1998.

Southern, Pat, and Karen R. Dixon. *The Late Roman Army*. London: Yale University Press, 1996.

Tatlock, J. S. P. 'The Dragons of Wessex and Wales'. *Speculum* 8 (1933): 223–35.

Tilley, Christopher. *A Phenomenology of Landscape*. Oxford: Berg, 1994.

Tuan, Yi-Fu. *Space and Place: The Perspective of Experience*. London: Arnold, 1977.

Williams, Mark. *Fiery Shapes, Celestial Portents and Astrology in Ireland and Wales 700–1700*. Oxford: Oxford University Press, 2010.

8

Representing the sacred: Printmaking and the depiction of the Holy Mountain

Christos Kakalis

Introduction

This chapter examines the religious dynamics embodied in the sacred topography of Mount Athos through the comparison of representations of it. Mount Athos is a peninsula in north-eastern Greece which, since 1988, has been classified as a world heritage UNESCO monument. As a semi-independent realm that belongs to the Ecumenical Patriarchate of Constantinople, it consists of a male monastic community organized into a network of different structures ruled by twenty coenobitic monasteries. Entrance regulations, allowing only a specific number of male visitors to enter and interact with the natural landscape, the architecture, and the ascetic life enhance the boundary between inside and outside. In this way, the Athonite topography has acquired a character of a distant, sacred/other place in which ascetics practise *hesychasm*, an austere way of life based on the dynamic combination of silent prayer and communal rituals. Mount Athos is thus a place between the profane and the sacred that has triggered geographical imagination ever since medieval times. Through the examination of printed copper engraving representations of Mount Athos that were mainly produced during the eighteenth and nineteenth centuries, the chapter unpacks the physical and metaphysical dynamics of a religious mountainous topos that has the power to be the protagonist even on printed cartography. I argue that the examined maps offered the recipient an experiential understanding of religious landscapes that was more expressive than conventional two-dimensional representational methods. As such, these prints became a means of international communication expressing the tangible connection between the Holy Mountain and the Athonite tradition.

The production of Athonite engravings in European countries with strong Greek or Orthodox communities, such as Venice or Vienna, was gradually taken over by printmaking workshops on Mount Athos, affecting the printed representation of the Athonite built and natural landscape and suggesting the power and agency of the mountain in its ability to affect those who came to worship there.[1]

In this chapter, I argue that the agency of the Athonite mountainous landscape impregnates the paper visualizations to a degree that the latter become an embodiment of the physical and spiritual qualities of the former. Besides adding to the meaning of these *representational loci*, the limitations of engraving technique in different cultural contexts (Western and Eastern European ones) have also affected their materiality suggesting an interesting interaction between making and worship that this chapter also aims to further unfold.

My methodology combines archival work, fieldwork on Mount Athos, and practice-based research on printmaking techniques to explore the meaning of the printed translations of the Athonite landscape as an important group of paper depictions of pilgrimage topography. The latter is represented not as a conventional, accurate, and abstract translation of the landscape (a composition of specific data in a particular coding, such as contour lines), but as a richer transposition of an experiential understanding of the physical and metaphysical qualities of the peninsula. In this way, the materiality of pilgrimage cartography testifies to the embodied religious significance of Athos.

Physical topos, Athonite location

Before engaging with the images themselves, it is helpful to have an understanding of the geographic location in which they are set in order to put the images into a geographical context. The geographical relief of the Athonite peninsula is mainly mountainous. The plains are to the rear (mostly at the north of the peninsula) and of a small surface and the coasts are extremely rocky and steep. These conditions of geographical isolation have led to a primitive, untouched landscape, inhabited by ascetics searching for solitude.[2] The first written evidence of the presence of ascetics on Mount Athos dates back to the ninth century.[3] It was in 943 that the boundaries of the peninsula as a monastic realm were officially inscribed by the emperor's ambassadors.[4] Gradually, a network of different monastic complexes was organized on Athos built during the middle and late Byzantine period: huts (*kalyves*), cells (*kellia*), *sketes*, and twenty coenobitic monasteries.[5]

The mountainous southern end of the peninsula (the area between Karmelion Mountain and the skete of Hagia Anna) rises into a peak of 2,033 metres height, characterizing the Holy Mountain due to its imposing presence and symbolic and ascetic meaning. In my fieldwork on Mount Athos conducted between August and September 2013, I came to understand the following: a number of ascetics have chosen to live there as cave/hermitage dwellers practicing *hesychasm*, an ascetic way of life with intense meditational qualities; the mountain itself is a natural magnet for ascetics' embodied attention; ascetic practices include an annual pilgrimage to the summit of the mountain on the day dedicated to Christ's Transfiguration (6 August) in which pilgrims from all over the world also participate; a chapel dedicated to the same Scriptural event is built where an all-night vigil is held between 5 and 6 August; and finally, that this feast commemorates the heart of *hesychast* life, the possibility of communication with the divine (*theosis*) through personal and communal worship. Little is known about the history of the chapel and the establishment of the annual pilgrimage to the peak. The previous one was built in 1895, and it is almost certain that it had replaced another before it, as a chapel is depicted in Pierre Belon's 1588 map of Mount Athos and later depictions of the peninsula, as described by human geographer Veronica della Dora.[6]

In addition, I observed how, in this ascetic landscape, monks also practice hesychasm. Hesychasm derives from the Greek word for calmness or tranquillity (*hesychia*). Its aim is the achievement of a state of stillness that involves the inner (silent) ceaseless invocation of the Jesus prayer ('Lord Jesus Christ, Son of God, have mercy upon me the sinner'), a kind of inner monologue that aims to enable direct communication with God. It may be practiced individually at specific times of the day (akin to a personal meditational technique), during communal rituals, or in spontaneous bursts of prayer during the course of the day. The repetition of individual and communal rituals is combined with daily tasks (cooking, cleaning) into an ascetic way of life that is based on a series of formal documents, called *Typika* and informal traditions, and also opens to the experience of pilgrims.

Religious *topos*, Athonite topography

The individual and collective experience of the Athonite landscape relates to a number of different levels of familiarity experienced in a field of activities and rituals by insiders and outsiders. The ritual qualities of monastic life interact with the temporary experience of the strangers. The synthesis of monastic structures and the mountainous landscape of the Athonite peninsula in which it is organized opens a field of experience for monks and strangers. The life of the monks is based on a strict daily programme which divides the day into periods of work and worship. On the other hand, the visitors approach Mount Athos carrying elements of their everyday life and past, and participate up to a point in the monastic life there.

In this phenomenal framework of the constant interaction between the individual and the world the Cartesian distinctive entities of *psychic* and *physiological* are unified through a holistic engagement of the subject to an intentional experiencing of a space. Acting specifically orientated in relation to objects, locations, and events, the individual is always an active agent who experiences space and time as interdependent parts of the whole of which he/she is part. Intentionality implies a motivating power that opens the subject to the possibility of a dynamic interaction with the environment. At the same time he/she experiences an *ec-static* (to use Martin Heidegger's term) temporality in which past memories and future expectations coexist in the present.[7] Through his/her intentional actions he/she is in a state of *waiting* during which, according to Yi Fu Tuan, 'the expected event appears to move towards [him/her] … and the co-ordinate spatial feeling is one of contraction'.[8] In parallel, the individual is able to recollect past events, uniting the three temporal dimensions into one. Place is thus conditioned by the notions of familiarity and participation as the person is invited to be engaged in its constitution: the happening of its organization and dwelling both as an individual and as a member of a community. In the case of Mount Athos this is really evident with personal ascetic endeavours being combined with the collective liturgical life of monastic communities.

In my fieldwork, undertaken between 2010 and 2016, it became clear to me that walking these paths of Athos was of itself an interaction with the different aspects of the religious landscape within the context of an immersive (religious, ascetic, or more touristic) experience. The theory is that the individual, monk, or male visitor, deciding to go from a hermitage to a monastery of the Athonite desert, follows a certain route, mostly unmapped, trying to reach his destination. Whether combined with a sacred/pilgrimage character or not, this process is an opening of man to natural and constructed things of the world and at the same time an opening of the things towards man. The intentional use of the path stands as a stage of preparation towards a possible future distinct experience, a possible entering into a place of both personal and collective significance. The body of the individual plays an important role in the whole process as it moves from place to place mapping the landscape through this movement. This was certainly the case for me when I undertook this walk. It was for me, an embodied encounter involving a dynamic interconnection of soundscapes, visionscapes, touchscapes, smellscapes, and tastescapes. The different sensual qualities of place directed my movement enhancing the meaning of my experience. Simultaneously, this experience merged with the experiences of other people enhancing also the meaning of the place, the meaning of art, architecture, and landscape that keeps changing depending on this organic understanding of religious topography. The sounds of the birds and the sea, the smells of the plantation, and the warmth of the rays of the sun combined with silent prayer or liturgical elements (chanting, censing, etc.) became a personal quest or a litany of a special day.

Sacred place, according to Michael Kunzler, is a 'corporeal-reality' that happens when a 'space between' opens during the reciprocal relationship between an I and a (divine) Thou. This is a gap, a distance that is bridged through individual and collective experience.[9] The individual's interaction with a concrete environment in which the divine may be manifested plays a nodal role. Therefore, according to Mircea Eliade, a sacred place, clearly demarcated from the profane space, is a 'centre', an *Axis Mundi*, where hierophanies and theophanies may occur, allowing the possibility of the connection between the levels of earth and heaven.[10] Whereas sacred place refers to a cosmic event, the profane world is a foreign chaotic space.[11] This dichotomy is expressed in a dialectical way, as different (built and natural) things can be active receptacles of the sacred while still part of their more profane environment.[12] This dialectical relationship between the sacred and the profane also supports the opening of the religious locales to the reception of the stranger: the outsider who enters carrying his own personal sphere and who interacts dynamically with the sacred environment, with the possibility of engagement in the hierophanic events occurring there.

The buildings and the natural landscape of Athos' peninsula co-form the active context of the liturgical movement of the individuals. The mountain of Athos that geomorphologically characterizes the peninsula is actively associated with the sacred through traditions, pilgrimages of monks and outsiders to its peak, and annual celebrations of the event of the Transfiguration of Christ (6 August). Even though it is not centrally located, this mountain is still Eliade's *Axis Mundi*, 'a region impregnated with the sacred, a spot where one can pass from one cosmic zone to another'.[13] This mountainous landscape has been the shelter of the ascetic practice of hermits for more than a thousand years now.

The different sacred locales built along its slopes are experienced through a ritualistic way of life that can be characterized as a liturgical one. Liturgy relates to the service(s) held in a church. In Eastern Christian theology, liturgy is also extended to every aspect of everyday life, trying to unite its material and immaterial components into a cosmic religious event of human experience.[14] Recollecting Jean Yves Lacoste's approach, this liturgical life is a movement of the individual from the familiarity of daily experience to his/her real condition of 'foreignness'.[15] As a foreigner, the individual tries to reach his/her homeland through liturgy. The body plays an important role in this process as liturgy involves the embodied, ritual experience of this movement towards a Homeland, the 'absolute knowledge' of the divine that in the case of Orthodox asceticism is never fully realized.[16] In this sense, religious space and time are experienced through the ritual movement of the body subjects aiming at a spiritual knowledge, the achievement of which relates to a corporeal realization of the world. Ritual becomes a means of liturgical experience. Its performance influences the building of a space that has to provide a shelter for the gathering of the individuals, according to certain symbolic and spiritual qualities. In addition, the concrete formation of a locale affects the participation in rituals by indicating different ways of (liturgical) inhabitation. At the same time, in the case of Mount Athos, practices of silent prayer are dynamically interconnected with the communal liturgies, as I found out during my fieldwork on Mount Athos.

The Athonite landscape, therefore, deals with the expression of different kinds of embodied experience. On the one hand, as mentioned above, the embodied experience of monks is conditioned by the notion of ritual and silent prayer, on which life in these ascetic structures is based. On the other hand, the journey of male outsiders and their freer movement along the footpaths of the peninsula is also an important aspect of life there. As my fieldwork showed, the system of paths that connects the different places of monastic activity of the Athonite landscape (monasteries, sketes, cells, desert, natural cavities) is set as a woven thread through the dense natural environment which changes according to the frequency of use and the climatic fluctuations. Male outsiders undergo a circular journey the beginning and end of which are clearly demarcated, enhancing its ephemeral interaction with the natural landscape and dynamically coexisting with the ascetic perception of the Athonites.

Mapping the Athonite topography

Considering the experience and complexity of this religious landscape, questions such as how it can be mapped effectively, how this landscape can be depicted in such a way that the lines and the components of the map will not just represent measured geographical data but will also reveal traces of its experience, symbolism, and depth of sacred connotations, can now be asked.

The traditional understanding of mapping, its materiality, and communicative dynamics is questioned here through a closer examination of a unique collection of mapping practices. Their symbolical imagination, their crafting, and their use are combined here to tell a story about 'maps' as narratives of sacred topoi that go beyond the mathematical 'accurate' representation of a place and can play an important role in the depiction and communication of sacred topographies. The commissioner, the maker, and the readers are combined through the way these translations of Mount Athos were perceived, printed, and offered. Gilles Deleuze and Felix Guattari distinguished between a map and a tracing to underline the experimental dynamics of cartography in relation to the real.

> What distinguishes the map from the tracing is that it is entirely oriented toward experimentation in contact with the real. The map does not reproduce an unconscious closed in upon itself; it constructs the unconscious. It fosters connections between fields, the removal of blockages on bodies without organs, the maximum opening of bodies without organs onto a plane of consistency ... The map has to do with performance, whereas the tracing always involves an alleged 'competence'.[17]

Along these lines, according to Edward S. Casey, etymologically, 'topography' combines the Greek word for place (τόπος-topos) with the one for writing (γράφειν-graphein), relating lived spatiality with the notion of inscription.[18] In the traditional use of the term, *topos* is connected to a specific mathematically defined location and *graphein* relates to 'the model of a [two-dimensional] flat surface on which are inscribed images as well as words'.[19] Thus, traditionally, topography is 'the science or practice of describing a particular place, city, town, manor, parish or tract of land; the accurate and detailed description or delineation of locality'.[20] This traditional definition raises a number of questions as to whether the information related to a landscape is restricted only to what is noticeable and countable, how the more transcendental aspects of reality are mediated, and whether the individual's memory, feelings, and spirituality interfere in the reading of the landscape.

Unlike tracings, which propagate redundancies, the examined mappings of Mount Athos expressed new or very distant pilgrimage worlds within past and present ones; they inaugurated the possibility of visiting sacred landscapes upon the hidden traces of a living context. Maps in this way were active agents of imaginary landscapes, rather than being passive records of the place. This stems from the belief that thought is inseparable from the medium in which it is formulated and expressed.

In this context, there is evidence for the *liminal* role of these maps as embodiments of both internal and external affairs of Athonite monasteries, adding to their symbolic meaning and further unfolding the depth of their creation and dissemination. Mount Athos had already been depicted in diverse representations up until its early printed communication via printed etchings. Represented as an ideal community in medieval O-T maps compared to Thomas More's *Utopia* and even included in the manuscripts of Ptolemy's *The Geography* where it resembled an island and was schematically depicted as a mountain, it was mainly thought to be a distant and ideal realm. During the early eighteenth century the mountain of Athos became the symbol of the peninsula depicted in printed bird's-eye view maps. A characteristic example is the map engraved by Allessandro dalla Via in the early eighteenth century (Figure 8.1). The size of the map is 745 mm × 1,070 mm and it was printed in Venice. In it, the east and west views of the peninsula are depicted as an elongated strip of land, with the double mountain of Athos in the middle. The map depicts the sea with a variety of sailing vessels, the land, and a symbolic realm above the land: the top of the mountain is flanked by the icons of the *Deisis* (the enthroned God between Mary and Saint John the Baptist) and the Mother of God. The latter follows the type of *Portaitissa*, an icon kept in the Iveron Monastery whose abbot commissioned the map. Below the sea, inlaid texts depict the pilgrimage to Athos. This image is a characteristic example of sacred cartography, describing sacred places through the combination of images and texts. Moreover, it was a 'map of authority', intended to be hung on a wall with the aim of impressing the viewer.[21] In the same period, two other similar maps of Athos were printed in Venice by unknown authors in 1708 and 1713.[22]

How many maps were produced during that period is unknown. Nevertheless, 1,100 different engraved images and 300 plates have been located across the world. The numbers indicate a flourishing of printmaking during that period as well as the existence of a network of relationships between the Ottoman Empire and the places where the maps were printed, mainly in the Danubian principalities, Venice and Vienna.[23] An intellectual and financial regeneration in the Balkan peninsula occurred during the eighteenth and early nineteenth centuries, while its countries were under Ottoman occupation. A dynamic network of relationships between its countries as well as countries that were

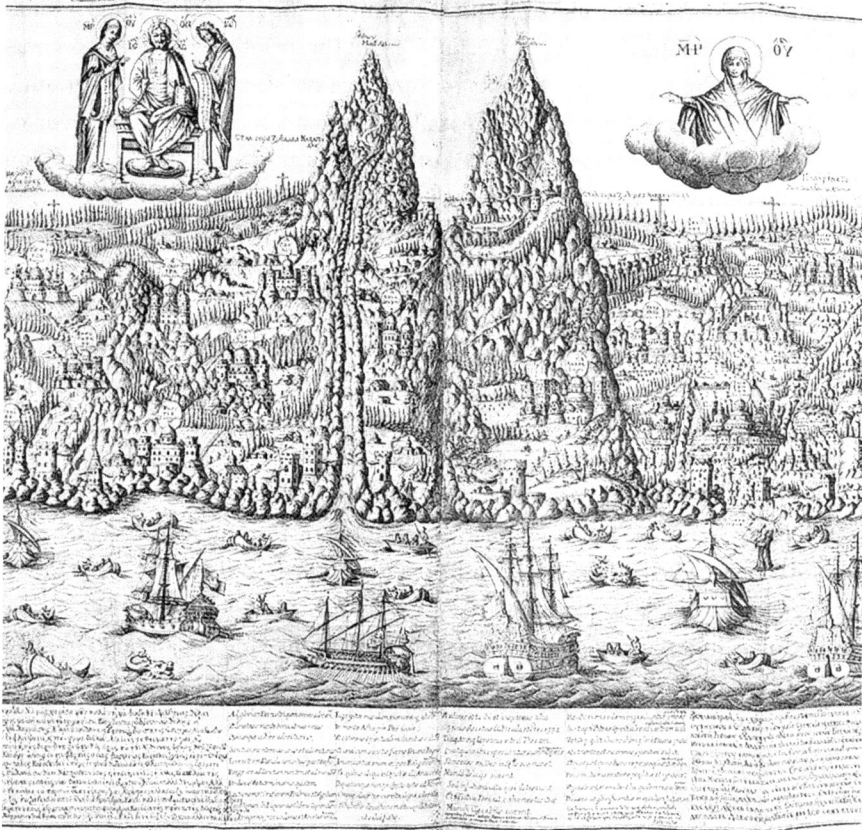

Figure 8.1 Copper engraving, Allessandro dalla Via, Venice, 1713. Courtesy of Athos Library.

outside the Ottoman Empire was gradually developed. Greece played a key role in it. According to sociologist Victor Roudometof, during this period 'social mobility and the division of labor impacted upon the always fluid nature of ethnic identity'.[24] A Balkan amalgamation of Greeks, Grecophones, and Hellenized populations was gradually formed.[25] The so-called 'Balkan Orthodox Christians' were Greeks, largely acculturated populations amalgamated into a kind of a Greek culture and populations that were at least under heavy Grecophone influences. Danubian principalities played a nodal role in this transnational environment as they were never under direct Ottoman rule and therefore their institutions were different from the Ottoman.[26] A Greek-Orthodox identity was therefore spread around Balkans and Europe through moving populations and commercial interactions.

Into this Greek-Orthodox context, printing flourished through book circulation facilitated by maritime commerce. The printing of the books was funded either by wealthy merchants or subscription systems.[27] A cartographic explosion was also taking place in parallel. The map became the conveyor of important meanings, related to the idea of 'nation' as gradually defined/changing during the centuries. Greek merchants who were buying and selling books printed in Vienna, Venice, Leghorn, and Trieste were also carrying printed maps. In order to acquire a map the client could either write directly to the publishers or refer to nodal commercial representatives in Iassy, Bucharest, Smyrna, Ioannina, and other towns.[28] In addition, pilgrimage mobility also intensified during this period, and Mount Athos was gradually transformed from an otherworldly, mythical place into an approachable pilgrimage topography.

In this context, after visiting Mount Athos in 1698, the Greek private doctor and astrologer of Constantine Brancovan, Ioannis Komninos, created a pilgrim's travel guide, the first edition of which was printed in 1701 in Snagov, which met with great success. The text was composed in verses describing the topography through an interrelation of physical and religious elements as experienced by the author.[29] In it the first graphic representation of the Holy Mountain depicted the west and east views of the peninsula as two separate drawings, one under the other. The later maps examined in this study, like the one of Alessandro dalla Via, were influenced by Komninos's first visualization. Even though these maps are not accurate and mathematical in their conception, they can be considered as maps as, according to the geographer George Tolias, they are a 'graphic display of empirically comprehended spatial analogies'.[30] They are not just tracings of a landscape, but non-conventional agents of a topography full of events of worship and pilgrimage, as well as of the religious and geopolitical movements of the period during which they were produced.

Heavy taxation since the 1600s forced the Athonite monasteries towards a downturn. In the seventeenth century only the wealthier monasteries (like the Vatopaidi, Iveron, and Chilandar) were able to survive and were able to support the other monasteries. A vicious circle of loan and debt became the economic reality for most of the monasteries. As historian Fokion Kotzageorgis characteristically argued, besides the financial problems that followed the establishment of the Ottoman Empire, 'Christian monasteries were one of the non-Muslim institutions during the Ottoman Empire that experienced a noticeable endurance through time'.[31] A strategic combination of a deep understanding of Ottoman law with effective diplomatic relations with the governors and the empire's Christian elites led many monasteries, including some of Mount Athos, to a prosperous management of their economies. A very well-thought-out and orchestrated network of fundraising expeditions, products' exchange, estate businesses, and the establishment of metochia (satellite monastic complexes) at key places of the Balkans was the basis for their sustainable maintenance and development.[32]

During this period some of the Athonite monasteries ordered maps, representations of their complexes, as well as other pious icons. These were used when monks travelled to Europe and the Danubian principalities for fundraising expeditions (*zhteiai*), but were also given as blessings to the pilgrims. The engravings were a result of the Greek-Orthodox network of interactions between the Ottoman Empire, the principalities, and Europe. The monasteries covered the printing expenses of these maps. According to Tolias, 'the fathers in charge of the fundraising tours, once in Moscow, Venice or Vienna themselves supervised the engraving and printing of the sacred maps and other prints of devotional matter, such as printed icons or indulgences (*sygchorochartia*)'.[33] The maps are therefore conveyors of the economic situation of Mount Athos, as well as the Greek-Orthodox identity created during the eighteenth and nineteenth centuries in the Balkans. These 'maps of authority' were hung on the wall along with the description of the monks asking for donations and attracting pilgrims. Given also as a blessing to pilgrims and donors, the maps reflected the external Athonite economy situation of that period; the maps were, hence, display devices of monastic economies. The travelling and hanging possibilities of these maps were embodied in the folding lines inscribed on their surface as a result of its use in the passage of time. Along with the symmetrical organization of the theme, they suggested important communicative dynamics that materialized the relevant display processes.

According to della Dora, these depictions also carried important elements of the spiritual meanings of a topography with which very few of the viewers would have the opportunity to interact. 'The Edenic island became a climax, a ladder for physical and spiritual ascent. It became a liturgical space where the pilgrim performed a sort of procession.'[34] The peak of the mountain with the chapel of the Transfiguration on it had become a 'geographic icon' which was able to transfer both the ascetic life of the monk and the possible journey of the outsider.[35]

In this sense, Komninos's guide is not only a bearer of the geopolitical interactions between Athos and Wallachia, it is also an expression of spiritual meanings of a pilgrimage topography, embodying traces of the Athonite internal, hesychast economy of Athos as experienced by the author:

So, if you wish, do ascend Athos from there

Otherwise get up early and descend to Lavra.

Walk fast, go to Kerasia

[and] as you climb up, spend one night at Panaghia.

Then quickly do ascend to Athos with greatest eagerness.

......

Then descend once again to Panaghia.[36]

Text and images are combined to suggest a possible immersion of the individual in what Komninos has described as 'the mountain of quietness' (*oros hesychias*).[37] Physical and spiritual were combined to also express the sacred qualities of the place.

Challenging conventional cartography, the examined bird's-eye views highlight the significance of metaphor in experience. The different localities depicted in their middle zones are combined through their coexistence in the same physical and metaphysical landscape. The doubling of the central mountain plays a key role, creating, according to della Dora, 'a gateway to the heavenly kingdom'.[38] The depiction of the ascent to the top of the mountain illuminates the ascetic character of the topography, connecting it to its future-eschatological perspective through a 'threshold' created between the two mountains. This process is depicted as also including the possibility for a stranger to walk up the mountain, narrating the reciprocal relationship between the sacred and the profane in pilgrimage.

The mountain's conversation in copper

Engraving involves a process of mirroring and projection that depends to a great extent on the engraver's hands. This is elucidated in the case of the examined prints with the doubling of the mountain in the middle suggesting its possible folding. Controlling his hands forces the engraver to inscribe the lines, directing the burin (tempered steel chisel) while prefiguring the intensity of the shadow and the representational accuracy of the final result. Printmaking expressed in the representation of the mountain of Athos is an action, an encounter between the engraver as the translator, the reader (viewer) of the map, and the mountain. The engraver translates and his burin voices the story of the landscape, traced in a different way each time the paper is pressed on the plate. This is always a reciprocal relationship with the agency of the mountain. The engraver and the mountain are in a dynamic interaction through the way the latter is revealed on paper by the former.

Combining craftsmanship with an opening to different representational narratives, engraving is still considered on Mount Athos as a way of producing meaningful religious images. Icon painting is still practiced in the same tradition of expressing a sense of sacred stillness, and printmaking invites the engraver to deploy iconographic methods: controlling the relationship between the solid and the void through burin hatchings, mirroring and projecting, almost re-addressing the questions suggested during the eighteenth and nineteenth centuries. The Athonite prints of this period stand as liminal travelling landscape objects, between internal and external worlds, and allowing for their constant interaction via the diverse lenses of their interpretation. The print is in-between the mountain and its religious symbolism as experienced by ascetics and pilgrims.

As a means of representation, copper engraving technique, influenced by the relevant historical and social context of these European countries, has contributed to the narrative qualities of these translations. While wood engraving was more common in the early printing attempts (during the fifteenth and sixteenth centuries), with only two examples in the case of Athonite depictions, copper engraving has probably been the most popular printing method, reaching its peak during the eighteenth and nineteenth centuries when the greatest production of prints of Mount Athos happened.[39] Relatively soft and rust-proof, copper is a material that can be easily used for this process. Hundreds of engraved lines create a printed image. The engraver holds the burin almost in parallel with the plate, carefully pushing it into the copper and guiding it along the scheme already traced on the plate carving out a groove. Engraving allows for a variation of detail, depending on the number and thickness of the engraved lines. The closer the lines, the finer the shading becomes. After the lines are carved, ink is spread on the plate and is carefully wiped to leave the ink held in the engraved lines. The amount of ink carried eventually by the plate depends on the depth of the lines made by the engraver. Rollers on the printing press force dampened paper onto the engraved plate, printing the image onto the latter. In this way the agency of the depicted landscape as a palimpsest of stories of individual and collective identity is included in the process of crafting as a key definer of the depth and boldness of lines, distances between them, intensity of shading, use of text, and dynamic processing of the physical depth of the copper plate and paper.

Western Athonite prints are characterized by a sense of naturalism and intense use of perspective, visualization techniques that were not followed in Eastern Christian culture. Perspective as a means of transmitting theological ideas has formed a common ground in Western European art since 1500. The lines were closely engraved on the copper plate to produce perspectival illusions of depth. The monasteries were usually placed on the peninsula almost at their exact locations, slightly distorted to give a sense of organic incorporation in the landscape. There were no detailed representations of the complexes, as usually only the general forms and abstract traces of the network of paths that connected them were transferred. The compositions were characterized by the darker parts of depth depiction that was challenged at the same time by the unfolding of the two sides of the peninsula, something that changed its three-dimensionality and elucidated the temporal qualities of the journey around it.

Gradually print workshops were established on Mount Athos, especially around its capital, the village called Karyes. These workshops started producing prints of a style that can be characterized as 'Athonite', a style that stands between Western aesthetics and (post)Byzantine iconographic tradition. A creative interaction between the printmaking workshops in Western Europe and the ones of Mount Athos was gradually developed. The first images produced on Athos were based on Western ones and in parallel, prints made in Vienna or Venice for Athonite monasteries were based on Athonite images.[40]

Athonite engravings started gradually adhering to more Byzantine or post-Byzantine ways of rendering, with the elimination of the dimension of depth and perspective, and often with an absolutely simplified, almost naive, vision of the landscape. This is characteristically expressed in an image, probably printed around 1770 on Mount Athos that is considered to be one of the earliest engraved plates made there (Figure 8.2). Lack of depth, flat white surfaces, and an almost laconic delineation of the path leading to the peak of the mountain flanked by repeated similar rocks placed one after the other are the key elements of the representations. The monasteries are represented either through their facades naively placed on the mountain, almost added as in a collage, or through their more organic incorporation, following Western precedents and adding perspectival hatching selectively. The paths are also inscribed on the slopes of the peninsula through simple lines, notating the connection between the monasteries. The Athonite use of print methods, different from the ones used in the earlier (Western) depictions of Athos, possibly testifies to the creators' deliberate decision to include elements from Christian Orthodox

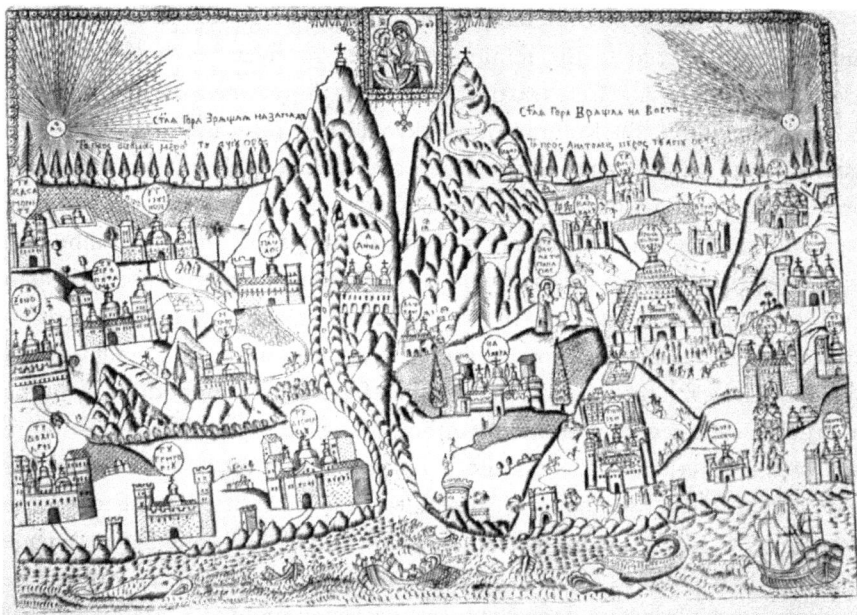

Figure 8.2 Copper engraving, Mount Athos, 1770. Courtesy of Athos Library.

iconographic tradition, enhancing the translation of the theological qualities of the mountainous peninsula.

According to Orthodox theology, the static present moment enclosed by Byzantine iconography attempts to convey the eternal presence of God through the deployment of an iconic stillness. The visual interaction with the icon is included in the possible ways of the devotees' personal and collective worship, also enhanced by the way the icon is conceived and synthesized. The linear perspective is usually reversed, with the vanishing point towards the side of the viewer. The represented faces and landscapes emerge from the painting and invite the devotee to engage in an active relationship. According to Christian orthodox tradition, the vanishing point coincides with the heart of the viewer. This aims to highlight the important role that he/she plays in Christian life. The use of one background colour (usually gold) contributes to the process, replacing to an extent any other additions and allowing the iconographic syntheses to adjust to the offered surfaces without the Byzantine (reversed) perspective being changed. The lack of shading (lack of black and white combined with the use of gold) is intended to depict the idea of the Transfiguration, the still transformation of one's being through communication with the eternal Sun (God).[41]

In the Athonite prints the lines were curved at longer distances and their number was reduced to the minimum needed to create an intelligible and meaningful synthesis. However, this Athonite style revisited the much earlier Athonite 'maps', like the Komninos's proskynetarion. This cannot be considered as a decline of printmaking as long as there are still monasteries that commission prints from outside Mount Athos. The engraver narrates the topography, using an iconic language in the translation of the meanings that the place embodies. Moreover, printmaking involves manual work, something vital for Christian Orthodox religious imagery, in which actual making and craftsmanship are considered as essential for its 'liturgical efficacy, full iconic potential and symbolic power'.[42] The examined maps, therefore, are also embodiments of the internal, ascetic economy of Mount Athos, as well as past and possible future pilgrimage experiences of the visitors. Engraving as a process of making has contributed to the realization of these ideas, especially if emphasis is on the difference between the maps produced outside the peninsula and the ones made in Athonite workshops. Almost paradoxically, engraving becomes in this case a religious practice when deployed to map a sacred mountain. The sacredness of the mountain transforms the map into an iconic depiction of a religious landscape and at the same time iconographic techniques seek to deliver this transformation.

Conclusions

The comparison of these two printed representations of the Athonite landscape, characteristic of the two periods related to the geography of their production, uncovers a number of different qualities of sacred cartography. On the one hand, it underlines their communicative dynamics both as display devices of economic exchange between different parts of the Ottoman Empire and as traces of the survival techniques that Athonite monasteries have deployed to maintain their status and manage a fruitful development of their economic state during that period. In parallel, the mappings are also bearers of the pilgrimage and hesychast qualities of Athos, through visualization particularities (doubling of the mountain, emphasis on the footpath towards the peak, etc.) and addition of textual experiential descriptions. Printmaking played an important role in these communicative dynamics, as from the engraving to the printing, the idea of depth imbued the visual result with different qualities either to attract the eyes of the readers through Renaissance perspectival methods or to transmit the sacred messages of the topos in the crafting endeavour of the monks-makers to produce more 'iconic' results. Through the lens of the printmaking process, this chapter touches the particularities of these expressions to underline their significance as embodiments of important qualities and shows how material religion reveals the power of the mountain to replicate itself in print. In this way, the chapter unpacks the way Mount Athos exerts agency via its printed representations as an insight into material religion. The materiality of the map meets the materiality of the mountain through crafting. Hesychast ideology is communicated through the replication of the mountain and it is communicated effectively because of its important religious connotations and their activation in ritual and non-ritual movements there. If place is the dynamic field of the bodily experience of space and time, then the chapter examines the representational potentials of the Athonite topography as an agglomeration of different (religious) places that are interrelated through a fabric of interwoven practices as materialized in the studied mappings. Printmaking revisits the mountain, seeking to document and represent it not in an accurate, mathematical way but in a way that the cultural and symbolic agency of the mountain as a hierophanic topos is expressed, triggering the imagination of the viewer and inviting him/her into an active dialogue with the landscape. Mount Athos as placed in its physical, historical, and religious landscape has a power to inform its representation on paper. The mountain's meaningful presence on the map is the result of the interrelation of its hierophanic agency with the communicative agency of the visualization practices.

Notes

1 Ντόρυ Παπαστράτου, *Χάρτινες Εικόνες. Ορθόδοξα Θρησκευτικά Χαρακτικά 1665–1899* (Athens: Athos Library, 1986).

2 Dimitrios Kotoulas, 'The Natural Environment', in *Simonopetra – Mount Athos*, ed. Stilianos, Papadopoulos (Athens: ETBA, Hellenic Industrial Development Bank, 1991), 47–56.

3 Dionysia Papachrysanthou, *Ο Αθωνικός Μοναχισμός – Αρχές και Οργάνωση/ Athonian Monasticism – Origins and Organization* (Αθήνα/Athens: Μορφωτικό Ίδρυμα της Εθνικής Τράπεζας της Ελλάδος, 1992), 31–9.

4 Graham Speake, *Mount Athos: Renewal in Paradise* (New Haven, CT: Yale University Press, 2002), 58–9.

5 Papachrysanthou, *Ο Αθωνικός Μοναχισμός*.

6　Veronica della Dora, 'Preliminary Taxonomies, Edenic Visions and the Cosmographic Dream: Pierre Belon's Mapping of Mount Athos', *Griffon* 8 (2006): 47–61, at 50.

7　Martin Heidegger, *Being and Time*, trans. John Macquarrie and Edward Robinson (Oxford: Blackwell, 1962), 378–401.

8　Yi Fu Tuan, 'Space and Place: Humanistic Perspective', in *Philosophy of Geography*, ed. S. Gate and G. Olsson (Dordrecht: Reidel, 1979), 400.

9　Michael Kunzler, *The Church's Liturgy* (London: Continuum, 2001), 24, 25.

10　Mircea Eliade, *Patterns of Comparative Religion* (London: Sheed and Ward, 1958), 373.

11　Mircea Eliade, *The Sacred and the Profane: The Nature of Religion*, trans. Willard R. Trask (Orlando: Harcourt, 1987), 29.

12　Mircea Eliade, *Images and Symbols: Studies in Religious Symbolism* (Princeton, NJ: Princeton University Press, 1952), 84, 178.

13　Eliade, *Patterns of Comparative Religion*, 99–100.

14　Hans Urs von Balthasar, *Cosmic Liturgy: The Universe According to Maximus the Confessor* (San Francisco, CA: Communio – Ignatius Press, 1988), 165–73.

15　Jean Yves Lacoste, *Experience and the Absolute: Disputed Questions on the Humanity of Man*, trans. Mark Raftery-Skeban (New York: Fordham University Press, 2004) (first publication in French: 1994), 12.

16　Lacoste, *Experience and the Absolute*, 8, 33; Marco Totti, 'The Inner Dimension of Pilgrimage to Mount Athos', in *The Monastic Magnet: Road to and from Mount Athos*, ed. Rene Gothoni and Graham Speake (Bern: Peter Lang, 2008), 116.

17　Gilles Deleuze and Felix Guattari, *A Thousand Plateaus: Capitalism and Schizophrenia* (Minnesota: University of Minnesota Press, 1987), 12.

18　Edward S. Casey, *Representing Place: Landscape Painting and Maps* (Minneapolis: University of Minnesota Press, 2002), 160.

19　Casey, *Representing Place*, 160.

20　Casey, *Representing Place*, 160.

21　Giorgos Tolias, 'Athonian Sacred Cartography: The Beginning', in Όρους Άθω, Γης και Θαλάσσης Περίμετρον. Χαρτών Μεταμορφώσεις *(Mount Athos: Between the Earth and the Sea. Its Transformations through Maps)*, ed. Euaggelos Livieratos (Thessaloniki: Εθνική Χαρτοθήκη/Ethniki Chartothiki, 2002) (in Greek), 158–9.

22　Tolias, 'Athonian Sacred Cartography', 158–9.

23　Παπαστράτου, Χάρτινες Εικόνες.

24　Victor Roudometof, 'From Rum Millet to Greek Nation: Enlightenment, Secularization and National Identity in Ottoman Balkan Society, 1453–1821', *Journal of Modern Greek Studies* 16, no. 1 (1998): 12.

25　Roudometof, 'From Rum Millet', 14.

26　Roudometof, 'From Rum Millet', 14.

27 Roudometof, 'From Rum Millet', 22.

28 Roudometof, 'From Rum Millet', 10.

29 Veronica della Dora, *Imagining Mount Athos: Visions of a Holy Place from Homer to World War II* (Charlottesville: University of Virginia Press, 2011), 1.

30 George Tolias, 'Maps Printed in Greek during the Age of Enlightenment 165–1820', *e-Perimetron* 5, no. 1 (2010): 4.

31 Κοτζαγεώργης, Φ. 'Ταμοναστήριαωςτοπικέςο θωμανικέςελίτ', in *Μοναστήρια, ΟικονομίακαιΠολιτική*, ed. Η λίαςΚολοβός, 163–90. (Κρήτη: Πανεπιστημιακές εκδόσειςΚρήτης 2011), 130–62.

32 Κοτζαγεώργης, 'Τα μοναστήρια ως τοπικές οθωμανικές ελίτ', 163–4.

33 Tolias, 'Maps Printed in Greek during the Age of Enlightenment 165–1820', 12.

34 della Dora, *Imagining Mount Athos*, 92.

35 della Dora, *Imagining Mount Athos*, 92–3.

36 Ioannis Komninos, cited in della Dora, *Imagining Mount Athos*, 92.

37 Komninos, cited in della Dora, *Imagining Mount Athos*, 92.

38 della Dora, *Imagining Mount Athos*, 95–6.

39 Markos Kampanis, 'The Printmaking Tradition of Mount Athos', *Orthodox Arts Journal*, 9 March 2015, http://www.orthodoxartsjournal.org/the-printmaking-tradition-on-mount-athos/ (accessed 14 October 2019).

40 Kampanis, 'Printmaking Tradition of Mount Athos'.

41 George Florofsky, *Issues of Orthodox Theology* (Athens: Artos Zois, 1973), 160–2; Vladimir Lossky and Leonid Ouspensky, *The Meaning of the Icons* (New York: St Vladimir's Press, 1982).

42 Fr. Silouan Justiniano, 'The Degraded Iconicity of the Icon: The Icon's Materiality and Mechanical Reproduction', *Orthodox Arts Journal*,https://www.orthodoxartsjournal.org/the-degraded-iconicity-of-the-icon-the-icons-materiality-and-mechanical-reproduction/ (accessed 3 May 2018).

Bibliography

Casey, E. *Representing Place: Landscape Painting and Maps*. Minneapolis: University of Minnesota Press, 2002.

Deleuze, G., and F. Guattari. *A Thousand Plateaus: Capitalism and Schizophrenia*. Minnesota: University of Minnesota Press, 1987.

della Dora, V. *Imagining Mount Athos: Visions of a Holy Place from Homer to World War II*. Charlottesville: University of Virginia Press, 2011.

Eliade, M. *Images and Symbols. Studies in Religious Symbolism*. Princeton, NJ: Princeton University Press, 1952.

Eliade, M. *Patterns of Comparative Religion*. London: Sheed and Ward, 1958.

Eliade, M. *The Sacred and the Profane: The Nature of Religion, the Significance of Religious Myth, Symbolism and Ritual Within Life and Culture.* New York: Harvest/ HBJ book, Harcourt Brace Jovanovich, 1959.

Justiniano, S. 'The Degraded Iconicity of the Icon: The Icon's Materiality and Mechanical Reproduction', *Orthodox Arts Journal* (2013), https://www. orthodoxartsjournal.org/the-degraded-iconicity-of-the-icon-the-icons-materiality-and-mechanical-reproduction/ (accessed 3 May 2018).

Κοτζαγεώργης, Φ. 'Τα μοναστήρια ως τοπικές οθωμανικές ελίτ', in *Μοναστήρια, Οικονομία και Πολιτική*, ed. Ηλίας Κολοβός, 163–90. Κρήτη: Πανεπιστημιακές εκδόσεις Κρήτης, 2011.

Kunzler, M. *The Church's Liturgy.* London: Continuum, 2001.

Lacoste, J. *Experience and the Absolute: Disputed Questions on the Humanity of Man*, translated by Mark Raftery-Skeban. New York: Fordham University Press, 2004 (first publication in French: 1994).

Papastratou, D. *Χάρτινες Εικόνες. Ορθόδοξα Θρησκευτικά Χαρακτικά 1665–1899.* Athens: Athos Library, 1986.

Roudometof, V. 'From Rum Millet to Greek Nation: Enlightenment, Secularization and National Identity in Ottoman Balkan Society, 1453–1821'. *Journal of Modern Greek Studies* 16, no. 1 (1998): 12.

Tilley, C. *A Phenomenology of Landscape: Places, Paths and Monuments.* Oxford: Berg, 1994.

Totti, M. 'The Inner Dimension of Pilgrimage to Mount Athos'. In *The Monastic Magnet: Road to and from Mount Athos*, edited by Rene Gothoni and Graham Speake, 109–22. Bern: Peter Lang, 2008.

Tuan, Y. 'Space and Place: Humanistic Perspective'. In *Philosophy of Geography*, edited by S. Gate and G. Olsson, 387–427. Dordrecht: Reidel, 1979.

Tolias, G. 'Maps Printed in Greek during the Age of Enlightenment 165–1820'. *e-Perimetron* 5, no. 1 (2010): 1–48.

Part Five

Contemporary conversations

9

Are Himalayan peaks sacred?: The paradoxical and polylogical construction of mountains

Lionel Obadia

Introduction

This chapter tackles the issue of representations of the mountains of the Himalaya, and the ways in which fantasies produced by Western people about Asian mountains challenge the local people's conceptions and imagination regarding these peaks. Mountains are a site for everyday life and experiences for different categories of people: villagers, tourists, trekkers, pilgrims, porters (of goods), and farmers, among many others. Yet, these people do not share the same views and feelings about mountains, especially when it comes to the issue of the sacred. Indeed, while the Himalayan region is renowned for its place at the heart of a religious cosmology, for local people at least, at the same time it is deeply affected by mass tourism, development policies, and conservation programs. Referring to the Himalaya as 'sacred mountains' is therefore problematic, although not exactly false. This chapter's focus is on deconstructing such generalizations on the basis of ethnographic fieldwork, through interviews and observations of practices among different categories of mountain dwellers and itinerant visitors that I undertook between late 1999 and the mid-2000s.

To this end, I provide a review of the literature on mountains and on the issue of sacredness, with a focus on anthropological perspectives on the Himalaya more specifically. After a concise look at the methodology for this study, I retrace the origin and evolution of the fantasy surrounding the Himalaya, first in the Western world and second, from a local point of view, in order to deconstruct generalizations about the sacredness of the highest mountains in the world. Following this reflection, I address processes of secularization in this region, looking at their sources and the ways in which external non-religious influences have an impact on local societies and their representations of the environment. The chapter ends with the analysis of the unexpected process of resacralization of the mountains, in the context of intercultural contacts, development policies, and increasing mobility in what was formerly a 'remote' and 'mystic' area. Specifically, this chapter will challenge three different aspects of the reflection relating to 'sacred mountains': first, the alleged universality of the symbolism of verticality of Divine Nature; second, the so-called unity of the meaning assigned by mountain societies of this region to their environment; third, the main point, the sacredness of the mountains that is almost systematically associated with the social and ecological-geological systems of the regions.

Mountains, symbols, beliefs: Rethinking the relationship?

In the Western imagination, the Himalaya has been envisioned as a sacred place where human beings have sacred experiences.[1] While the Himalaya and their most famous peaks (Sagarmatha, Kailash, Annapurna) were hence conceived as 'sacred' and the whole chain as a sacred region, no clear explanation has ever been provided for what was sacred about it.

Anthropologists of the Himalayan zone have drawn attention to the fact that the sense of sacredness of one or more mountains must include the local representations of the peaks.[2] Moreover, Western scholars like Sherry Ortner or Vincanne Adams have explored the differences between *local* and *Western* visions of the Himalayan Mountains, and the way they interrelate in everyday practices in the context of interactions between Western and Nepalese mountaineers.[3] Ortner and Adams put their emphasis on the images of mountain people and the way they are shaped by orientalism (on the Western side) and occidentalism (on the Himalayan side). Obviously, the issue of sacredness explored in their work has only been examined marginally. The subject nevertheless deserves a specific study, since local conceptions of the sacred in the Himalaya are more complex and variable than what has usually been assumed. Furthermore, the sacredness of the mountains is, in this case, not a symbolic property in a specific cultural context, but also the by-product of the interplay between two above-mentioned projective imaginations, orientalism, and occidentalism. Finally, the secular influence brought about by tourism, trekking, and mountaineering is unpredictably responsible for a kind of resacralization of the mountains.

This reflection on mountains partakes in a global 'spatial turn' in social sciences and humanities: a focus on spaces at large as they return to the forefront of the agenda of social sciences, and on issues in deterritorialization, defined as loss of sense of enduring location and the relocation of societies and cultures.[4] Religious studies have been impacted by this turn: it prompted not only a new emphasis on the geography of religion, after Park, but also a momentum to reinvent places in the context of identity claims and competition, and to introduce what Lily Kong described as new poetics and politics of space, the narratives of spaces, and strategies to appropriate them.[5] Asian and especially Indian and Nepalese mountains served as paradigmatic examples or illustrations of sacred mountains, according to official Hindu and Buddhist traditions, that have deeply transformed the belief systems of ancient pre-Aryan local cults. These are cults existing before the expansion of *Arya* people and the establishment of Brahmanism and later Hinduism in South Asia from soils to mountains. The old tradition of worshipping soil spirits has been reframed in religions venerating the gods of the peaks, accompanied with the representation of paradises located in the mountains or above them.[6] While the representation of Himalayan peaks seems to have long drawn on a complex mosaic of meanings, made of layers of various traditions, this line has not been pursued and the Himalaya are still envisioned according to globalizing and stereotyped conceptions of sacred places unified in the Hindu or Buddhist cosmology. Thus in my research I have sought to deconstruct this image and account for the complexity of representations and practices of the mountains, to shed light on the ways they are constructed in rather different ways and for different reasons by the inhabitants of the mountains, local highlanders, and foreign mountaineers. More precisely, ethnographies of Nepal contribute to understanding the fabric of the sacred in and of the mountains of the Nepalese Himalaya, from the trekking and mountaineering roads to Sagarmatha.

It is nowadays a quite well documented fact, from authors such as Samivel (aka Paul Gayet-Tancrède), that landscapes, and especially high peaks, have nourished various symbolic expressions of human imagination, be it considered as the product of the 'human mind' in general or shaped by the imagination of a given culture.[7] There is ample evidence in religious traditions that humankind has been utterly fascinated by peaks, since the early times of human civilizations and before the secularization process of the eighteenth-nineteenth centuries in Europe, when religion held a hegemonic position in the world, when mountains were seen as sacred. This is, for example, the approach taken by Edwin Bernbaum when he explored, on a comparative basis, the meanings associated with mountains around the world, in different cultures, including Asian ones, in order to identify key and common aspects: myths, worship, form, and location in the cosmological frame.[8] High landscapes and mountains have, however, been embedded in different repertoires of the sacred. Yet it is far from being a general principle that the sacredness of the mountains is all-embracing and applies to entire mountain regions and to all aspects of the cultural and psychic life of the peoples inhabiting mountainous regions. In this chapter, I want to deconstruct such generalizations and to highlight the complexity of the notion of the sacred and the way it applies to the mountains, in the case of the Himalaya, that has been often used as an illustration of these all-encompassing views. It would be senseless, however, to assert that the mountains of the Himalaya are *not* sacred. Yet, the way they are sacralized reveals a more intricate definition of the sacred and a more complex use of the mountains.

Spaces, Religions, Nature

From the early works of Pierre Deffontaines, one of the pioneers of human geography in the mid-twentieth century, to those of Park, mentioned earlier, sacred landscapes and spaces have been studied from the perspective of a dynamic and reciprocal relationship between the natural (biotic and abiotic) environment and the social and cultural systems that are shaped by and are shaping each other.[9] Still, there is a great temptation to reduce the variety of local agencies and arrangements between social-cultural organizations or systems on the one side, and biotic and geologic environments on the other side to a limited number of shared features or invariants; even the most convinced promoters of these views, such as Philippe Descola, have been circumspect regarding such approaches.[10] It is all the more the case for mountain environments and this is what inspired the writing of an anthology of beliefs in mountains by the French essayist Samivel that contributed to perpetuating the intellectual legacy of Mircea Eliade's general theory of religious space for whom mountains are, whatever the cultural context, the *axis mundi* of a universal cosmology.[11] Luckily, the complexity of contextual factors has been reintroduced in the comparative studies on mountains, such as Bernbaum's more recent perspective.[12] However, Asian mountains (the five sacred peaks of the Chinese and Tibetan worlds, the summits of the Indian and Nepalese Himalaya, the revered heights of Japan) are such exemplary illustrations of the above-mentioned correspondence between sacredness and geological verticality that they are repeatedly alluded to in scientific papers, as well as in non-academic literature dealing with mountains, religious symbolism, and sacred geographies. Some scholars have nevertheless urged caution about the tendency to accept uncritically relationships between mountain environments and sacredness in terms of universal archetypes, like Bernbaum for whom 'mountains are sacred for a variety of reasons, depending on the various ways people view them'.[13] They have rightly emphasized the convoluted connections between symbols, practices, and environments: mountains and peaks can be alternatively abstract symbols of verticality, objects of worship, contexts for rituals, references in mythologies, and topoi of cosmologies.[14] This symbolic approach fosters the expression of sophisticated theoretical (and even theological) speculations and as such conveys the richness of human symbolism or 'universal' cultural representations relating to the mountains or high environments. But their theoretical preconceptions and tendency to adopt general and official interpretations of mountains prevent them from capturing the actual heterogeneity of these meanings and images, and above all to accurately acknowledge the social and historical processes by which these visions have been constructed and transformed. Because of a theoretical a priori and the tendency to present general and official views of the mountains, such a perspective fails to capture the actual heterogeneity of these significations or representations, and above all, the social and historical processes by which they have been constructed and transformed. This is all the more obvious in the case of multicultural environments, such as the Nepalese Himalaya that is the main focus of this chapter.

Local ethnographic studies can oppose more relevant views than these generalizing approaches. They are significantly, and regrettably, less conducive to broad interpretations, but more capable of unveiling the depth of particular ideological or symbolic systems established by Asian mountain dwellers. The ethnographic perspective has thus contributed, to a certain extent, to renewing the terms of the theoretical debates in the comparative anthropology of the mountains. In light of this, the case studies presented in the collective volume *Montagnes sacrées d'Europe* for France, or in the *Sacred Mountains* of Edwin Bernbaum for the United States, among others, unfold the various ways by which peaks and mountains are symbolically pictured and practically appropriated by human societies, depending on the local geological configurations and local social and cultural issues.[15] In general, the significance of sacred places decreases when limited only to phenomenological or structural global approaches. From an anthropological perspective, however, asking the questions such as *who* thinks them and *how* means that mountains are 'good to think with'.[16]

To put an end to the criticisms addressed to the previously mentioned symbolist approach, the last intellectual pitfall to underscore, in the ethnographers' point of view, is the propensity to impose the idea of a correspondence between particular geological and geographic environments (mountains) and particular symbolic systems (cosmic world views). Such a perspective sees mountains as reliant on cultural systems prevailing among the population living there. This crystallization of the meaning allocated to mountains on the model 'one society = one cultural/religious system of worldview = one typical environment' is already obsolete in anthropology today. Yet, anthropology is still an explicit reference in the publications promoting the all-embracing sacredness of the mountains. The context of globalization and the massive and fast developments of mobility and tourism in the Himalaya foster encounters between people and the hybridization of cultural frameworks and representation on a worldwide scale. This intermingling of different mentalities and world views about the mountains on a local scale confirms the outmoded character of the above-mentioned threefold model. It also suggests the need to shed new light on the representations and practices of the mountains, and to interrogate the issue of sacredness of the Himalayan peaks within a fresh perspective.

Methodology

A variety of sources has been used to frame this reflection. First, between late 1999 and the mid-2000s, over a total of twelve months, I collected first-hand ethnographic data in several fieldwork trips based in the villages located in the foothills of Sagarmatha. This consisted of fieldwork inquiries in the region of the Solukhumbu (north-east Nepal) while living in the villages and among the villagers, recording conversations and noting down observations of everyday life. I am a white, Western, urban male, who at the time of my research, was in my late thirties and who, according to the local views on foreigners, was also supposed to be a 'rationalist' – a psychological and cultural feature that could explain my ongoing interest in beliefs and symbols related to the sacred, and the many questions I asked of them. Being a foreigner (*videsh*) is not a huge hurdle for ethnographers in the region. The latter have significantly taken into account their ethnocentric bias, the ways images of the Asian Other structure the ethnographic immersion and interaction. They have also explored the projective fantasies of locals about foreigners, and the ways they influence their communication with them. Moreover, among the different categories of *videshi* in which foreigners were put, I had the good fortune of being identified as a 'physician', since I had spent time in outposts of Western medicine and domestic spaces for studying traditional healing and was regarded as friendly to the community. Unlike trekkers and mountaineers who just walked through the villages on their way to the peaks, I stayed in the settlements: eventually I was accepted in the village of Karikhola and became familiar with it.[17] The local residents were not the only people I encountered in this study. Travellers come to the region for sport tourism (trekking, mountaineering, and other high-altitude sports) and for cultural/spiritual tourism (to visit holy places in the mountains or the local Buddhist communities). So my study included making daily observations of profane and religious rituals and conducting interviews with local residents, mainly Sherpa, Magyar, Chhettri, and Gurung ethnicities, and also visitors to the region from other Nepalese ethnicities, *jathi* or castes as well as foreigners who were mostly from Japan or Western countries. Because the Nepalese Himalaya are precisely situated on the routes of sport tourism and cultural/spiritual tourism, I also conducted interviews with local visitors of the region (other ethnicities and *jathi* or casts from Nepal) as well as foreigners (Westerners and Japanese people mainly). Since I had to travel along the same routes, I had direct contact with these different categories of people.

'Sacred' Himalayan landscapes and mountains: Archaeology of a representation

The first mapping of the Himalayan regions by Westerners dates back as early as the sixteenth century by the Spanish Antonio Monserrate.[18] It was followed by the first systematic exploration of the Tibetan region in the first third of the eighteenth century by the French Jean-Baptiste Bourguignon d'Anville, and expeditions in other sites of the Himalaya all along the nineteenth century.[19] In the early twentieth century, scientific expeditions (geologists, geographers, botanists, and later anthropologists) have become more regular and systematic. Since then, the peaks of the highest chain of mountains of the world have inspired a large body of texts, and nowadays hypertexts on the internet, most of which maintain that these mountains are somehow sacred.[20] This is both a true and relevant assertion when it is based on the parallel study of the Hindu and Buddhist cosmologies, for which several Himalayan peaks, and especially the mythical mount Meru (whose precise and definitive location is still discussed by specialists), are considered as *axis mundi* of the cosmic and physical universe. It is, however, not a satisfying intellectual stance for anthropologists to conclude that, on this scriptural ground, the Himalaya *are* sacred. The reference to sacred texts that attributes a sacred status to the Himalaya partakes of a strange tautology: this religiocentric bias that has been pervasive in studies of Asian societies in general causes them to be typified as 'spiritual countries'.[21] This scriptural reductionism, therefore, can be understood as a reason for the excessive focus on the sacred. But the Himalaya have also been studied from the perspective of ecology, geology, and adaptation of societies to their environment without automatically referring to sacredness as a key factor to explain the specific status of these mountains. These works are mainly known in academic circles. However, in view of the recurrence of the reference to the sacred in books, articles, TV broadcasts, movies, online pages, and other media devoted to the Himalaya (e.g. *National Geographic* in the United States or its French counterpart *Geo*), wide audiences in Western countries seem much more interested in this spiritual dimension of Asian societies, and more particularly the ones from the mountain regions. Sacredness and mountains are consubstantial in this literature, and this link calls for a deconstruction of the moral geographies of orientalism in the Western mind, and the appeal to Asian traditions, based on the Western fascination with 'the East'.[22]

First, this reference to the sacred attributed to the mountains is generic on the lexical level but vague on the semantic one. As an extensive and all-embracing term, it applies to the mountains on the grounds of the popular association between place of residence, belief, and environment. For the average Western reader living in a secularized country, the inhabitants of the Himalaya are, by contrast, seen as 'naturally' religious, engaged in something like a cult of mountains, since the Western assumption is that their rituals are performed in a context of high altitude and since the symbol of mountain is central to their cosmology.[23] The sense of exoticism emerging from these images has purportedly been instrumentalized by Western tour operators advertising the merits of a 'mystical' or 'initiatory' experience in the 'sacred mountains' and selling tours as a destination for tourists, promoting at the same time the aesthetics of high landscapes and the spirituality of the local populations.[24] Second, the Himalaya is not any kind of mountains. Reflecting upon the nature of the sacredness in this area requires an investigation in the orientalist imagination and the ways the Western projections on the Orient are shaped by fantasy and imaginary visions.

The founder of modern cultural criticism, Edward Said, paved the way for a reflection on the ways 'the Orient' epitomizes an imagined counter-model in the case of Near East orientalism (Arab and Muslim world).[25] Nevertheless, a Far Eastern (Asian) orientalism is imbued with rather different images, especially since the end of the nineteenth century when Asian traditions, and above all Buddhism, became fashionable.[26] Shrouded in a halo of mysticism and spirituality, the mountains of Nepal, Tibet, India, and China are at the heart of a powerful imaginary topography, and during the last century, from the Society of Theosophy founded in 1875 by Helena Blavatsky (1831–1891) and Henry Olcott (1832–1907) to the twenty-first century's New-Age movement, they have been established as a zone where the sense of the sacred was more 'condensed' than anywhere else in the world, especially in the case of Tibet.[27] The Himalaya therefore served as remote storehouse for spiritual fantasies for Westerners and, as Pascal Bruckner observed, the site for 'spatial therapy' for those who had undertaken, and still do, a trip to the East with the hope of encountering a master or experiencing 'wisdom'.[28]

An indigenous point of view

These views, limited to Western idealizations, do not account for local conceptions and uses. As Molyneaux pointed out, 'Symbolic centers of the world [epitomized by the mountains] are potentially as numerous as social groups.'[29] In this case, the populations dwelling on the Everest foothills of Nepal are mostly *bothia* of Tibetan origin. They belong to a sect practicing *Mahayana* ('Great Vehicle' or Northern form of) Buddhism. The Himalaya and especially the Everest peak are, in principle, the natural theatre for rituals in accordance with their cosmology. The high landscapes of the Himalaya are more than a configuration of biotic (living) and abiotic (geological) elements. They are the physical supports of religious representations, the 'palaces' or 'residences' of celestial or superhuman entities such as *bodhisattva*, *deva*, *dakini*, and beyond, more global cosmographic representations of the universe made of a central axis and layers of 'worlds'.[30]

It is an illusion to believe that there exists a unified expression of what is sacred in this area. Moreover, Hindu, Buddhists, Shamans, and animists look at the mountains differently, even if all their cosmologies include a mountain symbol. Many important studies in the region have already widely and explicitly demonstrated that, from the domestic scale to the whole village unit, the cultural ecology of the peoples in the Himalayan regions is conditional on their particular religious systems and not only on the official tradition to which they are supposed to adhere.[31]

The toponymic identity of the whole chain of the Himalaya comes originally from a Sanskrit terminology (*Hima*: 'of the snow', *alaya*: 'the place'), and according to the scriptural tradition, each peak refers to a mythological feature or a divinity of the Hindu pantheon: among others, *Durga*, the 'universal mother' also known as *Parvati*, 'born from a mountain', is the daughter of the Himalaya; *Shiva*, God of destruction, lives on Mount Kailash. For the Hindus, coming from the south of Nepal, and Buddhists and animists in the north, these are the same mountains, and, given the number of times it is mentioned, the mythological Mount Kailash is of primary importance. They are, however, significant according to different cosmological traditions.[32] This is particularly so with the higher and more sacred peak, anglicized as Everest as it was named after the British explorer George Everest in 1865, but for the Nepalese known as Sagharmata ('culminating point of the sky or Earth') or Jomolongma ('Goddess of the skies') in Tibetan or Sherpa languages.

If contrasts exist between traditions, others can be observed within a single tradition. For instance, if in Buddhism, all spaces are virtually sacred, for Buddhists, depending on where they live, some spaces are sacred while others are not.[33] The world of the high valleys and peaks of the Nepalese Himalaya looks like a mosaic of geological forms, to which meanings are assigned. For the Sherpas, but also for their Tibetan neighbours, understanding the complexity of the environment is a long and complex endeavour that requires attention to details. When they tried to teach me the sophisticated local cultural grammar of the mountain environments, I made several mistakes revealing hidden or discreet aspects of their belief systems. One day for instance, I was sitting on a slope, watching a ritual for local divinities performed in a small gully where a dozen people were praying and chanting. When I tried to get closer to the scene, I inadvertently trampled the side of the bank and was (lightly) admonished by the whole community for disrespecting the spirits of the site. Similarly, at the wider scale of the whole village, now, popular cosmographic conceptions distinguish the anthropomorphized space of the humans from the supernatural space of the forests.[34]

In order to avoid an attack from an evil or animal spirit dwelling in what they called 'the jungle', I had to learn the routes to follow and the sites not to cross when I walked from one village to another. When I asked for information regarding the beliefs connected with the surrounding peaks, I was informed by Pasang (Figure 9.1), a Sherpa and my friend and host in the village, that 'this one, you mustn't go to, the deu-deuta [local gods or spirits] would punish you and you would be in danger', but, when pointing to a peak next to it, 'This one? No, nothing special, this is just a mountain like any other.'

Figure 9.1 Pasang and another Sherpa 'admiring' a mountain in the northern region of Nepal, 2002. Photo: Lionel Obadia.

I repeated the experience in different contexts – among the Sherpas, the Magars, and the Tibetans (refugees) in Northern Nepal – and was given the same ambivalent answers, sometimes confirming the sacredness of one high place, sometimes not. For the Nepalese mountaineers, therefore, only certain mountains are sacred or supernatural sites: many others are nothing more than neutral rocky and woody landscapes. In his study carried out among the young Sherpas, the German anthropologist Kurt Luger clearly underlined this ethnographic evidence: for foreign visitors, the landscape of mighty mountains arouses fascination and exaltation, an experience that helps to understand why it is called 'sacred', whereas local populations have limited interest in the same landscapes that seem to them invariably dull (in a chromatic sense) and mundane (aesthetically speaking).[35]

Furthermore, my ethnographic study of the mountains unveiled a non-unified system of belief applied to a unified space, but a diversified array of places (located) and routes (ambulatories) distributed throughout the whole mountain environment: remote temples (but close to paths), sites for burning the dead in isolated locations at high altitude, urbanized places (monasteries), natural sacred sites (caverns) that can be associated with fixed rituals (ceremonies) or mobile ones (pilgrimages). In addition, as Katia Buffetrille found, the Buddhist influence

Space, Place, and Religious Landscapes

Figure 9.2 Mani walls in the mountains of Nepal, 2002. Photo: Lionel Obadia.

in the Himalayan region of Tibetan and Nepalese cultures greatly contributed to the transformation of cultural representations of the mountains.[36] The symbolic shaping of the environment assumed a wide variety of forms: cairns, *chorten* (or *stupas*, Buddhist votive monuments), huge rocks carved with mantras, *Mani* walls (walls assorted with carved mineral plates, covered with mantras) (Figure 9.2) to mention a few of the more visible Buddhist signs in the mountain environment.

In the case of this region, and in the whole country of Nepal, Shamanic and animist traditions have also resisted the expansion of the major religions of Hinduism in the south and Buddhism in the north. In the shade and at the margins of Buddhism specific rituals and beliefs unfold, but in a particular spatial and temporal frames: nightly, outdoors or domestic rituals characterize Shamanic activities, whereas Buddhist ritualism is mainly daily and circumscribed in the space of the monastery.[37]

Other spaces are only sporadically invested despite their powerful potential for symbolization. Some are characterized by verticality, for instance, passes, where votive cairns are systematically erected and decorated with 'prayer flags', *lung-ta*. Others are characterized by their liminality, like meadows in between the anthropomorphized space of villages and the supernatural sites of the forests (Figure 9.3).[38] In such places, it is risky to adopt a casual attitude, under threat

Figure 9.3 Mountain village in the Himalaya. Photo: Lionel Obadia.

of being spiritually sanctioned, as happened to me, during my fieldwork, when the villagers repeatedly mentioned the attacks of spirits I was supposed to have annoyed with my naive behaviour in the first months of research.[39] Between these places, there are extensive zones bereft of any symbolic projections. One can logically conclude, on the basis of these empirical elements, that the Himalayan mountains, at least in the case of northern regions of Nepal, are not only *subject* to a sacredness (whose subtle sophistication is apprehended only by the religious elites) but also identified sites for sacred rituals involving the whole group, including the average illiterate villager or farmer. Consequently, it seems useful to distinguish between a sacredness *of* the mountains and the sacredness *in* the mountains: in the first case, mountains are the subject matter of the sacred beliefs; in the second one, they are the background for sacred rituals. To expand the point a little, the difference between the two can be established empirically in the case of a sacred geography, scriptural or symbolic, in which peaks are sacred per se, and in the case of a geography of the mountains, when one can identify sites where rituals are performed. In the first case, the sacred is extended to the whole mountain, but with a rather vague conception of the sacred (relating to a cosmology or a mythology). In the second, it is embodied in sites and places where religious acts are performed; these sites are boundaries that mark out the distinction between spatialized rituals and ordinary profane practices. This difference in the scale and location of the sacred merges with a difference in the degree of sacralization of spaces in broad terms, in the case of the sacredness of mountains, and in particular natural boundary features (routes, rivers, passes, grottos) or human-made ones (circles, fields, and, of course, temples and places of worship). My empirical data demonstrated that there was no direct correspondence between these regimes of sacredness and the mountains that are subject to them.

A secularized nature? Development, tourism and nature preserves

The cultural and religious meanings attached to the Nepalese Himalayan mountains, however, reach beyond the narrow repertoires of 'modern' Western orientalism and 'traditional' local cultural frameworks of the villagers. Indeed, other layers of symbolic meanings and social uses of the Himalaya have been added by the introduction of secular ideas, through tourism, ideologies of development, and sustainability. The 1950s opened a new chapter in the cultural and economic history of Nepal, due to major political changes at the national and continental levels. In 1951, the fall of the Rana regime, which had excluded foreigners from the Kingdom of Nepal for a whole century, quickly and massively transformed the economy and social organization of high mountains.[40] Since then Nepal has been submerged by 'floods' of tourists, especially in the north.[41] Tourism is a very important economic factor and keeps increasing every decade, reaching a total of 5 per cent of the gross domestic product in the mid-1990s.[42] It has, however, also been responsible for a rapid environmental degradation to such an extent that every administration since 1976 has launched programs for the preservation of natural resources, and has constructed protected areas and parks, in order to safeguard biodiversity.[43] The Sagarmatha region comprises one of these parks. This conservation policy, along with the development of tourism and the engagement of the local population in this new economy, contributed to a transformation of the representations and uses of the mountains in the Himalaya.[44] First, as Bruckner observed, 'spiritual tourism' was prevalent in the Kathmandu Valley in the 1960s, pursued by Western baby boomers in search of 'wisdom'.[45] But that was soon supplanted by other forms of tourism, driven by less existential motivations. In the 1970s and 1980s, as David Zurick pointed out, mountaineering, trekking, rafting, and other nature sports flourished along the same routes and injected more secular influences from the West into the local cultures, which in turn adapted their economy to these new practices.[46]

Since then, mountains have become playgrounds for tourists seeking thrills or entertainment, in addition to the previously existing sacred and less sacred representations.

Tourism, however, is not exactly nor even entirely secularized in this region: a spiritual or religious tourism is still important for local (Nepalese or Indian, Buddhist or Hindu) populations for whom a long-standing tradition is to visit religious sites located in the mountains, be they sites for pilgrimage or cave places of worship.[47] Residents of the valley, ordinary laymen, or religious virtuosi (yogi, sadhus, Brahmans, Lamas) circulate the mountains towards these religious sites on the same roads used by contemporary Western spiritual seekers (those direct descendants of the 1960s counterculture) looking for spirituality. As Robert Thurman and Tad Wise observed, on these mountain paths one can also meet scholars in Tibetology or Himalayan cultures who have adopted the faith of the people whose belief systems they were studying, and who see their journey in the Kailash mountains as a metaphor for their initiation into Buddhism.[48]

The massive industry of mountain tourism in Nepal that has been booming for the past fifty years has infused local cultures with secular visions and uses of the mountains, at the risk of damaging the symbolic frameworks associated with the mountains, by replacing them with natural and sporting ones.[49] In most of the cases I and other ethnographers recorded, the motivations of trekkers and mountaineers was limited to modern international sports values and practices: they only wanted to reach a mountaintop or to hike the most famous treks in the world.[50] The indigenous populations, living in the heart of international circuits of mountain tourism, quickly understood the opportunity to set up and control the local economy of trekking and mountaineering. Paradoxically, according to Ortner, this commitment to trekking is contrary to the idealized images they are subjected to, and moreover, the most famous of them, the Sherpas, were not originally interested in mountaineering.[51] The Sherpas and Tibetans that tourists encounter in the mountain villages and routes still follow their religious traditions and invite their trekking and/or mountaineering 'patrons' (*sabh*) to the almost unavoidable ritual of attaching prayer flags *lung-ta* on the posts on roadsides. This is a custom that Western travellers perform with interest and curiosity, but with hardly any effect on their view of the mountains, except that they henceforth understand that, for the porters or guides, there is something sacred connected with them. Despite spending time and going through experiences together, foreign trekkers/mountaineers and local communities are engaged in a dissymmetric relationship (patron-employee, foreigner-local, rich-poor) and, contrary to what Michel Raspaud, an historian specializing in Western expeditions in the

Himalaya, stated, they do not really encounter each other on a cultural level.[52] Ortner and Adams both paved the way for an anthropological analysis of the cultural imaginary of mountaineering. Adams's research, in particular, showed that the indigenous people of the Himalaya (the Sherpas) reinvented themselves in a mimetic relationship and therefore *performed* on a public stage the identity of Buddhist mountaineers to conform to the image created by Westerners while at the same time maintaining privacy around other aspects of their cultures.[53] As a result, James Fischer's ethnographic studies in the Himalayan foothills revealed that the continuous presence of secular Western populations of tourists led to a revival of religious adherence of mountain people, an unexpected outcome of the continuous flow of tourists and other secular influences.[54] The issue, in summary, is that mountains have been sacralized by local people whose religiosity is both invented by foreigners and reinvented through contact with foreigners and by outsiders, whose imagination shapes mountaineers in the guise of spiritual actors.

A resacralized mountain: Paradoxical outcomes of tourism

Adding further to this argument, mountaineering and trekking are, as sports, profane or secular practices. Yet, because of the physical effort involved, there is, at the very heart of these athletic practices, a certain sense of asceticism and loneliness. Furthermore, the aesthetics of the landscape can arouse feelings that can be likened to a 'sacred experience' recounted by high-altitude climbers (mountaineers of high mountains). Raspaud compared the ascent of high peaks to a 'shamanic initiation'.[55] Although such an idea may seem provocative, the analogy does not clearly explain the essential nature of the sacred in question. The advent of sacred feelings, independent from any system of belief, emerging from physical effort, is by nature discreet, intimate, and free from any tradition. As such, it is radically contrary to those of the ritualized and culturally codified sacredness of the Buddhist, shamanic, and animist Nepalese mountaineers.

The reflection could be supported by the already complex demonstration that the Himalayan mountains are crossed and constructed by various imaginary frameworks, mixing exported secular references (mountains as a natural place for sport or development activities) and local religious ones (mountains as the site where gods and spirits dwell, or where cultic sites are located), with exported spiritual references (the mystical experience of high peaks). In this complex distribution of the sacred and the secular, the residents are supposed to own 'sacredness' more than those who observe them – a view congruent with the orientalist fiction of the Himalaya regarded as 'spiritual' region by secular views (occidentalist). As Adams has observed, local populations are still subsumed to the Western stereotyped and romanticized figure of the 'brave' and 'spiritually inclined' mountaineers of Nepal, living in harmony with their natural environment. This is an outcome of the concealed orientalism of modern views of the 'genuine' cultures and peoples, immersed in an enchanted world, the one of the magical Himalaya.[56]

An excessive focus on orientalism and the imaginary construction of the Himalaya as sacred dismisses another aspect of the local reality: the local secular cultural forms. Indeed, the relationship the Sherpas have with their counterparts in the mountain regions of Nepal is also based on very down-to-earth ecological and economic concerns that are not always religious by nature. According to Barbara Brower, the forms of social organization, architecture, modes of residence, land ownership, agriculture, and economic exchanges are the ordinary activities of the Sherpas and the Tibetans, for whom the mountain is above all a place for living, for identity claims, and economic production.[57] As Barbra Aziz has shown, even for monks living in the mountains, religious practices or activities regarding the sacred are far from being their only livelihood.[58] Ordinary laypeople, according to Christoph von Fürer-Haimendorf, are engaged in nonreligious activities on a daily basis.[59] Yet, and as already mentioned above, these laypeople observe many rituals through which they take part in the sacralization of their environment.[60] Ortner pointed out that, while initially codified by religious values, the social and cultural practices of the Sherpas (to stay with the same example) are also elements of an identity performed and constructed in ordinary practices, of which sacred symbols or acts are only a part.[61] Moreover, in Nepal, like in Burma, mountainous terrain is not systematically interpreted in sacred terms, but also given, as Edmund Leach noted, a label of ethnicity.[62] The Nepalese semantic categories of *madhesi* ('plain people') and *pahari* ('mountain people'), according to Rajendra Pradhan, are used to distinguish 'civilized' groups (Hindu) from 'tribal' ones (Buddhists and other believers) on the basis of a complex moral and political geography of ethnicities.[63] Finally, a last point must be discussed in this reflection on the blurred frontier between the sacred and the secular in this region of the world: the cultural ecology of these populations of the Himalaya is exactly identical to the cultural imaginary embedded in it. Their sense of ecological responsibility is a mix of secular references (local and exported ones) and religious values (local ones). My examination of the latter seems to confirm that, here again, the Buddhist mountaineers, supposedly respectful of their 'sacred' environments, are neither entirely eco-friendly nor religiously respectful of their 'holy' mountains.[64]

Conclusion: Ambivalent and paradoxical intermingling between sacred and secular in the Himalaya

Following the research of other anthropologists who have worked in the same region, I have tried to dig into the complexity of the representations of the mountains and the complex interplay between them. Unlike others, I have chosen to narrow the focus onto the issue of the *sacred*, and the ways the different representations confronted and intersected with one another, and created a mosaic of contrasting ideas related to sacredness. Further, as a result of my research, I would like to suggest a revision of the simplistic classical models of 'Himalaya-as-sacred-mountains' on the grounds of an empirically informed reflection of how actors make mountains sacred (or not) rather than on how texts or myths depict them.

There is a strange paradox in the previously discussed intermingling between imaginary frameworks and practices in the Nepalese Himalaya. The *local sacralization of the mountains* is indeed far more heterogeneous than one could expect at first sight. The *projective and exported sacralization* of the same mountains brought by human and cultural flows, and more precisely stemming from secular (Western) societies, induces homogenizing effects. This conjunction thus refers to two parallel but distinct forms of sacredness, both associated with the same mountains, and inspired at the same time by secular ideologies (development, ecology, and tourism) and local cultural systems, which include significant religious elements but which do not absolutely and consistently grant religious meanings to the mountains. The ethnographic approach to these modes of (re)sacralization of this part of the Himalaya also unveiled the existence of secular forms of thought and practice, either exported or vernacular. Far from eliminating the religious conceptions of 'sacred mountains', secular and imported ideas and practices were instead absorbed and appropriated by Himalayan societies. This was considered by authors such as Ortner, and Paul Rogers and John Aitchison, to be an adaptive response to the challenges of modernity.[65] This cultural absorption of foreign thoughts is happening without apparent major contradiction for the indigenous peoples' own cultural conceptions, since they also are, in a certain way, driven by secular preoccupations. Neither tourism nor development programs nor policies of conservation have deeply secularized the Himalaya: the Asian mountains remain firmly rooted in local or 'traditional' expressions of sacredness that are both integrated in policies of conservation.[66] They are also reactivated (*mutatis mutandis*) by foreign secular influences and exported ideas of the sacred (analogical, imaginary) from 'modern' societies. Observing closely the plurality of representations projected on these mountain regions, from an ethnographic point of view, requires one, in my opinion, to adopt more careful interpretations of the sacred mountains of Asia. Contrary to the persistent essentialist overgeneralizations, the representations and uses of the valleys and peaks of the Nepalese Himalaya are not subjected to unified systems of meanings. They look like complex combinations of significations projected on the mountains by the different actors living permanently or sporadically there. Rather than immutable systems of significations and beliefs, then, I observed active, dynamic meanings, sometimes antagonistic, sometimes complementary, but always negotiated between social actors in this context.

A focus on sacredness and the differences it entails does not perpetuate an old-fashioned essentialist phenomenology of the mountains, but rather facilitates the understanding of the dynamics of meaning production and sharpens the focus on challenges for the societies of the Himalaya. A cultural interpretation of the Everest region also leads to the conclusion that mountain spaces are complex ones, incorporating a multiplicity of references and frameworks used by the many actors of the mountains, the encounters of particular cultural imaginations, and the constitution of hybrid networks of meanings. This is a place where indigenous secularity and Western sacredness improbably mix together, where indigenous sacredness and Western secularity merge. As a very final conclusion, and again, against the temptation to develop simplistic general and transcultural theories of sacred mountains, from my research it seems more than ever necessary to consider the mountains at the level of ideas and practices of ordinary people living there, not simply in the abstract world of cosmologies. Therefore, I would argue that mountains appear as they are empirically: socially produced spaces in the context of the heterogeneous polylogy of cultures and people dwelling in or traversing them.

Notes

1 John Snelling, *Sacred Mountain* (London: East-West Publications, 1991).

2 Ramesh raj Kunwar, *Fire of Himal: An Anthropological Study of the Sherpas of Nepal Himalayan Region* (New Delhi: Nirala, 1999), 35–53.

3 Sherry Ortner, *High Religion: Cultural and Political History of Sherpa Buddhism* (Princeton, NJ: Princeton University Press, 1989); Vincanne Adams, *Tigers of the Snow and Other Virtual Sherpas: An Ethnography of Himalayan Encounters* (Princeton, NJ: Princeton University Press, 1996).

4 Doreen Massey, *For Space* (London: Sage, 2005), 9–15.

5 Chris Park, *Sacred World: An Introduction to Geography and Religion* (London: Routledge, 1994), 18–19; Lily Kong, 'Mapping "New" Geographies of Religion: Politics and Poetics in Modernity', *Progress in Human Geography* 25, no. 2 (2005): 211–33, at 219–20.

6 H. G. Quaritch Wales, 'Sacred Mountains in the Old Asiatic Religion', *Journal of the Royal Asiatic Society of Great Britain and Ireland* 1, no. 2 (1953): 23–30, at 29.

7 Samivel (Paul Gayet-Tancrède), *Hommes, Cimes et Dieux* (Paris: Arthaud, 2005), 23.

8 Edwin Bernbaum, *Sacred Mountains: Themes and Teachings* (Berkeley: University of California Press, 1997).

9 Pierre Deffontaines, *Géographie et religions* (Paris: Gallimard, 1948), 10; Park, *Sacred World*, 2–7.

10 Philippe Descola, *Par-delà Nature et Culture* (Paris: Gallimard, 2005), 532–52.

11 Mircea Eliade, *The Sacred and the Profane: The Nature of Religion* (Boston, MA: Houghton Mifflin Harcourt, 1959), 20–4.

12 Edwin Bernbaum, 'Sacred Mountains: Themes and Teachings', *Mountain Research and Development* 26, no. 4 (2006): 304–9, at 307.

13 Edwin Bernbaum, *Sacred Mountains of the World* (Berkeley: University of California Press, 1967), 94.

14 Samivel, *Hommes, Cimes et Dieux*, 11–19; Bernbaum, *Sacred Mountains of the World*, 93; Jean-Pierre Roux, *Montagnes sacrées, montagnes mythiques* (Paris: Fayard, 1999), 21.

15 Serge Brunet, Dominique Julia, and Nicole Lemaître (eds), *Montagnes sacrées d'Europe. Montagnes sacrées d'Europe* (Paris: Publications de la Sorbonne, 2005); Bernbaum, *Sacred Mountains of the World*.

16 Pierre Albert, 'Les montagnes sont-elles bonnes à penser en termes religieux?' in *Montagnes sacrées d'Europe*, ed. S. Brunet, D. Julia, and N. Lemaître (Paris: Publications de la Sorbonne), 65–72, at 65.

17 Lionel Obadia, 'Le rôle des catégories locales dans la conduite d'une enquête ethnographique dans le Solukhumbu (Himalaya népalais)', in *L'ethnographie comme dialogue. Immersion et interaction dans l'enquête de terrain*, ed. Lionel Obadia (Paris, Publisud, 2003), 175–201.

18 *The Commentary of Father Monserrate, S.J. on His Journey to the Court of Akbar* (Delhi: Asian Educationnal Service, 2003).

19 Jean Baptiste Bourguignon d'Anville, *Oeuvres: Mémoire et abrégé de géographie ancienne et générale, Tome II* (Paris: Levrault, 1832).

20 See, for instance, the list established by http://mountain.org/.

21 Stefan Feuchtwang, 'India and China as Spiritual Nations: A Comparative Anthropology of Histories', *Social Anthropology* 17, no. 1 (2009): 100–8, at 100–1.

22 Harvey Cox, *Turning East: Promise and the Peril of the New Orientalism* (New York: Simon & Schuster, 1977), 146–69.

23 Gérard Toffin, *Man and His House in the Himalayas: Ecology of Nepal* (New York: Sterling), 228.

24 Michael Stausberg, *Religion and Tourism: Crossroads, Destinations and Encounters* (London: Routledge, 2011), 103.

25 Edward W. Said, *Orientalism* (London: Routledge & Kegan Paul, 1978), 20–2.

26 Lionel Obadia, *Bouddhisme et Occident. Bouddhisme et Occident. La diffusion du bouddhisme tibétain en France* (Paris: L'Harmattan,1999), 40–51; Lionel Obadia, *Le bouddhisme en Occident* (Paris: La Découverte, 2007), 31–3.

27 Monica Esposito (ed.), *Images of Tibet in the 19th and 20th Centuries*, Études Thématiques 22 (Paris: École française d'Extrême-Orient, 2008), 5–6.

28 Pascal Bruckner, *Le sanglot de l'Homme blanc. Tiers-Monde, Culpabilité, Haine De Soi* (Paris : Le Seuil, 1983), 159.

29 Brian Molyneaux, La terre et le sacré (Koln : Tachent, 2002), 24.

30 Katia Buffetrille, *Pèlerins; lamas et visionnaires. Sources orales et écrites sur, les pèlerinages tibétains* (Vien : Arbeitskreis fur tibetische und buddhistische Studiens Universitat Wien, 2000), 23–5.

31 Gérard Toffin (ed.), 'Paysages et divinités en Himalaya', *Etudes Rurales* no. 107–8 (1987): 9–133; Niels Gutschow et al. (eds), *Sacred Landscape of the Himalaya*, Proceedings of the conference held in Heidelberg, 25–27 May 1998 (Wien: Verlag der Österreichischen Akademie der Wissenschaften, 2003).

32 Agehananda Bharati, 'Actual and Ideal Himalayas: Hindu Views of the Mountains', in *Himalayan Anthropology: The Indo-Tibetan Interface*, ed. J. Fischer (Paris: Mouton), 77–82, at 80.

33 Michael Boord, 'Buddhism', in *Sacred Place*, ed. J. Holm and J. Bowker (London: Pinter, 1994), 8–9.

34 Toffin, Gérard, ed. 'Paysages et divinités en Himalaya'. *Etudes Rurales* no. 107–8 (1987): 9–133.

35 Kurt Luger, *Kids of Khumbu: Sherpa Youth on the Modernity Trail* (Kathmandu: Mandala Book Point, 2000), 109.

36 Katia Buffetrille, 'Reflections on Pilgrimages to Sacred Mountains, Lakes and Caves', in *Pilgrimage in Tibet*, ed. A. McKay (Leiden: Curzon Press, 1998), 21–2.

37 Lionel Obadia, 'Festivités religieuses, publiques et discrètes. Mondialisation, tourisme, et mimesis chez les Sherpas du Nord Népal', *Anthropologie et sociétés* 34, no. 2 (2010): 177–97, at 188–90.

38 Marie Lecomte-Tilouine, 'Hommes – divinités de la forêt à travers le miroir au Népal Central', *Etudes Rurales* no. 107–8 (1987): 55–69, at 68.

39 Lionel Obadia, 'The Conflicting Sherpas' Relationships to Nature. Tradition, Protection, and Destruction: Indigenous or Western Ecology?', *Journal for the Scientific Study of Religion and Nature* 1, no. 4 (2008): 117–35, at 126.

40 Christoph Von Fürer-Haimendorf, *The Sherpas Transformed: Social Change in a Buddhist Society of Nepal* (New Delhi: Sterling, 1984), 64–80; Terry Cox, 'Herding and Socio-Economic Change among the Khumbu Sherpas', *Kailash* 12, no. 1–2 (1985): 63–79, at 77–8.

41 James Fischer, *Sherpas: Reflection on Change in Himalayan Nepal* (Berkeley: University of California Press, 1990), 108–52.

42 Pradyumna Karan and Hiroshi Ishii, *Nepal: A Himalayan Kingdom in Transition* (Tokyo: United Nations University Press, 1996), 78.

43 Barbara Brower, *Sherpa of Khumbu: People, Livestock, and Landscape* (New Delhi: Oxford University Press, 1991), 99–100.

44 Stan Stevens, 'National Parks and ICCAs in the High Himalayan Region of Nepal: Challenges and Opportunities', *Conservation & Society* 11, no. 1 (2013): 29–45, at 39–40; Isabelle Sacareau, 'Les transformations d'une haute montagne par le tourisme: le massif des Annapurna dans l'Himalaya du Népal', *Annales de géographie* 605 (1999): 1–45, at 31–7.

45 Bruckner, *Le Sanglot de l'Homme Blanc*, 176–7.

46 David Zurick, 'Travel and Sustainable Tourism in the Peripheral Economy of Nepal', *Annals of the Association of American Geographers* 82, no. 4 (1992): 608–28, at 620–5.

47 Tony Bleie, 'Tourism in the Central Himalayas: The Case of Manakamana Temple in Gorkha, Nepal', *Mountain Research and Development* 23, no. 2 (2003): 177–84, at 177–8.

48 Robert Thurman and Tad Wise, *Circling the Sacred Mountain: A Spiritual Adventure through the Himalayas* (New York: Bantam Books, 1999), 133.

49 Isabelle Sacareau, *Porteurs de l'Himalaya: Le trekking au Népal* (Paris: Belin, 1997), 138 and following.

50 See, for instance, Bill O'Connor, *The Trekking Peaks of Nepal* (Mountaineering Books, 1998), 9–19.

51 Sherry Ortner, *Life and Death on Mt Everest: Sherpas and Himalayan Mountaineering* (Princeton, NJ: Princeton University Press, 1999), 30.

52 Michel Raspaud, 'La vision des vainqueurs. Himalayisme et choc des cultures', *La Création Sociale. Sociétés, Cultures, Imaginaires* 5 (2000): 127–46, at 139–45.

53 Adams, *Tigers of the Snow*, 172.

54 Fischer, *Sherpas*, 137–8.

55 Michel Raspaud, 'L'expérimentation de la haute altitude en Himalaya', *Babel. Langages – Imaginaires – Civilisations* 8 (2003): 87–110, at 99–110.

56 Adams, *Tigers of the Snow*, 53.

57 Brower, *Sherpa of Khumbu*, 12–50.

58 Barbara Aziz, *Tibetan Frontier Families: Reflections of Three Generations from D'ing-ri* (New Delhi: Vikas, 1978).

59 Christoph von Fürer-Haimendorf, *The Sherpas of Nepal: Buddhist Highlanders* (London, Butler & Tanner, 1964).

60 Kunwar, *Fire of Himal*, 1964.

61 Sherry Ortner, *Sherpas through Their Rituals* (Cambridge: Cambridge University Press, 1978), 154.

62 Edmund Leach, *Political Systems of Highland Burma* (London: G. Bell, 1954), 281–2.

63 Rajendra Pradhan, 'Ethnicity, Caste and a Pluralist Society', in *State of Nepal*, ed. K. Mani Dixit and S. Ramachandaran (Lalitpur: Himal Books, 2002), 16–17.

64 Obadia, *Conflicting Sherpas' Relationships to Nature*, 125–7.

65 Ortner, *High Religion*, 99–117; Paul Rogers and John Aitchison, *Towards Sustainable Tourism in the Everest Region of Nepal* (Kathmandu: IUCN Nepal, 1998), 88–91.

66 Xiaoli Shen, Zhi Lu, Shengzi Li, and Nyima Chen, 'Tibetan Sacred Sites: Understanding the Traditional Management System and Its Role in Modern Conservation', *Ecology & Society* 17, no. 2 (2012): 13.

Bibliography

Adams, Vincanne. *Tigers of the Snow and Other Virtual Sherpas: An Ethnography of Himalayan Encounters*. Princeton, NJ: Princeton University Press, 1996.

Albert, Jean-Pierre. 'Les montagnes sont-elles bonnes à penser en termes religieux?' In *Montagnes sacrées d'Europe*, edited by Serge Brunet, Dominique Julia, and Nicole Lemaître, 65–72. Paris: Publications de la Sorbonne, 2005.

Aziz, Barbara. *Tibetan Frontier Families: Reflections of Three Generations from D'ing-ri*. New Delhi: Vikas, 1978.

Bernbaum, Edwin. *Sacred Mountains of the World*. Berkeley: University of California Press, 1967.

Bernbaum, Edwin. 'Sacred Mountains: Themes and Teachings'. *Mountain Research and Development* 26, no. 4 (2006): 304–9.

Bharati, Agehananda. 'Actual and Ideal Himalayas: Hindu Views of the Mountains'. In *Himalayan Anthropology: The Indo-Tibetan Interface*, edited by J. Fischer, 77–82. Paris: La Hague, Mouton, 1978.

Bleie, Tony. 'Tourism in the Central Himalayas: The Case of Manakamana Temple in Gorkha, Nepal'. *Mountain Research and Development* 23, no. 2 (200): 177–84.

Boord, Michael. 'Buddhism'. In *Sacred Place*, edited by J. Holm and J. Bowker, 8–32. London: Pinter, 1994.

Brower, Barbara. *Sherpa of Khumbu: People, Livestock, and Landscape*. New Delhi: Oxford University Press, 1991.

Bruckner, Pascal. *Le Sanglot De L'homme Blanc. Tiers-Monde, Culpabilité, Haine De Soi*. Paris: Le Seuil, 1983.

Brunet, Serge, Dominique Julia, and Nicole Lemaître, eds. *Montagnes sacrées d'Europe*. Paris: Publications de la Sorbonne, 2005.

Buffetrille, Katia. 'Reflections on Pilgrimages to Sacred Mountains, Lakes and Caves. In *Pilgrimage in Tibet*, edited by A. McKay, 18–34. Leiden: Curzon Press, 1998.

Buffetrille, Katia. *Pèlerins; lamas et visionnaires. Sources orales et écrites sur, les pèlerinages tibétains*. Vienne: Arbeitskreis fur tibetische und buddhistische Studiens Universitat Wien, 2000.

Cox, Harvey. *Turning East: Promise and the Peril of the New Orientalism*. New York: Simon & Schuster, 1977

Cox, Terry. Herding and Socio-Economic Change among the Khumbu Sherpas. *Kailash* 12, nos. 1–2 (1985): 63–79.

d'Anville, Jean Baptiste Bourguignon. *Oeuvres: Mémoire et abrégé de géographie ancienne et générale*, Tome II. Paris: Levrault, 1832.

Deffontaines, Pierre. *Géographie et religions*. Paris: Gallimard, 1948.

Descola, Philippe. *Par-delà nature et culture*. Paris: Gallimard, 2005.

Eliade, Mircea. *The Sacred and the Profane: The Nature of Religion*. Boston, MA: Houghton Mifflin Harcourt, 1959.

Esposito, Monica, ed. *Images of Tibet in the 19th and 20th Centuries*, Études Thématiques 22. Paris: École française d'Extrême-Orient, 2008.

Feuchtwang, Stefan. 'India and China as Spiritual Nations: A Comparative Anthropology of Histories'. *Social Anthropology* 17, no. 1 (2009): 100–8.

Fischer, James. *Sherpas: Reflection on Change in Himalayan Nepal*. Berkeley: University of California Press, 1990.

Fürer-Haimendorf, Christoph Von. *The Sherpas of Nepal: Buddhist Highlanders*. London: Butler & Tanner, 1964.

Fürer-Haimendorf, Christoph Von. *The Sherpas Transformed: Social Change in a Buddhist Society of Nepal*. New Delhi: Sterling, 1984.

Gutschow, Niels, Axel Michaels, Charles Ramble, and Ernst. Steinkellner, eds. *Sacred Landscape of the Himalaya*. Vienna: Austrian Academy of Sciences Press, 2003.

Karan, Pradyumna P., and Hiroshi Ishii. *Nepal: A Himalayan Kingdom in Transition*. Tokyo: United Nations University Press, 1996.

Kong, Lily. 'Mapping "New" Geographies of Religion: Politics and Poetics in Modernity'. *Progress in Human Geography* 25, no. 2 (2001): 211–33.

Kunwar, Ramesh Raj. *Fire of Himal: An Anthropological Study of the Sherpas of Nepal Himalayan Region*. New Delhi: Nirala, 1999.

Leach, Edmund. *Political Systems of Highland Burma*. London: G. Bell, 1954.

Lecomte-Tilouine, Marie. 'Hommes – divinités de la forêt à travers le miroir au Népal Central'. *Etudes Rurales* 107–8 (1987): 55–69.

Luger, Kurt. *Kids of Khumbu: Sherpa Youth on the Modernity Trail*. Kathmandu: Mandala Book Point, 2000.

Massey, Doreen. *For Space*. London: Sage, 2005.

Molyneaux, Brian. *La terre et le sacré*. Koln: Tachent, 2002.

Obadia, Lionel. *Bouddhisme et Occident. La diffusion du bouddhisme tibétain en France*. Paris: L'Harmattan, 1999.

Obadia, Lionel. 'Le rôle des catégories locales dans la conduite d'une enquête ethnographique dans le Solukhumbu (Himalaya népalais)'. In *L'ethnographie comme dialogue: Immersion et interaction dans l'enquête de terrain*, edited by Lionel Obadia, 175–20. Paris: Publisud, 2003.

Obadia, Lionel. *Le bouddhisme en Occident*. Paris: La Découverte, 2007.

Obadia, Lionel. 'The Conflicting Sherpas' Relationships to Nature. Tradition, Protection, and Destruction: Indigenous or Western Ecology?' *Journal for the Scientific Study of Religion and Nature* 1, no. 4 (2008): 117–35.

Obadia, Lionel. 'Festivités religieuses, publiques et discrètes. Mondialisation, tourisme, et mimesis chez les Sherpas du Nord Népal'. *Anthropologie et sociétés* 34, no. 2 (2010): 177–97.

O'Connor, Bill, *The Trekking Peaks of Nepal*. Seattle: Mountaineering Books, 1998.

Ortner, Sherry. *Sherpas through Their Rituals*. Cambridge: Cambridge University Press, 1987.

Ortner, Sherry. *High Religion: A Cultural and Political History of Sherpa Buddhism*. Princeton, NJ: Princeton University Press, 1989.

Ortner, Sherry. *Life and Death on Mt. Everest: Sherpas and Himalayan Mountaineering*. Princeton, NJ: Princeton University Press, 1999.

Park, Chris. *Sacred World: An Introduction to Geography and Religion*. London: Routledge, 1994.

Pile, Steven. 'The Strange Case of Western Cities: Occult Globalisations and the Making of Urban Modernity'. *Urban Studies* 43, no. 2 (2006): 305–18.

Pradhan, Rajendra. 'Ethnicity, Caste and a Pluralist Society. In *State of Nepal*, edited by K. Mani Dixit and S. Ramachandaran, 1–58. Lalitpur: Himal Books, 2002.

Raspaud, Michel. 'La vision des vainqueurs. Himalayisme et choc des cultures'. *La Création Sociale. Sociétés, Cultures, Imaginaires* 5 (2000): 127–46.

Raspaud, Michel. 'Le voyage en "oxygène rare" comme expérience initiatique. L'expérimentation de la haute altitude en Himalaya', *Babel. Langages – Imaginaires – Civilisations* 8 (2003): 87–110.

Rogers, Paul, and John Aitchison. *Towards Sustainable Tourism in the Everest Region of Nepal*. Kathmandu: IUCN Nepal, 1988.

Roux, Jean-Pierre. *Montagnes sacrées, montagnes mythiques*. Paris: Fayard, 1999.

Sacareau, Isabelle. *Porteurs de l'Himalaya: Le trekking au Népal*. Paris: Belin 1997.

Sacareau, Isabelle. 'Les transformations d'une haute montagne par le tourisme: le massif des Annapurna dans l'Himalaya du Népal'. *Annales de géographie* 605 (1999): 1–45.

Said, Eward, W. *Orientalism*. London: Routledge & Kegan Paul, 1978.

Samivel (Paul Gayet-Tancrède). *Hommes, cimes et dieux*. Paris: Arthaud, 2005.

Shen, Xiaoli, Zhi Lu, Shengzhi Li, and Nyima Chen. 'Tibetan Sacred Sites: Understanding the Traditional Management System and Its Role in Modern Conservation'. *Ecology and Society* 17, no. 2 (2012).

Snelling, John. *Sacred Mountain*. London: East-West Publications, 1991.

Stausberg, Michael. *Religion and Tourism: Crossroads, Destinations and Encounters*. London: Routledge, 2011.

Stevens, Stan. 'National Parks and ICCAs in the High Himalayan Region of Nepal: Challenges and Opportunities'. *Conservation & Society* 11, no. 1 (2013): 29–45.

The Commentary of Father Monserrate, S.J. on His Journey to the Court of Akbar. Delhi: Asian Educationnal Service, 2003.

Thurman, Robert A. F., and Tad Wise. *Circling the Sacred Mountain: A Spiritual Adventure through the Himalayas*. New York: Bantam Books, 1999.

Toffin, Gérard, ed. 'Paysages et divinités en Himalaya'. *Etudes Rurales* no. 107–8 (1987): 9–133.

Toffin, Gérard. *Man and His House in the Himalayas: Ecology of Nepal*. New York, Sterling, 2016.

Troillet, Jean. *L'aventure absolue*. Lausanne: Favre, 2001.

Wales, H. G. Quaritch. 'The Sacred Mountain in the Old Asiatic Religion'. *Journal of the Royal Asiatic Society of Great Britain and Ireland* no. 1/2 (1953): 23–30.

Zurick, David. 'Travel and Sustainable Tourism in the Peripheral Economy of Nepal'. *Annals of the Association of American Geographers* 82, no. 4 (1992): 608–28.

10

The Black Line of the Sierra Nevada de Santa Marta; a Red Line for a mountain

Alan Ereira

This chapter engages with the contemporary conversations with mountains via the Sierra Nevada de Santa Marta, the world's highest coastal massif, and refuge to some thirty thousand indigenous people who claim descent from the 'Tairona' culture. They regard it as the centre of creation. They believe they are responsible for sustaining its well-being and, through it, the whole earth. The least acculturated group is Kogi. Hidden, they protected their culture from conquest. Their spiritual leaders (*Mamas*) speak no Spanish and are trained for years, from infancy, in darkness. They are considered guardians of knowledge needed to maintain fertility. They work in the material world and in *aluna*, the cosmic thought space where they consult with the Sierra Nevada de Santa Marta. They make offerings at mid-mountain locations called *ezuamas*. Each *ezuama* invisibly connects to a lower site, and a designated *Mama* is its human manifestation. They appear to perform a form of earth acupuncture as advised in *aluna*. The Tairona made remarkable gold-copper objects, found throughout the Caribbean, Central America, and the northern Andes, to connect with *aluna*. Christopher Columbus found they were valued at two hundred times raw gold.[1] The Kogi believe these objects are central to species' survival. To protect the Sierra Nevada de Santa Marta from newly aggressive commercial exploitation and degradation its indigenous communities have jointly defined a circumscribed 'Black Line' within which they insist only indigenous rules should apply. This was agreed by the Colombian government and signed into law in August 2018, hours before President Santos left office. The Black Line is now a red line that the indigenous believe they have been asked by the Sierra Nevada de Santa Marta to defend.

Background

The Sierra Nevada de Santa Marta, on Colombia's Caribbean coast, is the highest coastal mountain in the world. Its indigenous people understand it not as a geographical feature but as a living entity. The Sierra is well known to mountaineers, students of biodiversity, mining contractors, enthusiasts for adventure holidays, and anthropologists of Latin America. It rises steeply from tropical beaches to two permanently snow-capped summits 5,770 metres high in just 42 kilometres. In 1892 the highest peak was christened Cristóbal Colon, representing it as a geographical monument to the father of colonization, but no one could say where that peak was until it was conquered by an American expedition in 1939.[2] To mountaineers, who assess peaks by 'prominence' above the start of the climb, it is ranked as the fifth in the world.

In terms of biodiversity this 17,000 square kilometres massif has a unique status. It is a UNESCO biosphere reserve.[3] It is also considered the most irreplaceable protected area in the world for threatened species.[4] Its astonishing capacity to support a huge variety of species with quite different needs is a consequence of its unusual structure. The massif is an equilateral triangular pyramid with each side measuring 80 kilometres, positioned at a collision point between the Caribbean and South American plates. S. Giraldo described it as a 'biogeographical island'.[5] It sits on its own tectonic plate quite unconnected to the Andes and has been forced upwards and rotated clockwise through 30 degrees.[6] The north face rises steeply from some 600 metres below the surface of the Caribbean. On the west it is sharply bounded by the plains of the Magdalena river valley and on the east by the narrow valley of the Cesar river and the Guajira desert. The surface is structured by thirty steep-sided river valleys originating from lakes of snowmelt. The variety of temperatures (tropical to arctic), precipitation (rainforest to desert), and saturation (mangrove swamp to tundra) creates a dense variety of microclimates, ecological niches that largely mirror the range of life-supporting land environments over the rest of the planet.

It inevitably has potential as a resource for rare metals. By November 2017 the Colombian government had granted 132 mining titles there and was considering 285 pending requests.[7] The exercise of these titles is challenged by indigenous people.[8] The main attraction noted by the exploratory mountaineers in 1939, apart from its sheer natural beauty and variety, was the opportunity for hunting birds and beasts such as jaguar, puma, bear, and docile creatures such as iguana and anteater which might have made rather unfortunate trophies.[9] According to their expedition's report, all that was needed to make the Sierra profitable and useful was an airport at about 2,000-metre altitude on the south side, and a comfortable resort hotel. The indigenous people, who were given the generic name Arhuacos, were described as uncooperative and lacking enterprise, so it was reported that they were unlikely to make good use of the place. In any case, the population appeared to consist of tiny groups that might total 1,500 people.[10] The report viewed them as having no more rights to the territory than did the iguanas, and they were said to be so degenerate that they could not be connected to the sophisticated culture described on the northern slopes by Spanish conquistadores. The Spanish had called that culture Tairona and apparently destroyed it in the seventeenth century.[11]

Tairona culture has now been brought back into focus by ecotourism to the Tairona National Park and treks to 'The Lost City' (*Ciudad Perdida*), the partly restored remains of a 'Tairona' settlement of stairways, stone paths, and 169 terraces with the foundations of buildings.[12] Discovered in the dense jungle of the Buritaca river valley in 1972 by professional tomb robbers, it was handed over to archaeologists in 1976. It is only 40 kilometres from Santa Marta, but because of the difficult terrain, the trek takes several days and is demanding. There used to be a risk of kidnap by armed guerrillas, but travellers have been safe since 2005. I am informed by Juan Mayr, who was the minister for the environment in 1998–2002 and who has sustained a long involvement with the Sierra, that the treks are now controlled and, in practice, taxed by the paramilitary forces that have supplanted the guerrillas. This information was given to me privately at a meeting in June 2019 when the paramilitaries had just announced that they were using armed force to 'take back control' of the Sierra from narco-traffickers, and they would not attack tourists. The site is the largest pre-Columbian settlement known in South America, six hundred years older than Machu Picchu. According to D. Wilson, it may have housed over seven thousand people and the indigenous people of the area now lay claim to it as ancestral and 'sacred' space.[13] As Andrés Ricardo Restrepo Campo and Sandra Turbay have noted, although some of them act as guides, the indigenous communities here are generally not comfortable with tourism today, any more than they were with mountaineering visitors eighty years ago.[14] The Lost City and hundreds of other Sierra sites are, according to the República de Colombia, Ministerio del Interior, Decreto numero 1500 de 6 Ago 2018, untouchable and connect directly to the source of life within and beyond the Sierra.[15]

Which brings me to those indolent, uncooperative inhabitants, who now hold a special place among anthropologists of Latin America. In truth the Lost City brought me very directly face to face with them. In 1988, as a BBC documentary film-maker doing a short shoot in Bogota, I was asked by my employers to see if there was a film to be made about the remains. That was when I learned that there were other related communities in other, effectively trackless river valleys of the Sierra, who think of themselves as the guardians of ancestral memory and caretakers of the world. There are four distinct cultures, called Kogi (or Kággaba), Arhuaco (or Ika), Malaya (or Wiwa), and the almost totally acculturated Kankuamo. I chose to seek contact with the Kogi, who were the least acculturated group, and the most shy of contact. Their isolation was not total. There was intercourse with Colombian peasant traders – Kogi would exchange cattle for machetes and cookware – and encounters with government officials and missionaries, but their spiritual leaders ('Mamas') would assess the gifts offered and if they felt they did not belong in their lands, would refuse them.

They had chosen to remain hidden, so far as possible, from the colonial invaders, but they eventually told me that they had recently decided their hidden offerings could no longer protect the world against the depredations of 'civilization'. I was told this when I was brought to meet the Mamas of seventeen communities. They had assembled at what was now a border town at about 1,500 metres called Pueblo Viejo, accessible by a steep climb and 'off-grid' but shared with a small group of farmers (colonos) and a settlement of nuns.

The modern world had begun to intrude aggressively since the 1970s with the arrival of large commercial marijuana operations, left-wing guerrilla armies, and right-wing paramilitaries. The government's presence was represented by Asuntos Indigenas, the Office of Indian Affairs, who ran a very basic lodge and clinic in Santa Marta, but it was not effectively sustained. To communicate with the local office I had first to pay off its unpaid telephone and pharmacy bills. The Mamas had decided that they needed to engage directly with the state but since they could not speak Spanish, and their own language Kaggaba was spoken by no one else, they needed to establish their own organization. To do this they needed Kogi who spoke Spanish and Kaggaba, or Spanish-speaking Wiwas and Arhuacos whose languages they could understand. The nineteenth-century missionary Rafael Celedon had attempted to produce a grammar of their language but failed to produce the religious texts he intended.[16] Furthermore, Gerardo Reichel-Dolmatoff, the godfather of Colombian anthropology, after many years in the Sierra and extensive publication, had never mastered Kaggaba. I consulted him before my first visit: he told me that his informants were not approved and that his notes had to be made secretly at night in a hammock with a torch in his mouth, from informants mumbling while chewing wads of coca leaf. He advised me that they were so difficult to approach that I should go to the Arhuaco instead. I found there were some Kogi who spoke fragmentary Spanish largely drawn from their experience of the conquest; their word for their own people was 'vasallos', 'vassals', the liminal meditative ceremony on arriving was 'confessio', 'confession', and the communal men's house was the 'cansamaria', which translates as 'worn out Mary' and appears to be derived from 'casa Maria', 'The House of Mary'. That may be part of a cynical remaking of Spanish, like their word for 'office' – *piscina*, swimming pool – instead of *oficina*.

So in 1987 they had founded the Organisación Gonawindua Tayrona (OGT). *Gonawindua* is the highest peak, the one we name after Columbus. 'Tayrona' is the archaeological designation of the culture that built the Lost City. They appointed Ramón Gil, a half-Wiwa, half-Kogi who spoke Spanish, as head of the OGT and called him *cabildo gubernador* – the council and the governor.[17] His training for the role had been initiated by a small group of Mamas several years before.[18] He told me that his grandfather had been a Wiwa Mama but his powers had not been passed down. Ramón said he had grown up 'wild', quite apart from the traditional world and had known little of it, living on the very permeable boundary between Wiwa and Colombian peasants. He had become a hustler and political activist, combating the settlers' incursions. Then Kogi Mamas appeared before him and told Ramón they had a special role for him. Completely shocked, he was removed from his wife and child and placed in a cave. Over fourteen months he was reshaped. He was taught cosmology and culture, Kogi history and philology, and their theory of translation, and emerged with the authority of the Mamas and the mountain at his back, to put a final end to the Colombian conquest.[19] My request had, it seems, arrived at the moment the Kogi were ready for it. It had gone through Asuntos Indigenas, who controlled access to the Sierra, and was taken to the Mamas by Ramón. He accompanied me to the Mamas, who were ready to consider this as a part of their effort to push back encroaching colonization.

Who are we

I was taken by night to the circular nuhue, the men's meeting house. Seated in their white woven robes around four fires, they listened to my explanation of television. They interrogated me about the experience of watching it (in what sense does the viewer experience a meeting with the person filmed?) and about the power of the film-maker (where is the truth in the result?). The next day, at a formal gathering in the square building missionaries had once erected as a church, I was asked if I had a machine that remembered what they would say. Three Mamas spoke; I never learned anyone's name but for external purposes they were Mamas Valencio, Bernardo, and Jacinto. They spoke in turn, telling the story of the world from its first conception as thought in the dark void of the cosmic mind, *Aluna*.

> In the beginning, there was blackness. In the beginning there was no sun, no moon, no people. In the beginning there were no animals, no plants. Only the Mother. The Mother was not people, she was not anything. Nothing at all. She was memory and potential. She was *Aluna*.[20]

Aluna thought through the experimental construction and collapse of various forms until there was a detailed blueprint for a workable structure with viable creatures. It was then made real. Past and future separated: between memory and potential was the present, the material world, and light. Reality was spun around a central spindle, the place of immanent creation, the mountain *Gonawindua* (Figure 10.1). Humans link the consciousness of *aluna* to materiality, and have to keep the world in balance.

Then, I was told, came a second creation of humans, younger brothers, who have no respect for the mother, for the earth, for the mountain. So they were expelled, across the sea. The lands where they now live are all mirrored in the mountain; it includes all kinds of places on the larger earth, and what happens there can be seen here. During the day I had been interrogated about the ecology of my home environment, and its equivalent, my place on the mountain had been established.

But then came Columbus. I was told the story of the conquest and destruction of indigenous people everywhere, and the retreat of the Mamas into the high Sierra to continue taking care of the mountain and the whole world. But the conquest is not over yet. Younger brother's advance continues. When it is complete, if it is complete, the Kogi Mamas, the mountain, and the world will all perish. Younger brother must learn, and must change.

So they took me in and took over my projected film about the Lost City. My account of this experience, and the efforts of the Kogi to use television to communicate their warning to the wider world, is documented in my book, originally published as *The Heart of the World* (1990) and in the materials available on the website of the Tairona Heritage Trust (www.taironatrust.org) which I subsequently established to channel support from their audience.

Figure 10.1 Drawing, approved by the Kogi, illustrating the threads that connect parts of the north face of the Sierra. Illustrator: Mauricio Montaña Maldonado.

What are the Kogi for

They turned the production into their own explanation of the immediate need for outsiders, who they call 'the younger brothers', to stop devastating nature and learn how to care for it. They set out to demonstrate the continuity and efficacy of their knowledge and guardianship from the time of the Tairona.[21] That claim is supported by archaeological evidence, which suggests that the Sierra had a much larger population before colonization, and that colonization was now diminishing the land's capacity to support life. According to Alvaro Soto, who was responsible for the excavation, the Lost City shows 'that it's possible to have a good density of population in a very beautiful environment like this one without destroying it'.[22] But now, according to the Kogi, the land itself was dying.

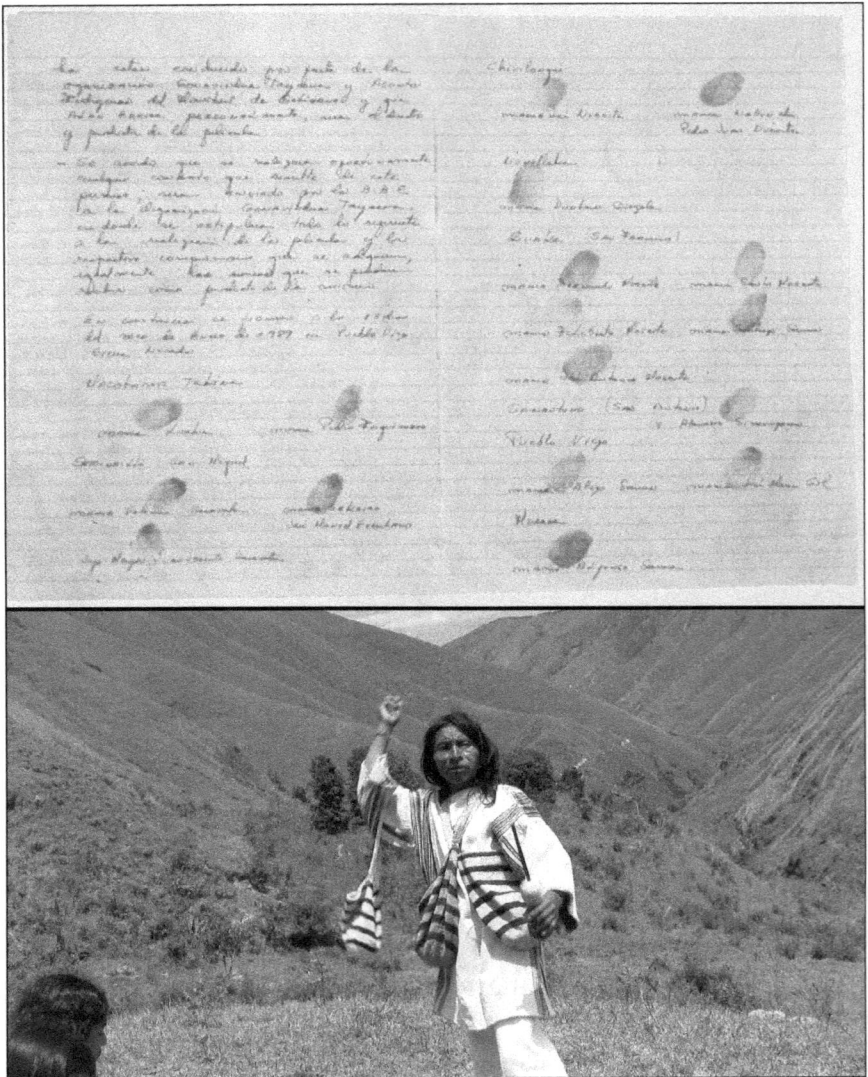

Figure 10.2 Top: Communal declaration and agreement to filming by the Mamas of seventeen communities, 1990. Image: Alan Ereira. Bottom: Mama Pedro Juan dramatically declaiming the statement made by Gonawindua to the world. Photo: Alan Ereira.

Their message was not the statement of any individual, any leader, or any town. To emphasize that fact, the Mamas of seventeen communities insisted on putting their fingerprints to a formal document written out by a government official (Figure 10.2, top). I was being presented with a terrible communal declaration made by a people who believe their purpose on the earth is to be its guardians, and who understand that they are experiencing its destruction. They spoke as the mountain.

> The Great Mother taught and taught. The Great Mother gave us what we needed to live and her teaching has not been forgotten right up to this day. We all still live by it. But now they are taking out the Mother's heart. They are digging up the ground and cutting out her liver and her guts. The Mother is being cut to pieces and stripped of everything. From their first landing they have been doing this.
>
> The Great Mother too has a mouth, eyes and ears. They are cutting out her eyes and ears. If we lost an eye we would be sad. So the mother too is sad, and she'll end and the world ends if you do not stop digging and digging.[23]

The language is significant. The Kogi do not see the exploitation of the land as the plunder of a resource, but as a physical assault on a living body. The viewer may choose to see that as a metaphor: it is easier to grasp. But that is not what is being said.

The obvious and somewhat bewildering questions that this posed were, what did the Kogi think the world actually is, why should they believe that they had ever been protecting it, what were the procedures they had been using to carry on this work, and what were they now trying to achieve? The seriousness of their intention was beyond question, as this was why they were taking the existential risk of exposure after centuries of defensive withdrawal. They had revealed that there were far more Kogi, in far more small towns, than any administrator, missionary, or anthropologist had supposed. Reichel-Dolmatoff, the anthropologist who most studied them, said in 1967 that they numbered perhaps two thousand.[24] By 1987 he had raised that to six thousand.[25] I learned from the Kogi that there were around eleven thousand, including many in towns which were effectively inaccessible except to themselves. They had been protecting themselves in the folds of the river valleys so that the Mamas could continue their work of healing the world. They were puzzled that we did not understand this. The most senior Mama ruminated,

> What would they think if all we Mamas died? Would they think, 'Well, so what?' What would they think? If that happened and all we Mamas died, and there was no-one doing our work, well, the rain wouldn't fall from the sky. It would get hotter and hotter from the sky and the trees and the crops wouldn't grow. Or am I wrong and they would grow anyway?[26]

The Kogi understand the Sierra to be the core of all creation, the spindle on which the world was spun, the heart of the living earth where all reality is reflected. So taking care of the Sierra is taking care of all existence, and that work is their *raison d'être*. Their act of deliberate exposure was, they believed, putting not just themselves, but all life at risk. Any substantial outside contact would, they concluded centuries ago, result in the collapse of their culture and the consequential death of the mountain and of the world. They developed a culture of silence in the face of intrusion.[27] But if they continued as before, the advancing intrusion of the unfinished Columbian conquest (as they put it) would kill the living world anyway. They felt they had no choice but to speak. Genuinely desperate and terrified by what we have been doing to our shared home, they had set about persuading their people to come out of isolation into direct and dramatic engagement with younger brother and his strange devices to deliver their warning. Ramón Gil spelt out formally the grim future to be expected in a world where the Kogis' work of stabilizing nature is no longer effective.

> The world is weak and diseased, The animals die, the trees dry up, people become ill. Many new illnesses will appear, there will be no cure for them, and the reason is that Younger Brother is violating fundamental principles, continually and totally. Drilling, mining, extracting petrol, minerals. Stripping away the world!
>
> We know that this is destroying all order and damaging the world. BBC, tell the Younger Brother, 'Open your eyes. Hear the Mamas' law and story. Learn how things really are.'[28]

What is a Mama

I found it hard to know what to make of the Mamas. Anthropologists referred to them as 'priests' or 'shamans', but that never seemed appropriate. A small number of investigators had tried to get close to them, such as Konrad Theodor Preuss in 1926, Tobón Uribe in 1986, and Reichel-Dolmatoff in 1976, produced an extensive literature, and described the Mamas as a priesthood.[29] Kogi with whom I discussed the notion of religious belief invariably considered the question and decided they were atheist. The Kogi have no organized religion and regard their engagement with transcendence as pragmatic, rather than a matter of faith or belief. They have no writing (indeed, they are very suspicious of it). Kogi Mamas, normally selected at birth, are trained to concentrate, meditate, perform ritual dance, and memorize the lore and knowledge of their ancestors.[30] This involves keeping the student (*kuivi*) from birth in a dark hut or cave for up to eighteen years, awake at night and sleeping by day, fed on white foods and warm water. He learns the arts of divination, including especially divining from the movement of bubbles, and how to make offerings to what are called the 'mothers' and 'fathers' of everything in the world. These offerings are spoken of as nourishment, and also as payments, *pagamentos*, meaning that they are required both to sustain life on another plane and to restore damage done there. All this was demonstrated in order to show how they have preserved their traditional knowledge. Once educated, he is a constant presence in the community and plays the role of trusted (indeed, infallible) adviser to families and the community, conveying what he learns from divination. 'Mama' means the sun. The Mama warms and illuminates everyone – and, as I was solemnly told by the Mama Jacinto, the Mama has a duty to care for the future of all kinds of creatures and all kinds of people, even the younger brother, 'although he has done us harm'.[31]

What is the mountain

To understand what a Mama does, and who he is, I had to learn to understand the Sierra from a Kogi perspective. That meant moving beyond the list of attributes I gave at the beginning, which enabled it to be analysed, tabulated, celebrated, and exploited from different perspectives. When younger brothers come to the Sierra as investigators, each brings a different expertise, applying their own way of knowing and experiencing, gathering, and utilizing what they want, and generally then leaving for a life elsewhere. For the Kogi, the great rock pile we call the Sierra Nevada de Santa Marta – the Snow Peak of the oldest colonial city of the Americas – is an entire cosmos. It is their only home. They, like the trees, ants, iguanas, rivers, and stones, are an integral part of the place. They cannot really grasp how younger brother fails to understand that we, too, are an integral part of the living world.

Spanish colonists invented this name, the Sierra Nevada de Santa Marta. It puts a label on a resource. The Kogi do not have a word for mountain. Falk Xué Parra-Witte has pointed out that they have a word for summits, *guinue*.[32] The closest they come is *Nulkujaluwa*, which starts with *Nuk*, 'everything', and is related to *Nuhuakalda*, the idea that underpins the earth. But its name, attached to, but certainly not limited to, the most significant summit, is *Gonawindua*.

Every Kogi understands *Gonawindua* to be alive, and to be the generating power that makes everything else alive. It is the constitution of the world, in every sense. It is the law. And it speaks. That is what the Mamas are for. To know and respond to what *Gonawindua* is saying.

This was spelt out to me by Ramón Gil. As Cabildo, Ramón reported to, and took instruction from, the Mamas. They report to, and take instruction from, *Gonawindua*. *Gonawindua* cannot be easily translated into any 'younger brother' language because it is not simply a word. Ramón explained that it is four ideas, *go na win dwa*, each of which is dense with meanings and which, when placed together, tell the story of the beginning of life. *Go* sets the stage for this narrative; it conveys 'something being born' or 'birth'. It also signifies 'in the beginning'. *Na* means 'something coming'; a Kogi may lift his head towards the east as astronomical dawn softens the darkness and exclaim *na!*. *Vin* means quickening: new life is signalling its presence, as a woman feels the first surprising movement in her stomach when she is four months pregnant. Then comes the eruption of life into the world that is *du:* or *dua* which means all living things, especially the tiny seeds of life, tiny sea creatures; *duas* signifies sperm and the spectacular spray of ejaculation that fills the sky, and that we call the Milky Way.[33] It is the word for the quickening of the world. It also means 'the mountain where the world began, the law-bringer'. The OGT say that

> *Gonawindwa* contains the origin sites of humankind. Here is the original placenta of our species and of all the knowledge placed in our hands. It is the navel of the Universe. It is where the totality of life is shaped; for us it is the beginning and it is history. And it is where life continues, transcendentally. (trans. Ereira)[34]

The great eruption of life that is *Gonawindua* began with a conception in the sense in which we use it, an idea. The mother of everything, the universal consciousness in which all ideas were conceived, is called *Aluna*. The first ideas of *Aluna* would be the living templates of material reality, the 'spiritual parents' of everything. They were and are bound by the laws that define the nature of things, laws which, one could say, structure the uncreated space in which *Aluna*, pure consciousness, lives. That space, the source of nature's laws, is called *Sé*.

At the time of making the film the Kogi thought that indigenous people had largely vanished from the earth, but once the film travelled among indigenous people worldwide, they were made aware of large communities in the lands of the younger brothers, who had to a large extent lost touch with their ancestral knowledge. They told me they were planning an international indigenous conference in the Sierra, in the hope that they could initiate a programme of recovery which might help reshape the world. It was intended to take place in Kogi territory, but then the Kogi decided to move it to an Arhuaco town, Nabusimake, 'Birthplace of the Sun'. They took me in their delegation, assuring the guerrillas who controlled access that I was a Mama and taking an impressive, if unusual, deaf-mute interpreter. Ramón controlled the agenda, and at the public meeting in Santa Marta which concluded the event, he spelt out the concept of original law which the Kogi wanted everyone there to internalize.

> The original laws, the fundamental principles, are in *Sé*. *Sé* has no beginning, it has always existed. It is spiritual existence, the spiritual principle of existence. *Sé* is not a person, not a thing. It is the sum of things. *Sé* is complex. *Sé* brought the material world into being, but it embraces far more than that. *Sé* organises everything so as to create harmony.
>
> When everything was dark, on a level which our view can not reach, the first spiritual Parents originated spirit and thought. They created everything in spirit, in the non material world. They were not people, not air, not anything, just idea.[35]

One of these first parents is Seizhankua, the active driving principle that now keeps movement flowing in the sky and on earth; Seizhankua is associated with the passage of time, which had yet to begin. All that there was were the threads of thought, which formed the woven cloth of past and future, memory and possibility. Ramón went on:

> Then Seizhankua crossed a thread of thought to make the centre and he lifted it. The peak Gonawindua appeared. There was a peak above and a peak below and it began to work as the motor of the world.

This separation of two layers was the beginning of reality, the opening of the gap between past and future. Gonawindua encompasses reality and idea, essence and existence, the blueprint and the manifest life of everything. Everything has its spiritual parent, and the whole is a single transcendent living being. In the words of Parra-Witte, 'Kogi perceive and relate to the mountains, valleys, waters, trees, rocks, and other landmarks of the Sierra Nevada as conscious, influential agencies with particular names, histories and significances. ... In the Sierra Nevada, the whole mountain range is considered an integrated living totality, the Mother's body, and globally the world's "Heart." '[36]

In 2013 the Mamas started on the extraordinary journey of supervising the recording and translation into Spanish of a thousand hours of oral statements, edited under the supervision of trusted non-Kogi into a Spanish text setting out the meaning of *Gonawindua* and the 'Law of Origin', their place and history.[37] They titled the work *Shikwakala*. The pattern of forces which control the movements of earth and sky is called *Shikwá*; it is seen as a non-material cosmos-spanning fabric, and those of its threads enfolding the Sierra are *Shikwakala*. But the book is not a treatise on the Kogi version of gravitational and electromagnetic forces. Its subtitle is *El Crujido de la Madre Tierra*, 'the creaking of Mother Earth', and the text opens with an explanation that when the fabric is damaged, as is happening now, 'Mother Earth trembles and cries'.[38] Their object is to show what that means and stop the damage. It is an effort to explain how they work with the living mountain of which they form part, and why our use of the land is catastrophic.

The work was published in 2018, and it is carefully organized to set out the case for the complete protection of the territory. So far it has only been privately distributed. They have been nervous about its effect and are very anxious about how it is read – partly because, as the text itself says, using Spanish 'inevitably means that we are producing a "mestizo" book. ... For example, for us, the territory is *Haba*, which is roughly translated into Spanish as *La Madre*. Because the deep meaning of an expression depends on that culture's vision of the world, this book should be understood as a dialogue between *Haba* and *La Madre*.'[39]

In 1973, the four peoples of the Sierra had physically marked the boundary of *Gonawindua*, with a group of Mamas walking what they call 'The Black Line'.[40] This invisible path around the whole Sierra links a large number of 'sacred' sites on its periphery.[41] In 1999, OGT contributed to an official declaration of the need for protection of the territory, but at that time the Kogi restricted themselves to saying that the territory was filled with sacred space.[42] Their constant demand to have the Black Line respected was an uphill struggle, partly because they never clearly articulated the meaning of this sacred space. It is only now, after they have declared that there are 'no more secrets', that the indigenous people of the Sierra have explained how these sites function.[43] At the end of 2018 they achieved government recognition by decree of the territory within the Black Line as filled with interconnected living features which are essential to their survival, and which, in the words of that decree, connect 'the spiritual principles of the world and the source of life'. It describes the waters of the mountain as the veins of a body.[44] In *Shikwakala*, the Kogi say that fundamental to describing *Gonawindua* is the understanding that for them, 'the ancestral territory is a living body, like a person. Its sacred places interact with everything related to the cycles of life, to health, behaviour, correct action, the territory's government, the work of the Mamas and of the traditional authorities, as well as constructions and crops. In short, they interact with all human and non-human life'.[45]

Parra-Witte concluded that the Kogi and the mountain can only be understood together 'as an organic composition'.[46] This has profound implications for their understanding and practice of medicine. The Mamas address medical issues in humans by direct engagement with *Gonawindua*. By the same token, what we understand to be their ecological advice and practice is their concern to take care of and heal its living body. An explanation of this was published by Camilo Arbeláez Albornoz. This remarkable medical practitioner lives in the Sierra and has worked for many years with Kogis helping them formulate a cross-cultural form of medical practice. He reported that the Mamas perceived an equivalence between the human body and the land. They carefully map the geography of the massif onto the symbolic form of a human; blood and bile have their exact equivalents within the earth. 'Both have sacred places, major and minor, the colour and consistency of their secretions have similarities, the signals they emit, ailments and diseases have precise territorial references …That is why the pollution of the mouths of the rivers, the destruction of the forests and the theft of sacred sites have caused many diseases. The relationship between body and territory begins with birth and is woven throughout life.'[47]

The Mamas work as bridges between *Aluna* and reality. It seems that *Aluna* has no direct presence in material reality; consciousness is memory and possibility, but material existence is the present, the place between. Birth and death involve life entering and leaving the world, and *Aluna* is the source of generative energy, so there must be transition between material reality and the transcendent. *Aluna* also requires a material agent to be present, so to speak, in the present, to take preventative action when the vigour of real life throws nature out of balance. The Kogi have a strong consciousness of the eruptive competitive energy of life, and the constant threat of chaotic disruption. Humans, endowed with consciousness, can, if trained, engage with *Aluna* and work as the agents of transcendental consciousness, acting directly in the world. Mama Valencio said, 'Human beings were made to care for the living things. The plants, the animals. This is why people were made.' That is what Mamas are trained to do.

The work is done at *Ezuamas*, locations that can be regarded as portals to *Aluna*. The word is used to convey a place of authority, so may be used for a government office, but its roots are 'hot' and 'one'.[48] An *Ezuama* is a primary hotspot, a dangerous and powerful vent into the living conceptual reality of *Gonawindua*. There the Mama directly encounters *Haba Aluna*, the Mother of everything, and the laws of *Sé* that are, roughly, like our idea of laws of nature. Every Mama who contributed to *Shiwakala* is identified not by his town but by the *Ezuama* where he has his seat. In the words of the text, 'There we find all the principles, standards and procedures of the Law of Origin to legislate and direct the administration of our ancestral territory and every aspect of the cultural life of our people. They are, in a manner of speaking, the cultural universities of our people.'[49]

The *Ezuamas* are situated on invisible fissures in space and time. These are the original 'Black Lines'. They radiate from the peaks, offering direct access to inner reality. They connect each river valley from top to bottom, and operate like a vascular system, with capillaries reaching out to lesser sites (Figure 10.1). The Mamas may therefore make 'offerings' at an *Ezuama* to affect connected sites many kilometres distant. Mama Shibulata stressed this at Seizua.

> So why is this place an ezuama? This is a place where we can connect. From here we can concentrate and understand where payments are needed all along the coast. We are told where work is required. When it is not possible to go down we concentrate here to make the payment from here. When it is not possible to go down.[50]

Those 'payments', represented by fragments of leaf, of cotton, of shell, held between thumb and forefinger, are the focus of a tremendous concentration. So the job of the Mama is to strive to comprehend, by concentration and observation, his place in the laws that shape reality. He participates in the laws of nature. In fact, he participates so closely that each lineage of the Kogi is

Figure 10.3 Three Mamas at the Ezuama of Seizua. Photo: Alan Ereira.

directly connected with particular *Ezuamas*, and certain individual Mamas are the permanent guardians of the sites, spending their whole lives there.

Some of the connections that pass through an *Ezuama* are more visible than others. They include underground flows, air currents, the movements of birds and animals, and so on. Much of the pragmatic understanding the Kogi draw from seeing the Sierra as a biological entity can be fairly readily translated into a holistic science that we can hope to learn to understand, for the benefit of the environment and therefore for ourselves. But there is another dimension to all this, the dimension of direct communication between *Gonawindua* and humanity, that is not so susceptible to our understanding.

The mountain speaks

The Mamas do what they do because they are instructed. The Mamas who took over Ramón Gil's life did not think that they were acting on their own initiative. They had been told what to do by *Gonawindua*, and they believe that there are times when their voices are not their own. I was given a startling demonstration of this in April 2009. I was invited to sit before the leader of the Mamas at an *Ezuama* around 3,000 metres high and listen to what I was told this mountain had summoned me to hear.

I had never before had a Skype call on behalf of a geographical feature. It had come three weeks earlier, and I had to scramble to get there from my home in London by the required date. I was told that a Kogi leader and healthcare expert, Jose Santos Sauna, was being installed as their new supreme political authority (*Cabildo Gobernador*) and had requested my presence on a journey of inauguration that would take him high into the mountain. I was required.

I barely knew Santos, but when our documentary film was shot in 1990 he had worked on translation. I flew via Madrid and Bogota to Santa Marta, now a major and prosperous coal port. I met my long-time helper, the American anthropologist Peter Rawitscher, and after a short night's sleep he took me in a Toyota land cruiser to load up with sacks of dried fish, the customary gift for a Kogi community. We then set off around the Tairona National Park and up a dry river valley into the foothills. In the past I had ascended with the luxury of a helicopter and I doubted my ability to make the climb without one, but Santos supplied me with his own mule and up we went for two days, dropping the fish at a lower community, then crossing high passes which were sometimes too steep for laden mules.

We arrived at Seizua, an *ezuama* with a small town where the circular houses are insulated with thatch to ground level, making them look like shaggy beasts in the mist. There were ritual meeting places of small stones and larger boulders, and I was taken through the customary process of arrival, standing before a seated Mama just outside the town, holding a cotton thread and explaining everything that had brought me to this point, everything I had felt and experienced, and what drove me. I spoke in English.

After a further communal interrogation, this time with translation, about the effectiveness and fate of that film, *From the Heart of the World*, a gathering began. There were some fifty men with white tunics and pantaloons seated on the grass, facing a wall of rock. In front of them were four white-robed women heavily draped with red necklaces. Facing them was the leading Mama, who spoke standing, with vigour and flamboyant extravagance (Figure 10.2, bottom).

I am Mama Pedro Juan, speaking in Seizua

Then he began. But he was not speaking alone. The four women seated at his feet, *Sakas* or female Mamas, were simultaneously reciting the same words. They all were in complete harmony, the Mother, *Haba Gonawindua*, breathing her words into the *Sakas*, amplified by the theatrical voice of the great Mama.

This was what I had been brought to hear.

The speech was long and impassioned. The Mama spoke of the mountain's essence as *Nulkukeje*, which embraces *Gonawindua* and the whole world, 'a Lord who knows the whole of the Law'. The Mother, *Haba Aluna*, said that its manifestation in physical reality, *Nulkujaluwa*, manifests the Law (what we call scientific laws, the laws of nature) and knows it. 'He was given responsibility not only for the *Ezuamas* but for everything down to the sea, to keep out everything that is damaging to it.' The *Ezuama* also 'knows the whole of the Law. It must warn those who are thinking of doing harm so that they understand that they cannot destroy the seas and everything that exists. They are not the owners of the world.'

The Mama declared that deforestation is wounding the living body, 'the Mother feels this like an amputation, or tearing out her heart. To that extent the Mother is like us', a suffering acutely experienced by the student Mamas in the dark, 'that do not eat red meat or conventional food, are the most important observers of the *Nukujaluwa*. We listen to them and know that the armed groups that are now here are making nature itself sick.'

This had brought the speech to its heart, the need to exclude outsiders from the mountain for the safety of the world. The mountain was demanding international respect for its boundaries. In return, the Mama said, younger brother could be shown how to manage the world's health without going there.

The Younger Brothers also have their *Ezuamas*, and some of them do prepare themselves, though in a different way. I believe that it is important to do this, and not only do it in theory but also in practice, and I want the Younger Brothers to listen to what we say and not continue causing damage, or nature itself will finish us off. That is why we speak to the Younger Brothers.

But that requires a change of behaviour. So the *Sakas* and the Mama, still speaking in unison while the men listened, spelt out what they felt impelled to say as the voices of the earth itself.

Originally there were no strange things like airplanes intruding, and this intrusion has an effect on nature. We must also tell you that *tuma* (ancestral divination stones) must not be taken out of the ground. We behave respectfully but the Younger Brothers do not. As soon as they see something in the earth they grab it. They are taking advantage of the frailty of nature, and the Mother does not resist, but ... This is what we Mamas want to make clear to the Younger Brothers.

The birds have gone from us, because the Parents of Teyuna (the humming bird, the Lost City and the spirit guardian of the tumas) have been taken. (They were made manifest in buried gold figurines that have been looted).

If Western society wants to have *sewa* (small stones for payments), if they want to work well and help us, there are stones that we can provide ... Tourists are gathering these stones and we say to them that they do not have authority to do that.

The sea also has stones and shells that we can gather. All the rivers that flow to the beaches come from *Ezuamas*. These rivers must not be damaged or they cannot carry anything down to feed the sea. The clouds are raised down there to complete the water cycle to the peaks. The lagoons high on the mountain are the Mothers of the sea and they supply its needs. The daughter of the lagoons is the sea, and like a daughter it supplies the lagoons through this cycle of the water ...

It is not possible to repair the damage that the Younger Brothers have done to the sacred sites. The Mother cannot survive this. So we now see the rivers drying out, avalanches, landslips, drought, unfamiliar weather, and all this is being brought about by the Younger Brothers. We can no longer feed nature with its ancestral sustenance, ...

There used to be different species of birds here. Nowadays there are almost no birds. Already there are no traditional foods. Previously we took care of the *Makú, Nulkujaluwa* and the sea without help. Now the Mother cannot be cared for by us alone, nor the Heart of the World. But as we said, we must look after these sacred sites.

Makú, which can represent the 'Father' of Thunder, is a transcendental force with powers over the world, and was here signifying the destructive force of the climate. In its defence, the mountain itself was setting out the Black Line as an absolute final boundary, what we might call a red line, a non-negotiable limit beyond which younger brother's behaviour is not just unacceptable but totally prohibited.

> We Mamas have analysed that you may not destroy the hills, but many sacred sites have been destroyed, cut into, and constructions erected over them. Can the Mother's existence continue?
>
> … Perhaps we did not work hard enough to make the Younger Brother understand. But we think that nature is going to support us so that the Younger Brothers understands us.

If Mama Pedro Juan was indeed giving utterance to the voice of the world, the world was now issuing an unequivocal threat,

> We Mamas know the function of each site, but the Younger Brothers do not listen. All this has been the cause of avalanches, destruction and massacres. This affects the Younger Brother as much as us. New diseases are appearing, travelling from place to place.

The death of the sea was imminent.

> One sacred site was the place of the Mother who had to take care of the sea, and we must take care of the sea just as of the Earth so that it produces fish, shellfish and everything. We human beings are her children. Now she is slowly fading. The Organisation Gonawindua Tairona and their Cabildo exist to make public declarations about all this since the Mothers cannot take care of things unaided.

And so we were brought back to the uncrossable line. Permission to enter the Sierra is now only to be obtained from the OGT, and the OGT does not speak of its own volition.

> Really the decision is made by the *Ezuamas*.

The new Cabildo of the OGT, Santos Sauna, is not a Mama and his inauguration was taking the form of a tour of the Ezuamas at which he had to learn to listen and listen to learn. He had been at pains to tell me that he had begun now to speak words that were not his own, but the voice of the mountain. This was how he negotiated (very successfully) with the other Santos, the country's president. The Mama ended his speech by stressing that the new Cabildo was '*not appointed by the organisation, but named by Nulkujaluwa* and by the mountains', and that the prohibition on non-indigenous access to the Sierra was demanded by the earth itself.

> The Mamas are not speaking out on their own initiative, but the sites themselves have begun to ask for this support. The *Ezuamas* used to be places where the Mamas alone held council, but now people simply walk wherever they want. There are sites where no-one can go. They have always been required to ask permission to go to sacred hills. These are sites that the Kogi of the Sierra Nevada believe may not be walked without permission of the Mama. You can only go there to make offerings, and only with prior permission. The mother suffers when people go without permission.

Failure to heed this would have consequences.

> We do not know who is going to fall sick first, but we are expecting pandemics, and because these are manifestations of the sickness suffered by nature itself, it is going to be hard to find drugs that can cure the coming sickness.
>
> All *Ezuamas* agree with this declaration …
>
> Ah!
>
> The world may begin to tremble.
>
> More and more indicators appear, like the birth of deformed children, as sacred sites are interfered with. That is our thought and this above all we will continue saying to the world.
>
> This is why we were born and live and this is what we declare. We invite other indigenous people and all people in the world to grasp the situation in which we now live.

That was the message of the mountain, spoken through the *Ezuamas*, articulated by four women and a man trained from birth in darkness. I was there to convey it. Eventually, the Mamas asked me to help them make a new film, called *Aluna*, in which they tried to make it heard. It did not make much of a splash.

Mama Pedro Juan's speech was made ten years ago. The Mama, who was in his prime, has suddenly died. The OGT still stands squarely behind the proclamation of the Black Line and the prohibition on uninvited incursions, but the political power to enforce it is lacking. Tourism has increased. A recent visit to the Kogi of the Palomino valley by artists, organized by Mia Pfeifer, found that their traditional work was entirely for tourists. Artisanal products were simply too profitable to keep. Their own bags are now woven with yellow plastic fibre, which is also used to tie together the beams of their houses and to make hammocks.[51] The artists were charged a fee by paramilitaries for being there, and local Kogi required them to pay for an electric saw to make a new loom.

The president who signed the Black Line decree did so as his final act before being replaced. Paramilitary power seems to have taken over. At the time of writing, the Black Line decree does not appear to have any effective force, and on 22 February 2019 the OGT felt compelled to publicly declare that 'the indigenous peoples are now intimidated by threats, extortion and even kidnapping by armed men who freely travel the mountain massif'.[52] Two indigenous individuals were said to have been kidnapped and held for ransom for ten days. Indigenous teachers and health workers are in danger. This is seen as the start of a possible larger assault on indigenous land and property. Control of the Black Line frontier is now in the hands, not of the OGT, but of the armed group. They said in their declaration, 'We used to go down quietly to perform spiritual works anywhere, but now, we do it with fear and we have to ask for permission from them to authorize us to go to places marked in the black line.'[53]

The warning was for the life of the world, a call to the defence of the Black Line. That was the reason for the historic act of producing a book, *Shikwakala*. They have now charged me with seeking its translation and international publication, and we are working together on developing a pilot project with UWTSD and UNESCO to share their knowledge with recognized scientific researchers, publicly demonstrating a 'new' approach to restoring the health of damaged territory. The end of the Kogi, the mountain, and the world is, in their mind, the same. The question they asked in our first film was,

> What would they think if all we Mamas died? Would they think, 'Well? so what?' What would they think? If that happened and all we Mamas died, and there was no-one doing our work, well, the rain wouldn't fall from the sky. It would get hotter and hotter from the sky, and the trees wouldn't grow and the crops wouldn't grow. Or am I wrong and they will grow anyway?

We may soon find out.

Notes

1   Marcos Martinón-Torres, Roberto Valcárcel Rojas, Juanita Sáenz Samper, María Filomena Guerra, 'Metallic Encounters in Cuba: The Technology, Exchange

and Meaning of Metals before and after Columbus', *Journal of Anthropological Archaeology* 31, no. 4 (2012): 439–54, at 446.

2   Thomas D. Cabot, Walter A. Wood, and Frank B. Notestein, 'The Cabot Expedition to the Sierra Nevada de Santa Marta of Colombia', *Geographical Review* 29, no. 4 (1939): 587–621.

3   Maria C. D. G Tribin, Guillermo N. Rodríguez, and Maryi Valderrama, *The Biosphere Reserve of the Sierra Nevada de Santa Marta: A Pioneer Experience of a Shared and Co-ordinated Management of a Bioregion: Colombia*, Working Paper No. 30 (Paris: UNESCO,1999), https://unesdoc.unesco.org/ark:/48223/pf0000118591 (accessed 18 Januray 2018).

4   Soizic Le Saout, Michael Hoffmann, Yichuan Shi, Adrian Hughes, Cyril Bernard, Thomas M. Brooks, Bastian Bertzky, Stuart H. M. Butchart, Simon N. Stuart, Tim Badman, and Ana S. L. Rodrigues, 'Protected Areas and Effective Biodiversity Conservation', *Science* 342, no. 6160 (2013): 803–5.

5   S. Giraldo, 'Lords of the Snow Ranges: Politics, Place, and Landscape Transformation in Two Tairona Towns in the Sierra Nevada de Santa Marta, Colombia' (unpublished PhD thesis, University of Chicago, 2010), 43.

6   Camilo Montes, Georgina Guzman, Germán Bayona, et al., 'Clockwise Rotation of the Santa Marta Massif and Simultaneous Paleogene to Neogene Deformation of the Plato-San Jorge and Cesar-Ranchería Basins', *Journal of South American Earth Sciences* 29, no. 4 (2010): 832–48, at 847.

7   Adriaan Alsema, 'Colombia Vows to Ban Mining in One of World's Highest Coastal Ranges', *Colombia Reports*, 27 November 2017, https://colombiareports. com/colombia-bans-mining-one-worlds-highest-coastal-ranges/ (accessed 19 January 2019).

8   Consejo Regional Indigena del Cauca – CRIC, 'Arhuacos Ganan Batalla Contra Empresa de Hidrocarburos Azabache', 23 February 2018, https://www.cric-colombia. org/portal/arhuacos-ganan-batalla-empresa-hidrocarburos-azabache/ (accessed 19 January 2019).

9   Cabot et al., 'Cabot Expedition', 594.

10   Cabot et al., 'Cabot Expedition', 611, 615.

11   Alan Ereira, *The Heart of the World* (London: Jonathan Cape, 1990), 138–41.

12   Álvaro Soto-Holguín, *The Lost City of the Tayronas* (Bogotá: Colombia I/M Editores Editorial Nomos S.A., 2006).

13   David J. Wilson, *Indigenous South Americans of the Past and Present: An Ecological Perspective* (Chicago: University of Chicago Press, 1999), 276.

14   Andrés Ricardo Restrepo Campo and Sandra Turbay, 'The Silence of the Kogi in Front of Tourists', *Annals of Tourism Research* 52 (May 2015): 44–59, at 48–9.

15   República de Colombia, Ministerio del Interior, Decreto número 1500 de 6 Ago, 2018, 3–4, http://es.presidencia.gov.co/normativa/normativa/DECRETO%20

1500%20DEL%2006%20DE%20AGOSTO%20DE%202018.pdf (accessed 14
August 2019).

16 Carlos Alberto Uribe Tobón, 'Pioneros de la anthropología en Colombia; el padre
    Rafael Celedón', *Boleten Museo Del Oro* 17 (1986): 3–31.

17 Yanelia Mestre Pacheco, Peter Rawitscher Adams, and 23 Mamas, *Shikwakala;
    El Crujido de la Madre Tierra* (Santa Marta: Organisación Gonawindua Tayrona,
    2018), 225.

18 Alan Ereira, *The Elder Brothers Warning* (London: Tairona Heritage Trust,
    2009), 42.

19 Ereira, *Heart of the World*, 44–5.

20 Ereira, *Heart of the World*, 115. This is not a uniquely Tairona vision; see for
    instance the Rig Veda creation hymn, 10:129.

21 *From the Heart of the World: The Elder Brothers' Warning* [video], YouTube
    (televised by the BBC 1990, uploaded 29 June 2018), https://www.youtube.com/
    watch?v=HfSnTUc52C8&t=9s; Ereira, *Heart of the World*.

22 *From the Heart of the World* (1990): 09.28–10.24.

23 *From the Heart of the World* (1990): 26.34–27.13.

24 Gerardo Reichel-Dolmatoff, 'Notas Sobre el Simbolismo Religioso de los Indios de
    la Sierra Nevada de Santa Marta', *Razón y Fábula* I (1967): 55–72, at 57.

25 Gerardo Reichel-Dolmatoff, 'The Great Mother and the Kogi Universe: A Concise
    Overview', *Journal of Latin American Lore* 13, no. 1 (1987): 73–113, at 73.

26 Mama Valencio in *From the Heart of the World* (1990): 28.22–28.27.

27 Restrepo Campo and Turbay, 'Silence of the Kogi in Front of Tourists', 48–9.

28 Ramón Gil in *From the Heart of the World* (1990): 36.06–36.46.

29 Konrad Theodor Preuss, 'Forschungsreise zu den Kágaba, Beobachtungen,
    Textaufnahmen und sprachliche Studien bei einem Indianerstamme in Kolumbien,
    Südamerika', *Anthropos* 21, no. 5/6 (1926): 777–96; Tobón Uribe, 'Pioneros de la
    anthropologia en Colombia; and Gerado Reichel-Dolmatoff, 'Training for the
    Priesthood among the Kogi of Colombia', in *Enculturation in Latin America: An
    Anthology*, ed. Johannes Wilbert (Los Angeles: UCLA Latin American Centre
    Publications, 1976), 265–88.

30 Gerardo Reichel-Dolmatoff, *The Sacred Mountain of Colombia's Kogi Indians*
    (Leiden: Brill, 1990), 5.

31 From the video *From the Heart of the World*: 38.10–38.40.

32 Falk Xué Parra Witte, 'Living the Law of Origin: The Cosmological, Ontological,
    Epistemological, and Ecological Framework of Kogi Environmental Politics'
    (Doctoral thesis, University of Cambridge, 2018), 167. https://doi.org/10.17863/
    CAM.22047.

33 Parra Witte, 'Living the Law of Origin', 117.

34 Organisación Gonawindua Tairona, https://gonawindua.org/organizacion/
    fundamentos/ (accessed 19 January 2019).

35 Ramón Gil, 'The Law of Sé: Linking the Spiritual and Material', in *Art and Cultural
    Heritage: Law, Policy, and Practice*, ed. Barbara T. Hoffman, trans. Alan Ereira
    (Cambridge: Cambridge University Press, 2006), 21–7, at 21.

36 Parra Witte, 'Living the Law of Origin', 20.

37 Mestre Pacheco et al., *Shikwakala.*

38 Mestre Pacheco et al., *Shikwakala*, 7.

39 Mestre Pacheco et al., *Shikwakala*,19.

40 Matthew T. Evans, 'The Sacred: Differentiating, Clarifying and Extending Concepts',
    Review of Religious Research 45, no. 1 (2003): 32–47.

41 Guillermo Rodriguez-Navarro, 'Traditional Knowledge: An Innovative
    Contribution to Landscape Management', in *Conserving Cultural
    Landscapes: Challenges and New Directions*, ed. Ken Taylor, Archer St. Clair,
    and Nora J. Mitchell (New York: Routledge 2015), 277–94, contains a summary
    identification of sites on the territorial boundary.

42 G. Sánchez Herrera, M. L. Hernández Turriago, G. Mayor-Aragón, C. Gómez-
    Rangel, I. P. Corredor Bobadilla, M. Y. Puentes Amaya, W. Blanco-Ortiz, M. Muñoz
    Díaz, J. M. Pinzón Cáceres, and R. Franke Ante, *Plan de Manejo 2005–2009,
    Parque Nacional Natural Tayrona* (Santa Marta: Ministerio de Ambiente Vivienda
    y Desarrollo Territorial/Unidad administrativa Especial del Sistema de Parques
    Nacionales Naturales, 2006), 74.

43 Personal communication from Cabildo Santo Sauna to me, April 2009.

44 Republica de Colombia, Ministerio del Interior, Decreto número 1500 de 6 Ago
    2018, Articulo 4 (b), (c), 9, 10 (accessed 14 August 2019).

45 Mestre Pacheco et al., *Shikwakala*, 230.

46 Parra Witte, 'Living the Law of Origin', 44.

47 Camilo Arbeláez Albornoz, 'Diversidad cultural: el mayor desafío a la salud
    pública contemporánea', *Palimpsestvs* 5, (2005), 42–51 at 47, bdigital.unal.edu.
    co/14236/1/3-8057-PB.pdf, accessed 5 March, 2019.

48 Parra Witte, 'Living the Law of Origin', 78.

49 Mestre Pacheco et al., *Shikwakala*, 113.

50 Mama Shibulata speaking at the *ezuama* of Seizua, 'Aluna' [video] YouTube (2012,
    uploaded 4 February 2018), https://www.youtube.com/watch?v=ftFbCwJfs1I,
    50.36–51.7 (accessed 5 March 2019).

51 Personal communication from Mia Pfeifer to me, January 2019; Mia Pfeifer,
    'FIBRA', http://www.miapfeifer.com/index.php?/selected-works/fibra/ (accessed 31
    January 2019).

52 Roger Urieles Velasquez, 'Amenazas, extorsiones y secuestros a indígenas en la
    Sierra Nevada', *El Tiempo*, 22 February 2019, https://www.eltiempo.com/colombia/

otras-ciudades/amenazas-extorsiones-y-secuestros-a-indigenas-en-la-sierra-nevada-330112 (accessed 5 March 2019).
53 Velasquez, 'Amenazas'.

Bibliography

Alsema, A. 'Colombia Vows to Ban Mining in One of World's Highest Coastal Ranges'. Colombia Reports, 27 November 2017. https://colombiareports.com/colombia-bans-mining-one-worlds-highest-coastal-ranges/ (accessed 19 January 2019).

Arbeláez Albornoz, Camilo. 'Diversidad cultural: el mayor desafío a la salud pública contemporánea'. *Palimpsestvs* 5 (2005): 42–51. bdigital.unal.edu.co/14236/1/3-8057-PB.pdf.

Cabot, Thomas D., Walter A. Wood, and Frank B. Notestein. 'The Cabot Expedition to the Sierra Nevada de Santa Marta of Colombia'. *Geographical Review* 29, no. 4 (1939): 587–621.

Campo, Restrepo, Andrés Ricardo, and Sandra Turbay. 'The silence of the Kogi in front of tourists'. *Annals of Tourism Research* 52 (May 2015): 44–59.

Consejo Regional Indigena del Cauca – CRIC. 'Arhuacos Ganan Batalla Contra Empresa de Hidrocarburos Azabache', 23 February, 2018, https://www.cric-colombia.org/portal/arhuacos-ganan-batalla-empresa-hidrocarburos-azabache/ (accessed 19 January 2019).

Ereira, Alan. *The Heart of the World*. London: Jonathan Cape, 1990.

Ereira, Alan. *The Elder Brothers Warning*. London: Tairona Heritage Trust, 2009.

Evans, Matthew T. 'The Sacred: Differentiating, Clarifying and Extending Concepts'. *Review of Religious Research* 45, no. 1 (2003): 32–47.

From the Heart of the World: The Elder Brothers' Warning [video], YouTube (televised by the BBC 1990, uploaded 29 June 2018), https://www.youtube.com/watch?v=HfSnTUc52C8&t=9s.

Gil, Ramón. 'The Law of Sé: Linking the Spiritual and Material'. In *Art and Cultural Heritage: Law, Policy, and Practice*, edited by Barbara T. Hoffman, translated by Alan Ereira, 21–7. Cambridge: Cambridge University Press, 2006.

Giraldo, S., 'Lords of the Snow Ranges: Politics, Place, and Landscape Transformation in Two Tairona Towns in the Sierra Nevada de Santa Marta, Colombia'. Unpublished PhD thesis, University of Chicago, 2010.

Le Saout, Soizic, Michael Hoffmann, Yichuan Shi, Adrian Hughes, Cyril Stuart, Tim Badman, and Ana S. L. Rodrigues, 'Protected Areas and Effective Biodiversity Conservation'. *Science* 342, no. 6160 (2013): 803–5.

Martinón-Torres, Marcos, Roberto Valcárcel Rojas, Juanita Sáenz Samper, and María Filomena Guerra. 'Metallic Encounters in Cuba: The Technology, Exchange and Meaning of Metals before and after Columbus'. *Journal of Anthropological Archaeology* 31, no. 4 (2012): 439–54.

Mestre Pacheco, Yanelia, and Peter Rawitscher Adams, and 23 Mamas. *Shikwakala; El Crujido de la Madre Tierra*. Santa Marta, CO: Organisación Gonawindua Tayrona, 2018.

Montes, Camilo, Georgina Guzman, Germán Bayona, et al. 'Clockwise Rotation of the Santa Marta Massif and Simultaneous Paleogene to Neogene Deformation of the Plato-San Jorge and Cesar-Ranchería Basins'. *Journal of South American Earth Sciences* 29, no. 4 (2010): 832–48.

Organisación Gonawindua Tairona. https://www.gonawindua.org/orden-de-la-naturaleza/ (accessed 19 January 2019).

Parra Witte, Falk Xué, 'Living the Law of Origin: The Cosmological, Ontological, Epistemological, and Ecological Framework of Kogi Environmental Politics'. Doctoral thesis, University of Cambridge, 2018. https://doi.org/10.17863/CAM.22047.

Pfeifer, Mia. FIBRA, http://www.miapfeifer.com/index.php?/selected-works/fibra/ (accessed 31 January 2019).

Preuss, Konrad Theodor, 'Forschungsreise zu den Kágaba, Beobachtungen, Textaufnahmen und sprachliche Studien bei einem Indianerstamme in Kolumbien, Südamerika'. *Anthropos* 21, no. 5/6 (1926): 777–96.

Reichel-Dolmatoff, Gerardo. 'Notas Sobre el Simbolismo Religioso de los Indios de la Sierra Nevada de Santa Marta'. *Razón y Fábula* I (1967): 55–72.

Reichel-Dolmatoff, Gerardo. 'Training for the Priesthood among the Kogi of Colombia'. In *Enculturation in Latin America: An Anthology*, edited by Johannes Wilbert, 265–88. Los Angeles: UCLA Latin American Centre, 1976.

Reichel-Dolmatoff, Gerardo. 'The Great Mother and the Kogi Universe: A Concise Overview'. *Journal of Latin American Lore* 13, no. 1 (1987): 73–113.

Reichel-Dolmatoff, Gerardo. *The Sacred Mountain of Colombia's Kogi Indians*. Leiden: Brill, 1990.

República de Colombia, Ministerio del Interior. 'Decreto número 1500 de 6 Ago 2018', http://es.presidencia.gov.co/normativa/normativa/DECRETO%201500%20DEL%2006%20DE%20AGOSTO%20DE%202018.pdf (accessed 14 August 2019).

Rodriguez-Navarro, Guillermo. 'Traditional Knowledge: An Innovative Contribution to Landscape Management'. In *Conserving Cultural Landscapes: Challenges and New Directions*, edited by Ken Taylor, Archer St. Clair, and Nora J. Mitchell, 277–94. New York: Routledge, 2015.

Sánchez Herrera, Gustavo, Marta Lucía Hernández Turriago, Gustavo Mayor Aragón, Camilo Gómez Rangel, Irina Patricia Corredor Bobadilla, Mary Yolima Puentes Amaya, Wilson Blanco Ortiz, Mirith Muñoz Díaz, Juan Manuel Pinzón Cáceres, and Rebeca Franke Ante. *Plan de Manejo 2005–2009, Parque Nacional Natural Tayrona*. Santa Marta: Ministerio de Ambiente Vivienda y Desarrollo Territorial/Unidad administrativa Especial del Sistema de Parques Nacionales Naturales, 2006.

Soto Holguín, Álvaro. *The Lost City of the Tayronas*. Bogotá: Editorial Nomos S.A., 2006.

Tobón, Carlos Alberto Uribe. 'Pioneros de la anthropología en Colombia; el padre Rafael Celedón'. *Boleten Museo Del Oro* 17 (1986): 3–31.

Tribin, Maria C. D. G., Guillermo N. Rodríguez, and Maryi Valderrama, *The Biosphere Reserve of the Sierra Nevada de Santa Marta: A Pioneer Experience of a Shared and Co-ordinated Management of a Bioregion: Colombia*, Working Paper No. 30. Paris: UNESCO, 1999. https://unesdoc.unesco.org/ark:/48223/pf0000118591 (accessed 18 January 2018).

Urieles Velasquez, Roger, 'Amenazas, extorsiones y secuestros a indígenas en la Sierra Nevada'. *El Tiempo*, 22 February 2019, https://www.eltiempo.com/colombia/otras-ciudades/amenazas-extorsiones-y-secuestros-a-indigenas-en-la-sierra-nevada-330112 (accessed 5 March 2019).

Wilson, David J. *Indigenous South Americans of the Past and Present: An Ecological Perspective*. Chicago: University of Chicago Press, 1999.

Index